A
CONCISE
DICTIONARY
OF
CULTS &
RELIGIONS

A
CONCISE
DICTIONARY
OF
CULTS &
RELIGIONS

WILLIAM WATSON

MOODY PRESS
CHICAGO

Library of Congress Cataloging in Publication Data

Watson, William G. (William Glenn)
    A concise dictionary of cults and religions /   by William G.
Watson
      p.   cm.
    Includes bibliographical references
    ISBN 0-8024-1726-4
    1. Religions—Dictionaries. 2. Sects—Dictionaries. 3. Cults—
-Dictionaries.   I. Title.
BL31.W38   1991
291'.03—dc20   90-22935
                                                  CIP

2 3 4 5 6 Printing/BC/Year 95 94 93 92 91

Printed in the United States of America

*To my wife for her support
during the hundreds of "after work" hours
spent in research and writing.*

*To Judy, a family friend,
who first challenged me to expand
a seminar handout into this book.*

*To Margie and Don,
whose encouragement kept me
sending the manuscript to publishers
until the right one was found.*

*And with grateful appreciation
to the late Dr. Walter R. Martin,
whose cassette tape series "World of the Cults"
catapulted me into a deeper study of cults
and a greater concern for those involved in them.*

Contents

Foreword   9

Preface   11

Dictionary of Cults and Religions   15

Bibliography
    General   264
    Comparative Religions   270
    Eastern Mysticism   271
    Jehovah's Witnesses   273
    Miscellaneous   276
    Mormonism   279
    New Age   282
    Occult   286

Ministries
    General   291
    Specific   295

Foreword

A perusal of William Watson's dictionary quickly illustrates a key point: We have a new vocabulary—almost a new language—that has appeared with the devastating immediacy of an earthquake. In only a few decades—a mere moment in human history—new words have come into being to name new concepts.

The new lexicon that we see in this dictionary is itself the clearest indicator that a profound ideological and religious changing-of-the-guard has taken place in our culture. Few of the terms and names recorded here existed before the 1950s.

If we performed a time-travel experiment mentioning New Age ideas to an audience of the 1950s, the hearers would be completely baffled. If you gave them this dictionary to flip through, telling them that such words and concepts would be in common parlance in thirty years, they probably would be deeply apprehensive about the changes on the horizon of their world. For in their hands would be the evidence of what Francis Schaeffer meant when he talked about a post-Christian era.

On our Access Counseling Line (415-540-0300) at Spiritual Counterfeits Project in Berkeley, we get calls from across America that cover the range of groups and concepts mentioned in William Watson's dictionary. Our Access files cover the main groups. The more esoteric groups and concepts are in our larger files. It is heartening to see how up-to-date this book is with recent terms and groups. It will be a great time-saver for us to use this dictionary for quickly accessible information. Be assured that we at SCP will have a copy of this dictionary next to our phone line in the Access room. It should be on the desk of every serious student of spiritual trends in the West. And doubtless it will have to be updated regularly as new hybrids develop.

Tal Brooke
President/Chairman
Spiritual Conterfeits Project

Preface

A *Concise Dictionary of Cults and Religions* is written from a Christian perspective most clearly expressed in the Apostles' Creed:

> I believe in God the Father, Almighty, Maker of heaven and earth.

And in Jesus Christ, His only begotten Son, our Lord; who was conceived by the Holy Spirit, born of the virgin Mary; suffered under Pontius Pilate; was crucified, dead, and buried; He descended into hell; the third day He rose again from the dead; He ascended into heaven, and sitteth at the right hand of God the Father Almighty; from thence He shall come to judge the living and the dead.

I believe in the Holy Spirit, the holy catholic [Christian] church, the communion of saints; the forgiveness of sins; the resurrection of the body; and the life everlasting. Amen.

Simply stated, Jesus is God. Human beings are not God and never will be—they are all sinners. Jesus' death on the cross completely paid the penalty for all sin. Salvation is not obtained by works but by faith in Jesus. These truths are revealed to us in God's written record, the Bible.

The beliefs of many of the groups listed in this dictionary are not classical Christian doctrines. Their various beliefs are stated to show areas in which these groups differ from orthodox Christianity. For purposes of this book, the words *cult, occult, sect,* and *religion* are used differently.

Cult is used in its general sense: a deviation, a counterfeit of classical Christianity, a group whose authority for cardinal beliefs is something or someone other than the Bible. Most deny the Trinity and the incarnation of Jesus Christ, that is, that He is and always has been God. Such groups also give emphasis to salvation by works. They may claim to be Christian, but by biblical standards they are not.

The word *sect* refers to a religious group that has veered away from the mainstream of a major religion but has retained a primary identification with that religion and does not deny its basic tenets.

A *religion* is a system of worship or living that centers on man's attempts to reach God or a state of enlightenment. It is an outward expression of the faith a person has in someone or something.

Occult comes from a Latin word meaning "hidden, secret, or mysterious." It refers to groups who openly credit Satan or the spirit world for their abilities. Satan, spirits, or gods and goddesses are worshiped and give power for the practitioners to cast spells or curses, divine the future, and communicate with the dead. Occultic groups are entirely opposed to Christ and Christianity.

The use of quotation marks around certain phrases or sentences within a given entry indicates material quoted from one of the sources referenced at the end of the entry or related entry.

Many entries in this dictionary reference a book in the bibliography, which is divided into eight categories. For example, "General: McDowell, pp. 123-30" will lead one to the *General* section of the bibliography in which is listed a book by Josh McDowell entitled *Handbook of Today's Religions*. When two or more books are listed in the bibliography by the same author, or by authors with the same last name, a shortened title (when necessary) follows his name in the entry. When no page numbers are given, the entire book is devoted to one group.

Most of the resources listed are in print. Some that are not have been included because of their timeless nature and possible availability in libraries.

Following the bibliography is a listing of ministries that specialize in cults and religions. These are groups that offer counseling for people involved in cults and sects or that provide information about such groups to churches through newsletters, tracts, books, tapes, or seminars. Ministries that focus on one or more areas are listed under Special Ministries.

This dictionary is not exhaustive. The groups and persons included are ones most likely to occur in America. Others have not been included because they are less influential or do not exist in America.

It is hoped that your study of cults, sects, and religions will lead you to study the Bible for a clearer understanding of what God says. The information given here is based on the latest research and information. By the time this book is printed, some changes may have occurred. Check with your local Christian bookstore for new books on the cults. If you need counseling, consult your pastor.

If you have never had the personal experience of accepting Jesus Christ as your Savior and Lord, consider the following: (1) God loves you and has a wonderful life planned for you (John 10:10). (2) You are a sinner, and your sin keeps you away from God (Romans 3:23; 6:23). (3) Trust Jesus to cleanse your life of sin, and He will do it (1 John 1:9). (4) You can accept God's gift of forgiveness and eternal life right now (John 1:12; Acts 16:31; Revelation 3:20).

If you want forgiveness for your sins, an abundant life, and the promise of eternal life with God, why not pray the following prayer (or one like it) right now? "Dear Jesus, I admit I am a sinner and I can't save myself. I need You. Thank You for dying on the cross in my place. Please come into my heart and forgive my sins and give me that abundant and eternal life You have promised in the Bible. Amen."

Did you pray that prayer sincerely? On the authority of God's Word, Jesus is in your heart right now. So that you can grow in your new Christian life, share what you have done with the pastor of a church and with family members and friends. Find a church where you can worship and study the Bible regularly. Begin having a time of daily prayer and Bible reading.

A

Abilitism

Teaches that each person is God individually and achieves enlightenment through meditation on questions asked in a relating exercise. Founded from a Scientology background in 1965 by H. Charles and Ava Berner. The headquarters and seminary are in Lucerne Valley, California, with centers in several other cities. Berner has written *The Ultimate Formula of Life*.

General: Ellwood, pp. 176-78.

Abode of the Message

This sect is a Sufi community near Lebanon Springs, New York. *See* Sufi Order.

Above All, Don't Wobble

The title of a book written by the late Bhagwan Shree Rajneesh in 1976. *See* Rajneesh International Foundation.

Abundant Life Church

What The Way International calls its meeting places. *See* The Way International.

Academy of Chinese Culture and Health Sciences

College of Chinese medicine in Oakland, California. *See* New Age Movement.

Academy of Parapsychology and Medicine

An organization that promotes research in psychic healing. *See* Holistic Health.

Action

The title of a sect magazine. *See* United Christian Evangelistic Association.

Actualism

A cult that teaches holistic health and that each human being is divine and "infinitely united with mother-father-creator God of cosmic creation consciousness." According to this belief, a person is able to mobilize the powerful potential of his divine nature.

Based in Valley Center, California, with teaching centers in New York City; Dallas and Houston, Texas; Tucson, Arizona; San Francisco, Los Angeles, Orange County, San Diego, and Escondido, California.

New Age: Khalsa, p. 27.

Acupuncture

This theory defines disease as an imbalance in the body's energy flow. Long needles are used to stimulate the body at points lying along various lines of energy flow. *See* Holistic Health.

Adam, E. B.

Cofounder of the Assembly of Yahvah in 1945. *See* Assemblies of Yahweh.

Adams, Frederick M.

Founder of the Goddess Kore cult. *See* Feraferia.

Adamski, George

Claimed to be the first human being to meet and converse with a UFO inhabitant from Venus. Author of *Cosmic Philosophy*, *Flying Saucers Farewell*, *Flying Saucers Have Landed*, *Inside the Space Ships*, and *Questions and Answers by the Royal Order of Tibet*. *See* George Adamski Foundation.

Adler, Margo

A member of the Covenant of the Goddess, second largest national witchcraft organization. She is the author of *Drawing Down the Moon*. *See* Witchcraft.

Advance

The title of a Scientology periodical. *See* Scientology.

Advertising Gifts and Premiums

The name of a mail-order company in California. *See* Synanon Foundation.

Aeromancy

Spiritualist method of divination that is done by observing ripples on a still body of water. *See* Divination.

Aetherius Society
Well-known UFO cult that holds regular meetings and encourages members to be channels of communication with extraterrestrials. This cult, founded in 1954 by George King, has been influenced by the teachings of Spiritualism, Theosophy, and the occult.
King, who calls himself the "Primary Terrestrial Channel" for the "Cosmic Intelligences," claims to be the psychic contact for Master Aetherius, a Venusian, who speaks through him. He further claims that Jesus and the apostle Paul speak through him and that he has ridden in a flying saucer with Jesus and the Virgin Mary.
Publishes the periodicals *Cosmic Voice* and *Spiritual Healing Bulletin* and is based in Hollywood, California. *See also* UFO Cults.
General: Ellwood, pp. 150-56; Larson, *New Book*, p. 105; Melton, *Encyclopedia*, p. 560; Rice, pp. 200-201.

AFC
Acronym of a front group related to the Unification Church. *See* American Freedom Coalition.

Afterlife: The Other Side of Dying
New Age book written by a Christian, Morton Kelsey. *See* New Age Movement.

Ahura Mazda
Supreme and good deity of Zoroastrianism, coequal and coeternal with Augra Mainyu, the evil god. *See* Zoroastrianism.

Aikido
One of the variations of kung fu. *See* Martial Arts.

Akashic Record
Spiritualist belief that every event that has ever happened still exists in the Universal Mind and may be perceived clairvoyantly. *See* Anthroposophical Society.

Alamo Christian Foundation
Cult that considers all other churches dead. It primarily preaches (from the King James Version of the Bible only) the wrath of God rather than love. (Love is considered a heresy.) If a person is in the Spirit, he does not sin, but salvation is lost if he leaves the Foundation. Former adherents tell of deplorable living conditions, mind control, slave labor, expropriation of property and income, and other illegalities. Young people

17

are told, "Parents are your worst enemies." The group's television broadcasts portray adherents as clean and well-dressed.

The cult operates as the Alamo Christian Church in Saugus, California, the Holiness Tabernacle Church in Dyer, Arkansas, the Christian Foundation of Canyon County, California, and the Music Square Church in Tennessee. There are also churches in Chicago, Illinois, and Brooklyn, New York.

The group was founded by Tony and Susan Alamo in 1969. Susan died in 1982 of a cancer that she had claimed would be healed by prayer. Tony planned to bring her back to life but finally buried her. Tony is president of the American Association of Non-Denominational Christian Schools and distributes materials through End Time Books.

General: Larson, *New Book*, pp. 245-47; Tucker, *Another Gospel*, pp. 357-59.

Alive Polarity

A New Age group that offers seminars on such subjects as "Health Building," "Marriage and Family Dynamics," "Fit 'n' Trim," "Spiritual Well-Being," and "Wholistic Polarity Therapy." The organization is based at Murrieta Hot Springs in Murrieta, California, and is directed by Marcia Peterson.

New Age: Khalsa, p. 29.

All and Everything

Book written by cult founder Georgei Ivanovitch Gurdjieff. *See* Gurdjieff Foundation.

All Things Made New

A 1975 book by John Ferraby with the subtitle *A Comprehensive Outline of the Baha'i Faith. See* Baha'i World Faith.

Allen, Brian

Has served as overseer of the Love Family holdings and is the son of actor Steve Allen. *See* Church of Armageddon.

Allred, Owen

Succeeded his brother, Rulon, as leader of the Apostalic United Brethren, a fundamentalist Mormon group. *See* Mormonism.

Allred, Rulon Clark

Founder of the Apostalic United Brethren, a fundamentalist Mormon group. *See* Mormonism.

Almost Armageddon
    Book written by Ellen Gould White. *See* Seventh-day Adventism.

Alpert, Richard
    Founder of the sect Ram Dass and a leader in the New Age movement. *See* Ram Dass.

Altered States of Consciousness (ASC)
    Phenomenon involving interruption or halting of "one's normal patterns of conceptual thought" and brought about by meditation, visualization, and chanting. *See* New Age Movement *and* Spiritualism.

Altschul, Benjamin
    Cult leader in Colorado. *See* Great Among the Nations.

Amalgamated Flying Saucer Clubs of America
    UFO cult that believes extraterrestrials are trying to help us reform and develop sufficiently to enter their universe. Founded in 1956 in Los Angeles, California, by Gabriel Green, who claimed he had received contacts from the planet Clarion. The group publishes *Flying Saucers International* magazine.
    General: Ellwood, pp. 145-49.

Ambassador College
    College in Pasadena, California, operated by the Worldwide Church of God. *See* Worldwide Church of God.

Ambassador College Press
    Publishing division of the Worldwide Church of God, located in Pasadena, California. *See* Worldwide Church of God.

Ambassador International Cultural Foundation
    A front group that operates under the auspices of the Worldwide Church of God. *See* Worldwide Church of God.

Amen, Ra Un Nefer
    Religious name of R. A. Straughn, founder of the cult called the Ausar Auset Society. *See* Ausar Auset Society.

America in Prophecy
    Book by Ellen Gould White that was first published in 1858 as *The Great Controversy. See* Seventh-day Adventism.

American Association of Non-Denominational Christian Schools
    Group headed by Tony Alamo, cofounder of the Alamo Christian Foundation cult. *See* Alamo Christian Foundation.

American Buddhist Movement
Operates the School of Enlightenment in New York City. The school offers training in Zen and Vipassana meditation, Buddhist philosophy and practice, and how to form a Buddhist study group. The group publishes the *American Buddhist Newsletter* monthly and the *American Buddhist Directory*, which lists every Buddhist group in the United States. *See also* Buddhism.
General: Melton, *Encyclopedia*, p. 774.
New Age: Khalsa, p. 30.

American Christian Press
Publishing division of The Way International, located in New Knoxville, Ohio. *See* The Way International.

American Constitution Committee
Front group of the Unification Church founded to propagate "the spirit of the U.S. Constitution." *See* Unification Church.

American Fellowship Services
One of three Way International splinter groups. *See* The Way International.

American Foundation for the Science of Creative Intelligence
Operates 350 teaching centers. *See* Transcendental Meditation.

American Freedom Coalition (AFC)
Front group of the Unification Church that works to advance a conservative agenda and to get conservative candidates elected to public office. The plans are to make it a third political party and to use it to gain a foothold in right-wing Christian circles. The group was begun in 1987 by Korean Col. Bo Hi Pak, Sun Myung Moon's chief lieutenant, and Gary Jarmin, a former official of the Unification Church. *See* Unification Church.

American Muslim Mission
Black sect of Islam that emphasizes black supremacy. The group is now led by Louis Farrakhan but was founded by Wallace Fard, former member of the Community of Islam in the West (originally the Nation of Islam).
General: Melton, *Biographical Dictionary*, pp. 74-75.

American Theosophist
Periodical of the Theosophical Society of America. *See* Theosophy.

Americana Leadership College
School that offers courses on spiritual growth techniques and counseling methods. *See* Inner Peace Movement.

Amnesty International
International social and political organization whose ideology meshes with that of the New Age movement. *See* New Age Movement.

AMORC
Acronym. *See* Ancient Mystical Order Rosae Crucis.

Amos, Clifford
Satanic cult cofounder. *See* Ordo Templi Satanas.

The Analects
One of the four books that contains the teachings of Confucius and is written by his disciples. *See* Confucianism.

Ananda
Religious sect that offers "Practice of Joy" sessions, which teach how to attain boundless energy and inward fulfillment. Worship includes chanting, meditation, Raja Yoga, and *Songs of Divine Joy* (by founder Swami Kriyananda). Group also offers Ananda Meditation Retreat, Cooperative Spiritual Living Program, and Yoga Teacher Training Program.
The sect was founded by J. Donald Walters (now known as Swami Kriyananda) and has a 650-acre "cooperative village" near Nevada City, California. Its business ventures operate under the name Yoga Fellowship, Inc., and gross two million dollars annually. *The Path: A Spiritual Autobiography* by Kriyananda shows the Hindu background of his teachings.
General: Larson, *New Book*, pp. 399-400; Melton, *Encyclopedia*, pp. 706-7.
New Age: Khalsa, p. 31.

Ananda Ashram
Cult headquarters in Monroe, New York. *See* Intercosmic Center of Spiritual Awareness.

Ananda Márga Yoga Society
A Sufi sect in which adherents seek to find "a dynamic blend of inner discovery and social action." Meditation and yoga are used to help persons achieve mental calm and self-realization. "All of creation is a manifestation of the Lord."
Members believe that they are the only ones qualified to control the world. Through their service branch, ERAWS

(Education, Relief, and Welfare Section), volunteers are encouraged to assist in offering meditation programs, establishing food cooperatives, teaching adult literacy programs, and doing drug and alcohol rehabilitation. Their Women's Welfare Department seeks to strengthen women physically and spiritually.

The sect was founded in 1955 in India by Shrii Shrii Anandamúrti. He was convicted as a murderer but later was found innocent and came to America in the 1970s. The group is based in Denver, Colorado, with its major training center in Steamboat Springs, Colorado. The monthly newspaper is the *Sadvipra*.

General: Larson, *New Book*, p. 110; Melton, *Encyclopedia*, pp. 707-8.

New Age: Khalsa, pp. 31-32.

Occult: Wedge, pp. 67-68.

Ananda Meditation Retreat
Sect program that offers training in yoga and meditation. *See* Ananda.

Anandamúrti, Shrii Shrii
Founder of Sufi sect. *See* Ananda Márga Yoga Society.

Anatomy of an Illness as Perceived by the Patient
Book written by Norman Cousins in 1979 that presents illness from a New Age standpoint. *See* New Age Movement.

Ancient, Arabic Order of Nobles of the Mystic Shrine
Masonic organization for Masons who have achieved at least the 32d degree in the Scottish Rite or who have become Knights Templar in the York Rite. *See* Freemasonry.

Ancient Mystical Order Rosae Crucis (AMORC)
One of several groups that claim to be representative of Rosicrucianism. The origins of this group can be traced to the mystery schools of learning established about 1500 B.C. in Egypt. H. Spencer Lewis, who initiated a revival of the order in the United States in 1915, was greatly influenced by Aleister Crowley, "a homosexual, murderer, and practitioner of black sex-magic" who called himself "Beast 666." Lewis tied AMORC to the occult, receiving a charter from Ordo Templi Orientis in 1921.

Parts of the Bible are accepted as "a beautiful poem," but other books are recommended in its place, such as *The Secret Doctrines of Jesus* and other writings of H. Spencer Lewis, *The Book of Jasher*, and books supporting reincarnation.

H. Spencer Lewis incorporated the Pristine Church of the Rose Cross and served as its bishop. The church was later dropped. By the time of his "transition" (death) in 1939, Lewis had established the Rose-Croix University, the Rosicrucian Research Library, and the Egyptian Museum, a popular tourist attraction. Lewis's son, Ralph M., succeeded him as Imperator of the Order.

AMORC is based in San Jose, California, and publishes *The Rosicrucian Digest*, a monthly magazine, and *The Rosicrucian Forum* for members. *See also* Rosicrucianism.

General: Larson, *New Book*, pp. 356-59; McDowell, pp. 221-24; Robertson, pp. 167-68; Tucker, *Another Gospel*, pp. 376-78.

Ancient Science of Soul Travel
Alternate name for the Hindu sect ECKANKAR. *See* ECKANKAR.

Ancient Wisdom
Book written in 1897 by Annie Besant and one of several favorites of New Agers. *See* New Age Movement.

And It Is Divine
Magazine of the Divine Light Mission sect. *See* Divine Light Mission.

Andrews, Lynn
Modern day shaman, who is known as "the Beverly Hills medicine woman." *See* Shamanism.

The Angels
Private police force of the late cult leader Jim Jones. *See* Peoples' Temple Christian Church.

Angels in the Flesh
Name for followers of Brother Julius. *See* Brother Julius' Followers.

Anglo-Israelism (British-Israelism)
A cult that identifies the ten lost tribes of Israel as the Anglo-Saxon nations, particularly Great Britain and the United States. Anglo-Saxons, therefore, are considered God's chosen race. *See* Identity Movement and Worldwide Church of God.

Anglo-Saxon Federation of America
Anglo-Israel group founded in 1928 by Howard B. Rand. The group publishes a newsletter and distributes Rand's

books from its headquarters in Haverhill, Massachusetts. *See* Identity Movement.

The Annals of Spring and Autumn
One of the classics of Chinese literature written by Confucius and included in the anthology *The Five Classics*. *See* Confucianism.

Anthem
Ayn Rand's 1938 novel, which propagated capitalism as God. *See* Ayn Rand.

Anthroposophical Society
Cult that teaches that human beings possess the truth within themselves (anthroposophy means "wisdom of man"). Believes that Jesus was human until He received the Christ-Essence at His baptism and that by means of a certain meditation technique people can also realize the Christ within.

This cult (also called Spiritual Science) is based in New York City and was founded in 1909 by Rudolph Steiner after splitting with Theosophy and Rosicrucianism. A "Christianized" form of this cult is called the Christian Community Church.

Steiner claimed the ability to read the Akashic Record; that is, every event that has ever happened still exists in the Universal Mind and may be perceived clairvoyantly. He claimed he could read this record in the evolution of plants, animals, and minerals.

The society founded the Waldorf Schools to awaken children's spiritual consciousness, and it provides other schools for "defective and maladjusted children and adults" and to teach "eurythmy, an art of movement to speech and music." Publishes Steiner's works and is related to the New Age movement.

General: Ellwood, pp. 106-10; Larson, *New Book*, pp. 111-12; Melton, *Encyclopedia*, pp. 626-28.
New Age: Khalsa, pp. 32-33.
Occult: Koch, pp. 11-18.

Apostalic United Brethren
Fundamentalist Mormon group founded by Rulon Clark Allred, who was later succeeded in leadership by his brother, Owen Allred. *See* Mormonism.

Appenhouse, Dorothy
Current president of the Theosophical Society of America. *See* Theosophy.

Applied Kinesiology
Belief that the "strength or weakness of certain muscle groups reflects the status of your internal organs, nutrition, emotional well-being, and even your spirituality." *See* Holistic Health.

Applied Scholastics
Group that offers "communications" courses to corporations. *See* Scientology.

Aquarian Age Church
Cult located in Arleta, California, that believes a person is "free to believe and develop spiritually as" he is *"inwardly directed."* Provides "Ageless Wisdom teachings, Meditation, and Spiritual Healing" in small group settings.
This group uses the writings of Alice A. Bailey and other theosophical writers.
New Age: Khalsa, p. 33.

The Aquarian Conspiracy: Personal & Social Transformation in the 1980s
Book by Margaret Ferguson published in 1980. It probably has done more in the past decade to promote New Age ideology on a popular level than any other book. *See* New Age Movement.

The Aquarian Gospel of Jesus the Christ
A New Age version of the life of Christ written by Levi Dowling in 1907. Teaches that all things are God and all things are one and that Jesus went to India to learn the "truth" before He began His ministry.
The book influenced Timothy Drew, the founder of the Community of Islam in the West, and has been an authoritative or Spiritualists. *See* New Age Movement *and* Spiritualism.

Aquarian Lights
Title of cult magazine. *See* International Church of Ageless Wisdom.

Aquarian Minyon
Jewish New Age group in Berkeley, California, that combines the practice of Jewish festivals and holy days with Kabbalah and New Age thought.
New Age: Khalsa, p. 33.

Aquino, Michael A.
A former lieutenant colonel in the U. S. Army who is founder and leader of the Temple of Set, a Satanic church in

California. Also author of *The Book of Coming Forth by Night*, apparently written after he had conjured up Satan. *See* Satanism.

Arcana Coelestia
Heavenly Mysteries Contained in the Sacred Scriptures. A book written by Emanuel Swedenborg in 1749. *See* Church of the New Jerusalem.

Arcane School
An organization, sponsored by the Lucis Trust, that trains people in New Age thought. Originally founded in New York City by Alice A. Bailey to investigate esoteric philosophy. *See* New Age Movement.

Arduin Grimoire®
Fantasy role-playing game, similar to Dungeons and Dragons®, that teaches occultic practices. *See* Occult.

A.R.E.
Abbreviation. *See* Association for Research and Enlightenment.

Arica Institute
Organization that emphasizes yoga, diet programs, chanting, religious dance, and exercises, all of which are designed to lead people to new levels of consciousness. One type of meditation used requires the student to focus on separate sections of the body for specified amounts of time. The group's background is primarily Sufism, but it includes elements of Shamanism, Buddhism, Confucianism, and the New Age movement.

Founded by Oscar Ichazo in Arica, Chile, in 1971 but now has headquarters in New York City. The Arica course lasts for six months and costs about $3,000.

General: Larson, *New Book*, pp. 113-14; Melton, *Encyclopedia*, pp. 685-86.

Arigo
Psychic surgeon and occultist in Brazil. *See* Psychic Surgery.

Arithmancy
Spiritualist method of divination that is done by reading numbers associated with a person's name and birth date. *See* Divination.

Armstrong, Garner Ted

Son of Worldwide Church of God founder Herbert W. Armstrong. He once helped his father with the church but was put out of the organization in 1978 because of alleged immoral conduct. Garner Ted formed his own group, based in Tyler, Texas, called the Church of God International. *See* Church of God International *and* Worldwide Church of God.

Armstrong, Herbert W.

Founder of the Anglo-Israelism organization that is best known by the name Worldwide Church of God. *See* Worldwide Church of God.

Armstrongism

Alternate name for the teachings of the Worldwide Church of God. *See* Worldwide Church of God.

Arthur Morgan School

School that gives emphasis to drawing out creative potential, envisioning a healthy planet, and actualizing that vision. "Based on Gandhi's philosophy that a 'school should be built by the children, should seek to be self-supporting, and should never be finished.'" Founded in 1961 by Elizabeth and Ernest Morgan in Burnsville, North Carolina.

New Age: Khalsa, p. 35.

As It Is

Book written by Robert de Grimston in 1967 that spells out his occultic philosophy. *See* Process Church of the Final Judgement.

Asatru Free Assembly

Occultic group that teaches that man is his own savior and can control his destiny by heroic action, defending his rights, and not compromising his beliefs. Also teaches reincarnation and the enjoyment of free sex without guilt.

The group was founded in Breckenridge, Texas, by Stephen A. McNallen in 1971. Background is Norse neopaganism (Norse gods and goddesses are worshiped). *The Runestone* is the quarterly newspaper.

Some related groups are: Odinist Fellowship, Odinist Committee in England, and Asatrufolks in Iceland. *See also* Witchcraft.

General: Larson, *New Book*, pp. 115-19; Melton, *Encyclopedia*, pp. 641-42.

Asatrufolks
   Norse neopagan cult in Iceland. *See* Asatru Free Assembly.

Ascended Masters
   Disembodied spirits who have reached the highest level of spiritual consciousness and now guide the spiritual evolution of mankind. Sometimes referred to as the "Great White Brotherhood," "enlightened masters," and "Universal Brotherhood." *See* New Age Movement *and* Spiritualism.

Asimov, Isaac
   Science fiction author and member of a New Age political action group. *See* Planetary Citizens.

Aspire
   Name of a daily devotional magazine published monthly by the Divine Science Federation International. *See* Divine Science Federation International.

Assemblies of Yahweh
   Several groups begun out of the Sacred Name Movement of the 1930s. In all these groups emphasis is placed on Yahweh as the only true name of God and as necessary for salvation. Jesus is called Yahsua and is equated with Zeus. The Holy Spirit is not seen as a person but a thing. The groups stress the importance of keeping biblical commandments, laws, feasts, holy days, food restrictions, and tithing.
   One group is based in Holt, Michigan, and was founded by C. O. Dodd in 1939. It publishes *The Faith* magazine and distributes literature through its Faith Bible and Tract Society. Congregations are located around the country.
   The Bethel group is based in Bethel, Pennsylvania, and was begun as an offshoot of the Seventh-day Church of God in the late 1920s. It rejects the concept of hell and recommends nonviolence and conscientious objection to military service. The group publishes the monthly *Sacred Name Broadcaster* and does its own translation of the Bible called *The Sacred Scriptures* (Bethel Edition). It also sponsors a radio program called "The Sacred Name Broadcast," featuring Jacob O. Meyer.
   The Assembly of YHWHOSANA was founded in the 1970s by Laycher Gonzales and is based in Boone, Colorado, with another congregation near Pueblo, Colorado. Members oppose the use of such diverse things as personal photographs ("graven images"), medical treatment, Social Security, banks,

Medicare, unemployment insurance, artwork, alcohol, tobacco, jewelry, dancing, dating, haircuts, and cologne. They do not use the names for months and days and do not celebrate Christmas or Easter.

The Institute of Divine Metaphysical Research was founded in 1931 by Henry Clifford Kinley after a "face-to-face conversation with God." The Scripture Research Association was founded by A. B. Traina in the 1940s in Brandywine, Maryland. He published his own translation of the Bible called *The Holy Name Bible*.

The Assembly of Yahvah was founded in 1945 by L. D. Snow and E. B. Adam. Congregations are in Winfield and Jackson Gap, Alabama. The group publishes *The Elijah Messenger*.

General: Larson, *New Book*, pp. 124-28; Melton, *Encyclopedia*, pp. 451-56.

Assembly of Yahvah

Sect founded in 1945 that now has congregations in Winfield and Jackson Gap, Alabama. *See under* Assemblies of Yahweh.

Assembly of YHWHOSANA

Sect based in Boone, Colorado, that was founded in the 1970s by Laycher Gonzales. *See under* Assemblies of Yahweh.

Association for Holistic Health

New Age group that supports holistic healing practices. *See* Holistic Health *and* New Age Movement.

Association for Humanistic Psychology

International New Age network that teaches human potential, personal growth, and holistic health. Founded by Abraham Maslow, the father of the Human Potential Movement. *See* New Age Movement.

New Age: Larson, pp. 240, 244.

Association for Research and Enlightenment (A.R.E.)

The metaphysical and Spiritualist organization founded in Virginia Beach, Virginia, in 1931 to research and preserve the works of Edgar Cayce. Cayce was known as the "sleeping prophet" because he gave his prophetic readings while he "slept." He also prescribed remedies for illnesses. He believed that God is a creative force, the universal "creative energy." According to Cayce, salvation comes by "self-transformation through belief in one's own intrinsic divinity." He also claimed to have written the book of Acts in a former life as Lucius.

Cayce taught reincarnation: "evolution of the spirit of man through many successive lifetimes on earth until finally the spirit has reached a perfection enjoined on us by Christ." Jesus, one of many sons of God in the land of Atlantis who went astray, took thirty reincarnations to make it. Under this view, Jesus had lived as Adam, Melchizedek, and the father of Zoroaster. (Cayce claimed to have also lived as the grandfather of Zoroaster.)

The A.R.E., presently headed by Hugh Lynn Cayce, Edgar's son, offers workshops on self-hypnosis, visualization, and psychic guidance, and promotes research in psychic healing. The major books and publications promoted or published by the organization include *There Is a River*, by Thomas Sugrue (official biography of Edgar Cayce), *Edgar Cayce: The Sleeping Prophet*, by Jess Stearn, *Many Mansions*, and *The Edgar Cayce Reader*.

General: Larson, *New Book*, pp. 129-34; McDowell, pp. 169-74; Tucker, *Another Gospel*, pp. 359-60.

Occult: Koch, pp. 57-59.

Association for Transpersonal Psychology

New Age-related group that teaches that all people are part of a "divine oneness." Ken Wilbur has led in this field. *See* New Age Movement.

Association of Unity Churches

Denominational name for the group of churches that adhere to the Unity School of Christianity. *See* Unity School of Christianity.

Astara Foundation

An eclectic cult that combines Egyptian mysteries, Spiritualism, Theosophy, yoga, Christianity, Masonry, Rosicrucianism, and the occult into a healing philosophy. It believes that God was most completely revealed in Christ, the "Light of the World," but denies the deity of Christ. Members "earn interest in peace of mind and enlightenment" so that, when they "fade from consciousness and go to the Valley of Rewards," they will receive "all they have deposited in the Cosmic Bank." They also seek the assistance of spirit guides of the Universal Brotherhood.

The group, with headquarters in Upland, California, was founded in 1951 by Robert and Earlyne Chaney, former Spiritualists. The textbook is *Astara's Book of Life*, and the monthly publication is *The Voice of Astara*.

General: Larson, *New Book*, pp. 135-38; Melton, *Encyclopedia*, pp. 597-98.

Astara's Book of Life
Textbook for the Astara Foundation cult. *See* Astara Foundation.

Astral Projection
Practice of projecting the soul to another location. Also called soul travel. *See* Spiritualism.

Astral Projection
Book written by Melita Denning and Osborne Phillips, Spiritualist cult leaders. *See* Order Aurum Solis.

Astral Travel
1980 book with the sub-title *Your Guide to the Secrets of Out-of-the-Body Experiences*. Written by Gavin and Yvonne Frost, founders of the Church and School of Wicca. *See* Witchcraft.

Astro-Soul
Advanced spiritual program that deals with astral projection, healing, communicating with departed souls, and exploring past lives. *See* Inner Peace Movement.

Astrology
Spiritualist religion that believes stars cause events to happen. Astrologers say, "The stars don't only forecast our future, but they also guide us to the coming of a new Spiritual Master." A person's future is charted by plotting the position of the stars and planets at the time of his birth using the *Ephemeris*. The resulting chart is called a horoscope. Jesus is seen as a superpsychic human being, not God.

Astrology was developed in Mesopotamia about 3000 B.C. Babylonian ziggurats were temples built for worship of the moon, stars, and planets. Modern astrological practice is based on this centuries-old understanding of astronomy. New and more recent astronomical discoveries are ignored. *See also* Divination.

General: Boa, pp. 119-29; Larson, *New Book*, pp. 139-45; McDowell, pp. 160-66; Tucker, *Another Gospel*, pp. 342-47.

See also Miscellaneous.

Astrology, Mundane and Spiritual
Astrological classic written by S. R. Parchment in 1933.
See Rosicrucian Anthroposophic League.

Atlantis
The name of a mythical island with a large, thriving population; described by Plato in two of his dialogues, *Timaeus* and *Critias*, as a paradise island beyond the Pillars of Hercules. Plato said it sank about nine thousand years before his time.

Several groups have picked up on this theory, including the Association for Research and Enlightenment, the Church Universal and Triumphant, ECKANKAR, Spiritualism, Theosophy, and various New Age groups. They claim the inhabitants of Atlantis were superhumans and that the survivors of the sinking island escaped to Tibet to become the ascended masters. These groups claim to communicate with such ascended masters. The 1980s movies *Cocoon* and *Cocoon II* contain references to Atlantis as well as to extraterrestrials.

Lemuria (also called Mu) is a similar mythical island in the Pacific or Indian Ocean. *See* Spiritualism.

Atlas Shrugged
Ayn Rand's 1957 novel that propagates an "elite intellectual and social caste system." *See* Ayn Rand.

The Atman Project
1980 book by Ken Wilber, leading figure in transpersonal psychology. *See* New Age Movement.

The Auditor
Title of a Scientology periodical. *See* Scientology.

Augra Mainyu
The Zoroastrian god of evil, who is viewed as being coequal and coeternal with the good god Ahura Mazda. *See* Zoroastrianism.

Augury
Spiritualist method of divination that is done by observing the flight of birds. *See* Divination.

Aum
Book by Sri Chinmoy. *See* Sri Chinmoy Centers.

Auras
Colorful fields of energy radiating from a physical body. New Agers claim an aura is a manifestation of a person's higher self, and they use the pattern of the aura to determine a

person's emotional, physical, and spiritual condition. Kirlian photography is used to capture auras on film. *See* New Age Movement.

Ausar Auset Society
Group that seeks to apply the occult truths of Rosicrucianism to Afro-Americans. It was founded by R. A. Straughn (known as Ra Un Nefer Amen) in the mid-1970s. Straughn, a black man, is a former member of the Rosicrucian Anthroposophical League. The society publishes *The Oracle of Toth* magazine. *See* Rosicrucianism.

Autobiography of a Yogi
1971 book written by Paramahansa Yogananda. *See* Self-realization Fellowship Foundation.

Automatic Drawing
Occultic practice, done while in a trance, of drawing pictures relayed from the spirit of a dead person. *See* Spiritualism.

Automatic Writing
Occultic practice, done while in a trance, of writing messages relayed from the spirit of a dead person. *See* Spiritualism.

Avatar
The general designation for a person considered to be the reincarnation of a Hindu deity in human form. Leaders of several Hindu sects claim to be avatars. *See* Hinduism.

Avesta
Title of the Zoroastrian scriptures. *See* Zoroastrianism.

AWAKE!
Monthly Jehovah's Witness periodical. *See* Jehovah's Witnesses.

Awakener
Regular Sufi publication. *See* Sufism Reoriented, Inc.

Awakening Heart Seminar
Human potential seminar. *See* Insight Transformational Seminars.

The Awakening Intelligence
Book by Jiddu Krishnamurti. *See* Krishnamurti Foundation of America.

Awareness Through Movement
Alternate name for Functional Integration, a method of holistic health developed by Israeli scientist Moshe Felden-

krais that uses approximately one thousand physical and meditative exercises related to yoga. Also called the Feldenkrais Method. *See* Holistic Health.

Ayn Rand
American writer who espoused the philosophy of objectivism and the "morality of rational self-interest." This philosophy "propagates a very elite intellectual and social caste system."

She taught that "capitalism is God, and the egotism of man is the driving force of God" and that "through science and technology, man can produce a utopia here on earth."

Ayn Rand wrote several novels promoting her views, including *We, the Living* (1936), *Anthem* (1938), *The Fountainhead* (1943), and *Atlas Shrugged* (1957). She also wrote nonfiction works, such as *For the New Intellectual* (1961) and *The Virtue of Selfishness* (1965).

See Gene Aven, *My Search* (Seattle: Life Messengers, n.d.).

Ayurveda
Said to be the oldest and most accurate form of holistic healing. It focuses on balancing the four "instincts" of life: religion, finances, procreation, and freedom. This balance is achieved through proper diet, the practice of yoga, and adherence to classical Hindu teachings. *See* Holistic Health.

B

Baba Lovers

Name for the followers of sect founder Meher Baba. *See* Sufism Reoriented, Inc.

Baba, Meher

Founder of the sect Sufism Reoriented, Inc., who from 1925 until his death in 1969 did not speak at all. *See* Sufism Reoriented, Inc.

Baba, Sai

Sect founder. *See* SAI Foundation.

Baba, Sathya Sai

Sect leader and avatar of Shiva and Shakti. *See* SAI Foundation.

Babbitt, Elwood

Medium from Massachusetts who claims to be a channeler of Mark Twain, Albert Einstein, William Wordsworth, Christ, Vishnu, and various gods. These channeled messages have been transcribed into such books as *Voices of Spirit* and *Talks with Christ*. Babbitt teaches that "you, in your own individuality, are a division of the Soul of Being, yet in all of your members you are united as one, the one and only great universe of Self." *See* New Age Movement.

Bach, Richard

Author of *Jonathan Livingston Seagull*, a best-selling book of the early 1970s. Reportedly the book was channeled to Bach by a being who came to him in the form of a seagull. *See* New Age Movement *and* Silva Mind Control.

Back to Godhead
   Colorful Hindu sect periodical. *See* Hare Krishna.
Bahá, 'Abdu'l
   Former leader of the Baha'i religion. *See* Baha'i World
Faith.
Baha'i Publishing Co.
   Publishing arm of the Baha'i religion, located in Wilmette, Illinois. *See* Baha'i World Faith.
Baha'i World Faith
   Religious sect that has its roots in Islam and pantheism.
Believes there is no Trinity, but that Abraham, Zoroaster,
Buddha, Jesus, and Muhammad were all equally messengers
from God. Jesus was a prophet of the Christians, one of nine
manifestations of the divine being. Bahá'u'lláh was the messiah and the source of revelation. Sin is the absence of good in
the life of the faithful. Salvation is achieved by prayer, personal sacrifice, and attending the Nineteen Day Feast on the
first day of each month of the Baha'i calendar. The goal is
universal brotherhood and to unite all religions into one: "the
earth is but one country and mankind its citizens." Worshipers recite the scriptures of all religions.
   Sacred writings are the works of Bahá'u'lláh (especially
Tablets); 'Abdu'l Bahá, his son; and Shoghi Effendi, his
grandson. *Star of the West* is the official publication. *All
Things Made New*, by John Ferraby, is another publication.
   The movement was founded by Mirza Husayn' Ali (today known as Bahá'u'lláh), a young Sufi in Iran in 1863.
Present world headquarters is in Haifa, Israel, and United
States headquarters is on the shore of Lake Michigan in Wilmette, Illinois, just north of Chicago. The governing body is
called the National Spiritual Assembly.
   The Baha'is own the Baha'i Publishing Company in
Wilmette and operate schools in Colorado Springs, Colorado;
Geyserville, California; Eliot, Maine; and Davison, Michigan. The song "Year of Sunday," by Seals and Croft, espouses the Baha'i viewpoint.
   General: Larson, *New Book*, pp. 146-50; Martin, *Kingdom*, pp. 271-78; Robertson, p. 163; Tucker, *Another Gospel*,
pp. 285-98.
   Miscellaneous: Beckwith; Miller.
Bahá'u'lláh.
   Founder of the Baha'i sect. *See* Baha'i World Faith.

Bailey, Alice Anne
Author whose works are used extensively in Spiritualism, Theosophy, and the New Age movement. Bailey, considered a New Age prophetess, based her writings on the teachings of Djwhal Khual, an ascended master. She founded the Arcane School and contributed the following books: *The Reappearance of the Christ, The Coming World Order,* and *The Externalisation of the Hierarchy.* See New Age Movement.

Ballard, Edna Wheeler
Cofounder of the I AM Movement. *See* I AM Movement.

Ballard, Guy Warren
Cofounder of the I AM Movement. Under the pen name Godfré Ray King he wrote *The Magic Presence* and *Unveiled Mysteries. See* I AM Movement.

Baraka Holistic Center for Therapy and Research
Organization that practices holistic medicine. *See* Movement of Spiritual Inner Awareness.

Barnett, Donald Lee
Founder of the Community Chapel in Seattle, Washington. *See* Fundamentalist Fringe Movements.

"Battlestar Galactica"
This movie and television series (now in syndication) contains images of Mormon theology and history. *See* Mormonism.

Be Here Now
1971 autobiography of Richard Alpert, New Age leader and founder of Ram Dass. *See* Ram Dass.

Be Still and Know
Book published by the Foundation of Human Understanding and its publishing arm, Foundation Press. *See* Foundation of Human Understanding.

Beacon Press
Publishing house of the Unitarian Universalist Association, located in Boston, Massachusetts. *See* Unitarian Universalist Association.

Belhayes, Iris
Channeler of Enid, a nineteenth-century "earthy" Irish woman. *See* Channeling.

Belk, J. Blanton
Executive director of the Moral Re-armament sect. *See* Moral Re-armament.

Bell, Arthur L.
Founder of Christ's Church of the Golden Rule. *See* Christ's Church of the Golden Rule.

Bell Bell
"Giggly six-year old from the legendary lost civilization of Atlantis," who is channeled by Taryn Krivé. *See* Channeling.

Bellweather
Metaphysical foundation set up by John Naisbitt, author of the book *Megatrends* and a New Age lecturer. *See* New Age Movement.

Bender, Deborah
Feminist activist and member of the Covenant of the Goddess, second largest national witchcraft organization. *See* Witchcraft.

Benjamine, Elbert
Founder of the occultic group Church of Light. Under the pen name C. C. Zain he wrote the twenty-one-lesson course *Brotherhood of Light Lessons*. *See* Church of Light.

Berg, Moses
Founder of the Children of God. (His original name was David Brant Berg.) *See* Children of God.

Berkeley Psychic Institute
Seminary of the Church of Divine Man in Berkeley, California. *See* Church of Divine Man.

Berner, Ava, and H. Charles
Founders of Abilitism, a Scientology-based cult. Charles wrote *The Ultimate Formula of Life*. *See* Abilitism.

Berry, Thomas
Jesuit priest and respected New Age author whose writing teaches that there is something sacred about everything. He encourages people to treat everything as honored and precious manifestations of God. *See* New Age Movement.

Bertran, J.
Founder of the Universal Harmony Foundation. *See* Universal Harmony Foundation.

Besant, Annie Wood
Successor to Madame Blavatsky and Henry S. Olcott as leader of the Theosophical Society. Besant wrote two books

used by the New Age movement: *Ancient Wisdom* and *Esoteric Christianity. See* New Age Movement *and* Theosophy.

Bethards, Betty
Spiritualist cult leader and author of *The Sacred Sword* and *Sex and Psychic Energy. See* Inner Light Foundation.

Bey, Hamid
Egyptian founder of the sect named Coptic Fellowship of America. *See* Coptic Fellowship of America.

Beyond and Beyond
Book by Bhagwan Shree Rajneesh. *See* Rajneesh International Foundation.

Beyond Hypnosis
1987 book by William Hewitt that presents "a program for developing your psychic and healing power." Used as a basis for SOAR, an educational curriculum that teaches children they can achieve anything they can imagine. *See* New Age Movement.

Bhagavad Gita
Most sacred and most widely read Hindu text. *See* Hare Krishna *and* Hinduism.

Bhajan, Yogi
Leader of the Healthy, Happy, Holy Organization, a Sikh sect. *See* Healthy, Happy, Holy Organization.

Bhaktivedanta Book Trust
A Hare Krishna publishing house. *See* Hare Krishna.

Biblical Research Center
Bible research group for The Way International. *See* The Way International.

Bilalian News
Periodical of the Community of Islam in the West sect. *See* Community of Islam in the West.

Bilalians
Alternate name for adherents to Community of Islam in the West. *See* Community of Islam in the West.

Bill, Annie C.
Founder of the Church of the Universal Design and author of the book *Science and Reality. See* Church of the Universal Design.

Bioenergetic Analysis
Psychotherapy that involves stretching the body in abnormal ways and measuring physical and emotional reaction to the stress. *See* Holistic Health.

Biofeedback
Method of bringing heart rate, skin temperature, and brain-wave pattern under control by mental concentration. Measurement instruments feed information back to the client. In some cases, biofeedback has been tried as a tool for creating altered states of consciousness. *See* Holistic Health.

Biorhythms
Tool for revealing human potential that was developed by Wilhelm Fliess out of his interest in mystical speculation and numerology. Physical, emotional, and intellectual cycles are plotted on a chart to warn of critical days when caution should be exercised. *See* Spiritualism.

Bird, Christopher
Coauthor of *The Secret Life of Plants*. *See* Plant Communication.

Bishop Devernon LeGrand's Church
Cult group led by Devernon LeGrand, who is known as "Reverend Doctor." He and his followers have been accused of rape and beating deaths, and of posing as nuns to solicit money. *See* James C. Hefley, *The Youthnappers* (Wheaton, Ill.: Victor, 1977), p. 161.

Black Hebrews
Sect of Judaism that is composed of blacks. *See* Thomas Whitfield, *From Night to Sunlight* (Nashville: Broadman, 1980).

Black Mass
Main ritual of Satanic churches that perverts the Roman Catholic mass and leads worshipers to blaspheme and ridicule Christianity. *See* Satanism.

Black Muslims
Alternate and more familiar name for the Islamic sect Community of Islam in the West. *See* Community of Islam in the West.

The Black Raven
Popular occult magic spell book. *See* Magick.

Blavatsky, Helena Petrovna
Cofounder of the Theosophy movement. *Isis Unveiled*, *The Secret Doctrine*, and her other writings are used in the New Age movement. *See* New Age Movement *and* Theosophy.

Blessing Quarterly
Periodical aimed exclusively at members of the Unification Church. *See* Unification Church.

Blessing, William Lester
Founder of the House of Prayer for All People. *See* House of Prayer for All People.

Blighton, Paul W.
Founder of the Holy Order of MANS cult. *See* Holy Order of MANS.

Blob, Charlotte
Founder of the UFO Education Center in Valley Center, California, which was set up to perpetuate the work of George Adamski. (Adamski claimed to be the first human to encounter aliens from Venus.) *See* George Adamski Foundation.

Bodhidharma
Founder of the Zen Buddhist sect around 600 B.C. *See* Zen Buddhism.

The Body of Christ
A communal group, also known as The Body, The End Time Ministry, and The Movement, in which members call themselves "manifested sons of God" and seek to become perfect. They are forced to switch loyalty from their families to the group, to disavow any affection for parents, children, spouses, even pets. They sign over their personal property and pensions to the group and raise their own food.

The group was founded in 1962 by C. E. Cobb, Sam Fife, and Dr. James Meffen, and follows the teachings of Fife. Its communes, generically called "wilderness farms," are located in Alabama, Florida, Georgia, Mississippi, Ohio, Texas, British Columbia, Guatemala, and Peru. The loosely connected settlements may have various specific names: in Dallas, the Dallas Northtown Church; near Eupora, Mississippi, the Church of Sapa. Many others are referred to as Christian Ministries. *See* James and Marcia Rudin, *Prison or Paradise?* (Philadelphia: Fortress, 1980), pp. 72-74.

41

Bon
    Pre-Buddhist religion of Tibet that included the practice of devil worship and witchcraft. *See* T. Lobsang Rampa.

The Book
    Book written by Bhagwan Shree Rajneesh and published by the Chidvilas Foundation. *See* Rajneesh International Foundation.

The Book of Ceremonies
    One of the classics of Chinese literature that was collected and edited by Confucius into *The Five Classics*. It teaches how to act the right or traditional way. *See* Confucianism.

The Book of Changes (I Ching)
    One of the classics of Chinese literature collected and edited by Confucius into *The Five Classics*. Used in divination. *See* Confucianism, Divination, *and* Martial Arts.

The Book of Coming Forth by Night
    Written by Michael A. Aquino after he had conjured up Satan. *See* Satanism *and* Temple of Set.

The Book of Enoch
    Written by Benjamin Purnell, founder of the Israelite House of David sect. *See* Israelite House of David.

The Book of Jasher
    Regarded as scripture. *See* Ancient Mystical Order Rosae Crucis.

The Book of Mencius
    One of the four books of Confucius's teachings. Written by Mencius, a student of the teachings of Confucius, who developed them into a system. *See* Confucianism.

The Book of Mormon
    One of the scriptural authorities of Mormonism. Written by Joseph Smith, Jr., in 1830. *See* Mormonism.

A Book of Pagan Rituals
    Popular book of neopagan rituals written in 1974 by Donna Cole and Ed Fitch. *See* Witchcraft.

The Book of Poetry
    One of the classics of Chinese literature collected and edited by Confucius into *The Five Classics*. He believed that reading poetry would help a man become virtuous. *See* Confucianism.

The Book of Shadows
Sacred book of witchcraft. Also can refer to a notebook of occult magic spells and rituals kept by people involved in Satanism. *See* Witchcraft.

Book of Toth
Egyptian occultic book that shares the wisdom of their gods. Tarot cards are based on this book. *See* Tarot Cards.

Booth, Harry L.
Cofounder of the now defunct Church of Satanic Brotherhood. *See* Satanism.

Boston Church of Christ
Leading group in the Discipling Movement. Based in Boston, Massachusetts. The pastor is Kip McKean. "Pillar" churches are located in Atlanta, Georgia; Chicago, Illinois; Denver, Colorado; London; New York City; San Francisco, California; and other cities around the world. *See* Discipling Movement.

BOTA
Occultic group acronym. *See* Builders of the Adytum.

Brahma
Major Hindu deity, the creator. *See* Hinduism.

Branham Tabernacle
Center of worship for followers of Branhamism in Arizona. *See* Branhamism.

Branham, William Marrion
Cult founder. Author of *The Seven Church Ages*. *See* Branhamism.

Branhamism
The doctrine of the Trinity is denied. Jesus was a created being, not the eternal son of God.

Founded by the late William Marrion Branham, a nontrinitarian preacher. In 1946 he supposedly saw an angel in a cave who gave him healing powers. His congregation in Jeffersonville, Indiana, became his primary channel for teaching. He predicted future events (some right, some wrong). His book, *The Seven Church Ages*, set the year 1977 for the beginning of the Millennium. He was killed in 1965 by a drunken driver.

Branham's followers believe the true church was restored through Branham's ministry. They distribute tracts and taped messages. Branham Tabernacle and the Tucson Taber-

nacle in Arizona are centers of worship. Spoken Word Publishers still prints his sermons.
General: Larson, *New Book*, pp. 156-58; Melton, *Encyclopedia*, p. 330.

Bread for the World
Hunger program. *See* New Age Movement.

Brooks, Nona Lovell
Cult cofounder and leading figure in the New Thought movement. *See* Divine Science Federation International.

Brother Julius' Followers
Brother Julius is also called the "Second Coming of Christ." Followers are called "Angels in the Flesh." (James C. Hefley, *The Youthnappers* [Wheaton: Victor, 1977], p. 161.)

Brotherhood of Light Lessons
Written by C. C. Zain (Elbert Benjamine) in 1934. A twenty-one-lesson course on the twenty-one branches of occult science. *See* Church of Light.

The Brotherhood of Spiritual Movements
Helps persons create and lead their own spiritual growth programs. *See* Inner Peace Movement.

Brothers of Our Father Jesus
Alternate group name. *See* Penitentes.

Brown, Edward H.
Cult leader. *See* Fraternitas Rosae Crucis.

Brown, K. Bradford
Episcopal priest and cofounder of a human potential seminar. *See* Life Training.

Brown, Patterson
Sect founder and former professor of philosophy. *See* Christ Brotherhood.

Buchman, Frank Nathan Daniel
Sect founder. *See* Moral Re-armament.

Buchmanism
Alternate sect name. *See* Moral Re-armament.

Buckland, Raymond and Rosemary
Teachers of Gardnerian Witchcraft credited with reviving witchcraft in America in the 1960s. Leaders of Saxon Witchcraft based in Charlottesville, Virginia. *See* Witchcraft.

Budapest, Zsuanna
Feminist activist. Member of the Covenant of the Goddess, second largest national witchcraft organization. *See* Witchcraft.

Buddha
Born Siddhartha Gautama in India. Founder of one of the major world religions. *See* Buddhism.

Buddhism
Nirvana, the absence of physical desire and suffering, is the final goal. Religious merit is gained by observing the precepts, giving generously to the monks, and worshiping the relics of the Buddha.

Began in India about 500 B.C. as a result of Hindus becoming disillusioned with beliefs of their religion, including the beliefs about the caste system and reincarnation. Founded by the Buddha (enlightened one), born Siddhartha Gautama, the son of a ruler. He renounced the princely life of pleasure and became a beggar seeking wisdom.

The original and conservative branch, Theravada Buddhism in India, reveres a group of three sacred writings called *Tripitaka*. Mahayana Buddhism, the liberal branch in China and Japan, is devoted to a massive 5,000-volume canon of scripture. Mahayana Buddhism has spawned Nichiren Shoshu and Zen Buddhism, both practiced in the West.

General: Boa, pp. 25-31; Larson, *New Book*, pp. 72-83; McDowell, pp. 304-24.

The Builders
Founded by Norman D. Paulsen. Described in his book *Christ Consciousness*. Has established communities in Salt Lake City, Utah, and on 700,000-acre Big Spring Ranch near Wells, Nevada. Operates a farm, ranch, and greenhouse. Background is the Self-realization Fellowship.

General: Melton, *Encyclopedia*, p. 505.

New Age: Khalsa, pp. 42-43.

Builders of the Adytum (BOTA)
Kabbalah and the use of Tarot cards are prominent features. Background is Eastern mysticism and the occult.

Founded in 1920 by Paul Foster Case, who believed he had been led to do it by a "Master of Wisdom." He moved BOTA to Los Angeles in 1933. After his death, Ann Davies succeeded him. Since her death in 1975, a panel of six ministers leads the group.

General: Ellwood, pp. 147-50.

Builders of the Dawn: Community Lifestyles in a Changing World

Written by Gordon Davidson and Corinne McLaughlin in 1986. *See* Sirius Community.

Burton, Robert

Leader of Fellowship of Friends. *See* Fellowship of Friends.

Butler, Richard

Sect leader. *See* Church of Jesus Christ Christian, Aryan Nations.

The Butterfly Rises

Written by Kit Tremain in 1987 describing her transformation through the channeling of Verna Yater, Kevin Ryerson, and others. *See* Channeling.

C

Cabot, Laurie
Officially christened witch of Salem, Massachusetts. *See* Witchcraft.

Caddy, Peter and Eileen
Founded the Findhorn Community in Scotland that serves as a prototype New Age learning center and think tank. *See* New Age Movement.

Cafh Foundation
Teaches that a person can, within himself, resolve problems that confront humanity. Provides activities in Boston, Massachusetts; New York City; Washington, D.C.; St. Louis, Missouri; and Los Angeles and San Francisco, California.
New Age: Khalsa, p. 43.

Camaron-Fraser, Laura
First woman Episcopal priest in the Pacific Northwest. Forced to resign when she admitted that a spirit named Jonah spoke through her. *See* Channeling.

Camp Gunnison
The Way Family Ranch at Gunnison, California. *See* The Way International.

Camp New Hope
Retreat center in Ulster County, New York. *See* Unification Church.

Candomblé
Alternate name for Macumba, spirit worship practiced in South America, primarily in Brazil. Also called Umbanda. *See* Voodoo.

Capnomancy
   Spiritualist practice of divination by reading the smoke from a fire or incense. *See* Divination.

Capra, Fritjof
   Physicist and "significant thinker" of the New Age movement. Author of *The Tao of Physics*, a union of science and Eastern occultic religions, and *The Turning Point*, a manifesto of New Age ideology. *See* New Age Movement.

Carlita
   Psychic surgeon in Mexico who operates in the dark. *See* Psychic Surgery.

CARP
   Acronym for the Collegiate Association for the Research of Principles, which recruits members from college areas. Raises money to support "international efforts," which allegedly goes into the leaders' coffers. Members must sell their quota of items on the street or be ridiculed by the group. *See* Unification Church.

CARP Monthly
   Periodical. *See* Unification Church.

Cartomancy
   Spiritualist method of divination by reading playing cards or Tarot cards. *See* Divination.

Cartouche
   Egyptian method of fortune telling. *See* Divination.

Case, Paul Foster
   Occultic group founder. *See* Builders of the Adytum.

Castaneda, Carlos
   Author of books on North and Central American Indian mythology. His writings, including *The Teachings of Don Juan*, popularized Indian philosophy, peyotism, the occult, and shamanism. In *Journey to Ixtlan* he taught that it is possible to talk with animals and trees. *See* Occult.

Cayce, Edgar
   A.R.E. founder called the "sleeping prophet." *See* Association for Research and Enlightenment.

Cayce, Hugh Lynn
   Current A.R.E. leader and son of Edgar Cayce. Author of the *Edgar Cayce Reader* (1974). *See* Association for Research and Enlightenment.

CDL Report
Publication of the Christian-Patriot Defense League. *See also* Christian Conservative Churches of America.

CE 3K Skywatchers
UFO cult in New York. *See* UFO Cults.

Celebration
Quarterly newspaper. *See* Universal Faith Church.

Center for Spiritual Awareness
New Age related group based in Lakemont, Georgia. Background is Hinduism. The *Bhagavad Gita* and the Bible are quoted. Yoga is practiced.

Serves as the education department of Christian Spiritual Alliance, Inc. Roy Eugene Davis is the president and director of the Center, which offers retreats and seminars. Publishes *Truth Journal* ten times a year. CSA Press publishes its literature. (Information gleaned from issues of *Truth Journal*.)

Center for UFO Studies
UFO cult in Evanston, Illinois. *See* UFO Cults.

Centering
Relaxation exercises practiced by New Agers in preparation for meditation. Sometimes combined with "prayer." *See* New Age Movement.

Centering the Heart Seminar
Human potential seminar. *See* Insight Transformational Seminars.

Centers of Light
One of five divisions. *See* Mark-Age.

Ceremonies of the Liberal Catholic Rite
Written in 1934 by Irving Steiger Cooper, first Regionary Bishop of the Liberal Catholic Church and a supporter of the Theosophical Society. *See* Theosophy.

Cerve, Wishar S.
Author of *Lemuria: The Lost Continent of the Pacific. See* Rosicrucian Fellowship.

Chakras
Kundalini Yoga teaches that seven centers of psychic energy in the body store energy from the universal life force. Various exercises and meditations awaken these centers, allowing the power to rise up the spine, an event called kundalini. This power can be manipulated to promote healing. The

ultimate result is enlightenment. *See* Yoga *and* Tantric Hinduism.

Chaney, Robert Galen and Earlyne
Founders of the Astara Foundation. *See* Astara Foundation.

Channeling
Also called trance channeling. Spiritualist method of communicating with ascended masters and other departed spirits in the spirit world. Some of the more notorious channelers are J. Z. Knight (Ramtha), Jach Pursel (Lazaris), Kevin Ryerson (John, Tom McPherson, others), Karen Glueck (Father Andre), the late Jane Roberts (Seth), Penny Torres (Mafu), and Verna Yater (Indira Latari and Chief White Eagle).

Other channelers include Darryl Anka, Elwood Babbitt (Mark Twain, Einstein, Jesus, Vishnu, others), Iris Belhayes (Enid), Rev. Laura Camaron-Fraser (Jonah), Linda Deen Domnitz (John Lennon), Virginia Essene, Taryn Krivé (Bell Bell), Thomas Jacobson (Dr. Peebles), Jean Loomis (Seth), William Rainan (Dr. Peebles), Azena Ramanda (St. Germain), Pat Rodegast (Emanuel), Eileen Rota (Pretty Flower), Jamie Sims (Leah), David Swetland (Matea), Alan Vaughan (Li Sung), Karen Vickers (Annie Besant, others).

The Butterfly Rises, by Kit Tremaine, tells of her transformation through the channeling of Verna Yater, Kevin Ryerson, and others. Features dialogues with Indira Latari as channeled by Yater.

Some channelers, like Barbara Rollinson-Huss, claim to be able to channel enlightenment from dolphins. *See also* Spiritualism.

New Age: Groothuis, *Confronting*, pp. 26-29; Larson, pp. 103-16; Miller, pp. 141-82.

Chidvilas Foundation
Publisher of the books and tapes of Bhagwan Shree Rajneesh and a newspaper, *The Rajneesh Times of India. See* Rajneesh International Foundation.

Children of God (COG)
Also known as Family of Love. Rejects American government, churches, schools, families, and jobs. Delights in the coming end of the world. Leaders use mind control, censor mail, and monitor phone calls. Members take biblical names.

Jesus was partly God. Hell is a place of reforming punishment; a dead person can be prayed out of hell. Worship services emphasize dancing, singing, and speaking in tongues. Other earmarks include communal living, rape, incest, polygamy, obscenity, sexual perversion, prostitution ("Flirty Fishing"), and the practice of Spiritualism. Witnessing material is pornographic. It has been called a "Religious Sex Cult."

Founded in 1969 by Moses Berg, formerly named David Brant Berg, son of a Christian evangelist couple. Moses is also called "MO" or Father David. Berg communicates his doctrines through "MO letters." Only the King James Version of the Bible is memorized, but verses are used out of context to say what MO wants. Mainline churches are rejected.

Headquarters is in Chicago. Background is the Jesus Movement. The *New Nation News* is its periodical.

General: Larson, *New Book*, pp. 159-65; McDowell, pp. 94-98; Tucker, *Another Gospel*, pp. 231-44.

Miscellaneous: Davis; Gordon.

Chinmoy Family

Book by Sri Chinmoy. *See* Sri Chinmoy Centers.

Chinmoy, Sri

Sect founder. Author of *Aum* and *Chinmoy Family*. *See* Sri Chinmoy Centers.

Chinook Learning Center

New Age seminar center in Washington state that teaches such subjects as "Spiritual and Cultural Transformation" and "Ritual and Ceremony" designed to bring about personal and global harmony. *See* New Age Movement.

Chirognomy

Spiritualist practice of divination by studying the shape of a person's hands. *See* Divination.

Chiromancy

Art of divining a person's character and fate from lines and marks on the palms and fingers. Also called palmistry. *See* Divination.

Chivalry and Sorcery®

Fantasy role-playing game similar to Dungeons and Dragons® that teaches occultic practices. *See* Occult.

Cho, Paul Yonggi

Pastor of the Full Gospel Central Church in Seoul, Korea, the world's largest Christian church with more than half a million members. *See* Positive Confession.

Christ Brotherhood
Founded by Patterson Brown, an ex-professor of philosophy. Takes in derelicts who pool their food stamps and try to live as true disciples of Christ. Patterson instills guilt in his followers. They do not acknowledge parenthood, requiring members to renounce their children.

General: Appel.

Christ Communal Organization
Focuses on joy, love, and celebration. Very little is said about Satan and evil. Manifestations of the Holy Spirit are emphasized. Use of drugs, alcohol, tobacco, and extramarital sex is discouraged. Owns several farms, a peach orchard, and a goat dairy.

Begun in the late 1960s in Southern California as an outgrowth of the Jesus Movement. Has set up nearly fifty communal living houses, each called ''House of Miracles.'' (James T. Richardson et al, *Organized Miracles* [New Brunswick, N.J.: Transaction, 1979].)

Christ Consciousness
New Age idea taken from Eastern mysticism and gnosticism that each person possesses the ''divine spark,'' which we must realize or attain. *See* New Age Movement.

Christ Consciousness
Written by Norman D. Paulsen in 1985. *See* The Builders.

The Christ Family
Also known as Freed Men of New Jerusalem. There are three prohibitions, replacing the Ten Commandments, that are keys to salvation: (1) no killing or violence; (2) celibacy—procreation is unnecessary since Armageddon will occur by 1984 (they missed it); and (3) materialism is wrong—no make-up or jewelry; all belongings are sold and the money given to the Family. They do not work.

The Bible is unnecessary; it is ''yesterday's newspaper.'' ''Give up the Bible. Jesus is here now; just go to him to find out what he wants.'' Members believe that they are the living Bible. Followers walk on foot coast to coast and sleep outside or in abandoned buildings. They take on biblical names.

Marijuana, tobacco, peyote, and other ''natural herbs'' are accepted as gifts from God. Women are subservient to male members.

Founded by Charles McHugh in 1969. McHugh had a "revelation" that he is the returned "Jesus Christ Lightning Amen." Hell is found on earth when a person breaks McHugh's prohibitions. (*Missions U.S.A.*, Atlanta: Home Mission Board, Southern Baptist Convention [March-April 1982]: 26.)

Christ Light Community

Practices ESP and other psychic phenomena, spiritual healing, and speaking in tongues. Provides "New Age Truth theological training, based upon universalized and Biblical Christianity." Background is metaphysics. Offers personal counseling, retreats, and seminars.

Founded by Gilbert N. and June Holloway in Florida in 1956. Moved to Deming, New Mexico, in 1967. Publishes a monthly newsletter. The parent corporation is New Age Church of Truth, Inc. (Taken from information sheets published by the Christ Light Community.)

Christ Truth Foundation

"The Teachings of Christ Truth reveal Your Creative Consciousness of GOD'S WORD unfolding as Your Higher SELF." Teaches how to develop a monthly mantra based on one's "soul's" name and birth date. Founded and directed by E. Blair McLean in Santa Barbara, California.

New Age: Khalsa, p. 49.

Christadelphians

Local "ecclesias" are run by male lay members. The Bible is recognized as the supreme authority, but they reject some of the most basic Christian doctrines. There is one Eternal God, but there are many Elohim, or created gods, who were once mortal men. Jesus was one of these. The Holy Spirit is not a person but "an unseen power emanating from the Deity." "Nothing will save a man in the end but an exact knowledge of the will of God . . . and faithful carrying out of the same." Heaven is the abode of God, but humans do not go there. The soul will simply go to sleep. Background is Unitarianism and Adventism.

Christadelphians do not vote, participate in war, or hold public office. Meetings are usually held in homes or rented halls.

Founded in 1848 by Dr. John Thomas, the son of an English Congregational minister. He practiced medicine in England and America but finally gave it up to propagate his religious views. In 1848 he wrote *Elpis Israel—An Exposition*

of the Kingdom of God, the classic exposition of his views. He also wrote *Eureka* (a commentary on Revelation) and *Christendom Astray* (a textbook). Robert Roberts took over leadership after Thomas's death. Based in Birmingham, England. The word "Christadelphian" means brother in Christ.
General: Tucker, *Another Gospel*, pp. 47-48.
Comparative Religions: Mead, pp. 72-73.

Christendom Astray
Textbook by John Thomas. *See* Christadelphians.

The Christian and the Supernatural
Written by Morton Kelsey to show that Jesus was greater than all the shamans, though similar. *See* New Age Movement.

Christian Community Church
"Christianized" form of a cult. *See* Anthroposophical Society.

Christian Conservative Churches of America
Founded by John R. Harrell in 1959 to blend Christianity and patriotism in opposition to Zionism and Communism. Background is Anglo-Israelism. Based in Louisville, Illinois. Three organizations are associated with the CCCA: Christian-Patriots Defense League, Citizens Emergency Defense System (a private militia), and Paul Revere Club. *See* Identity Movement.

Christian Defense League
Anti-black, anti-Jewish support group. *See* New Christian Crusade Church.

Christian Foundation
Located in Canyon County, California. *See* Alamo Christian Foundation.

Christian Healing
Written in 1909 by Charles S. Fillmore. *See* Unity School of Christianity.

Christian Ministries
Name given to many Body of Christ settlements. *See* The Body of Christ.

Christian-Patriots Defense League
Prepares Christian patriots for the coming collapse of North American governments. *See* Christian Conservative Churches of America.

Christian Science
Also called Church of Christ, Scientist. Founded in 1879 by Mary Baker Eddy based on the metaphysical teachings of Phineas Parkhurst Quimby.

Mrs. Eddy's *Science and Health with Key to the Scriptures* has greater value than the Bible. "The Bible is no more important to our well-being than the history of Europe and America." She also wrote *Retrospection and Introspection*, a doctrinal review.

The Trinity is not biblical; "the Trinity . . . suggests heathen gods." God is an impersonal being. Jesus was not God, not divine; only the Christ principle in Him was true deity. Sin is error, conquered by denying its power and existence. Salvation is deliverance from awareness of evil or pain. "Man as God's idea is already saved with an everlasting salvation."

Borrows from Hinduism its rejection of the reality of matter. Sickness and death are illusions, as are all material things. Healing is accomplished by thinking pure thoughts; one overcomes illness by refusing to think about it.

Publishes the daily newspaper *Christian Science Monitor* and sponsors public reading rooms. The *Christian Science Journal* and *Christian Science Sentinel* are periodicals used in the recruitment of new members. Produces the nightly news program "World Monitor" on the Discovery Channel. The Mother Church is in Boston. A self-perpetuating board of directors now governs the church.

General: Larson, *New Book*, pp. 166-71; Martin, *Kingdom*, pp. 126-65; McDowell, pp. 123-30; Robertson, pp. 132-46; Tucker, *Another Gospel*, pp. 149-76, 393.

Christian Science Journal
Periodical used in recruiting. *See* Christian Science.

Christian Science Monitor
Daily newspaper. *See* Christian Science.

Christian Science Sentinel
Periodical used in recruiting. *See* Christian Science.

Christian Science Theological Seminary
Formed as a result of a split-off from the Mother Church in Boston. *See* Divine Science Federation International.

Christian Spiritual Alliance, Inc.
Parent corporation. *See* Center for Spiritual Awareness.

Christian World Liberation Front
Begun in the 1960s in San Francisco. Background is the Jesus Movement. *Right On* is a regular publication. New Age: Newport, p. 147.

Christie, Louis
Cult cofounder. *See* Church of All Worlds.

Christopsychology
New Age book written by a Christian, Morton Kelsey, in 1984. *See* New Age Movement.

Christ's Church of the Golden Rule
Founded by Arthur L. Bell in San Francisco in 1934 as Mankind United, designed to bring about a worldwide utopia. (H. T. Dohrman, *California Cult* [New York: AMS Press, 1958].)

Chromotherapy
Use of color to heal. The patient sits under a certain color light or holds a colored object to heal a specific disorder. Also called color therapy. *See* Holistic Health.

Chrysalis
Journal published by the Swedenborg Foundation three times a year. *See* Church of the New Jerusalem.

Chuang-tzu
Chinese philosopher who developed and spread the teachings of Lao-tzu. Authored *Tao Tsang*, the 1,120-volume Taoist canon. *See* Taoism.

Church and School of Wicca
Witchcraft group in New Bern, North Carolina, founded by Gavin and Yvonne Frost in 1972. *See* Witchcraft.

"Church of Ageless Wisdom"
Typical name for a New Age church. *See* New Age Movement.

Church of All Worlds
Nature-oriented. Promotes the symbiotic relationship between earth and humans. Background is Spiritualism and pantheism.

Founded in 1967 by Tim Zell and Louis Christie in St. Louis. Priestess and president is Anodea Judith in Redwood Valley, California. She is also founder and director of LIFE-WAYS, a school for the study of consciousness and the healing arts in northern California.

Subsidiary organizations include Ecosophical Research Association, Forever Forests, Holy Order of Mother Earth (H.O.M.E.), and Nemeton. Ms. Judith's works are published by Llewellyn News Times. She has written *Wheels of Life*. *Green Egg* and *The Pagan* are magazines. Associated with the New Age movement.

General: Ellwood, pp. 200-204; Melton, *Encyclopedia*, pp. 642-43.

Occult: Larson, p. 165.

Church of Armageddon

Also known as the Love Family or the Love Israel Family. Founded in 1969 by Paul Erdmann (now known as Love Israel). Love Israel claims to be Christ's representative to gather God's true family. "I am love personified, so whatever I do is loving." "We are Christ" and "we are Israel."

Members shun medical care. Sickness is a sign of lack of faith. They follow Erdmann's teachings found in his book, *Love*. They observe strict dietary rules but consider the use of beer, marijuana, toluene, hashish, and electric shock as sacraments. Yoga is practiced.

Members take on biblical names, which they use until they merit "virtue" names such as Love, Logic, Understanding, and Strength. They give all possessions to the Family and renounce ties with their earthly families.

Present headquarters is in Seattle. Brian Allen (called Logic Israel), son of actor Steve Allen, oversees Family holdings, which include the following: a 160-acre ranch near Arlington, Washington; several houses in Seattle's Queen Anne Hill district; a colony in Hawaii; a fishing boat; and odds and ends given by joiners.

General: Larson, *New Book*, pp. 172-73; Melton, *Encyclopedia*, pp. 505-6; Tucker, *Another Gospel*, pp. 370-71.

New Age: Newport, pp. 146-47.

Church of Bible Understanding (COBU)

Jesus the Son is lower than the Father, and the Holy Spirit is lower still. The Church has "declared war on the powers of this world, including government, police, schools, parents, big business, the press, employers, neighborhoods, churches, friends, society, and most older persons." Focuses its evangelistic attention on teenagers who are estranged from their parents.

Begun as the Forever Family in 1971 in Allentown, Pennsylvania. The founder, Stewart Traill, assigned unorthodox meaning to orthodox Bible doctrines. Only Traill's teachings are authoritative for today.

Presently based in Philadelphia. The group numbers about 700, found mainly in nine eastern states and a mission in Haiti.

General: Larson, *New Book*, pp. 174-75.

Church of Christ, Scientist

Alternate cult name. *See* Christian Science.

Church of Christ, Temple Lot

Headquarters is in Independence, Missouri. Claims to be the original church founded by Joseph Smith, Jr. *See* Mormonism.

Church of Circle Wicca

Largest national witchcraft organization. Based in Mt. Horeb, Wisconsin. Publishes the *Circle Network News*. *See* Witchcraft.

Church of Divine Man

Related to the New Age movement. Its seminary is the Berkeley Psychic Institute in Berkeley, California.

New Age: Khalsa, pp. 40-41.

Church of Divine Science

Name applied to individual congregations. *See* Divine Science Federation International.

Church of God International

Founded by Garner Ted Armstrong in 1978 after he was ousted from the Worldwide Church of God for alleged immoral conduct. Garner Ted considers it a new beginning in God's work, though he says, "I'm preaching the same thing" as the Worldwide Church of God. The basic teachings of Herbert W. Armstrong are taught, though his apostolic authority is not accepted. The major difference is in recruitment policies. The Church of God International accepts new members more readily and without taking them through a lengthy indoctrination period.

Headquarters is in Tyler, Texas. Publications include *The International News* (a monthly newspaper), booklets, and cassette tapes. Radio and television programs are produced.

General: McDowell, pp. 114-15, 121; Melton, *Encyclopedia*, p. 438; Tucker, *Another Gospel*, p. 199.

Church of Illumination

The purpose is to harmonize philosophy with religion. Man has within him a spark of the Divine, the "Christos," which may be brought into consciousness. It then becomes an inexhaustible source of wisdom and power. In this process, the son of man literally becomes the Son of God. The Church is the tool for bringing the two natures (masculine and feminine) into a state of equilibrium.

Associated with the Fraternitas Rosae Crucis as its outer court. Founded in 1908 by Grand Master Reuben Swinburne Clymer. The Fraternity and the Church are now headed by his son, Emerson M. Clymer.

Comparative Religions: Mead, pp. 90-91.

Church of Israel

Formed in 1972 as a split from a Mormon splinter group (the Church of Christ at Holley's Bluff, Missouri), which had split off from the Church of Christ, Temple Lot. The Church of Israel, led by Daniel Gayman, replaced Joseph Smith's teachings with those of the Identity Movement.

Based in Schell City, Missouri. Divided into twelve dioceses, one for each of the twelve tribes of Israel. The Diocese of Manasseh (the United States) is the first one to be activated. Others are to be assigned to various European countries. Publishes *The Watchman*. See also Identity Movement.

General: Melton, *Encyclopedia*, pp. 462-63.

Church of Jesus Christ

Based in Bass, Arkansas. See Identity Movement.

Church of Jesus Christ Christian, Aryan Nations

Claims to be a "white racial theopolitical movement" designed to establish Aryan sovereignty over areas where Aryans have settled based on what they believe God teaches. Background is Anglo-Israelism.

Founded by Wesley A. Swift, a Ku Klux Klan organizer, shortly after World War II. After his death in 1970, Richard Butler started an independent branch at Hayden Lake, Idaho. Butler's connections with the Klan and Nazi groups make this one of the most notorious of the Identity Movement's groups. Publishes a newsletter, *Our Nation*.

In the mid-seventies a militant semi-secret group split off called the Order. Several members have been accused of murder, assault, and racketeering. See Identity Movement *and* Ku Klux Klan.

Church of Jesus Christ in Solemn Assembly

Fundamentalist spinoff. See Mormonism.

Church of Jesus Christ of Latter-day Saints
Official cult name. *See* Mormonism.

Church of Light
Practices astrology, directed thinking, ESP, and occult magic. Background is Egyptian mysticism and the occult. Founded in 1932 in Los Angeles, California, by Elbert Benjamine. Based on the twenty-one-lesson course *Brotherhood of Light Lessons*, by C. C. Zain, Benjamine's pen name.
General: Ellwood, pp. 183-85; Melton, *Encyclopedia*, p. 599.
New Age: Khalsa, p. 49.

Church of New World Religions
Based in San Francisco, California. "The Priesthood belongs to all individuals. . . . It is also something earned." Worship services follow the "New Age Christian Sangreal Sacrament Mass"; the liturgy is found in *New Age Priesthood*.
New Age: Khalsa, pp. 49-50.

Church of Religious Science
Founded by Ernest Holmes in 1927 as the Institute of Religious Science. One of the Mind Science groups. Background is gnosticism. *Science of Mind*, by Holmes, is the textbook. "When an individual recognizes his true union with the Infinite, he automatically becomes Christ." "If by Christian you mean that we are saved by the blood of Christ on the Cross, then we're not." Heaven and hell are merely mental states.
General: Larson, *New Book*, pp. 306-7.
Miscellaneous: Harm.

Church of Sapa
Body of Christ settlement near Eupora, Mississippi. *See* The Body of Christ.

Church of Satan
First of the three main Satanist churches. Headed by Anton Szandor LaVey in San Francisco. Became recognized in America in 1966. LaVey's *Satanic Bible*, *The Satanic Rituals*, and *The Compleat Witch* are the sacred writings. The *Cloven Hoof* is a regular publication.
There is no God, just "a universal force, a balancing factor in nature, too impersonal to care one whit whether we live or die." Anti-Christ. Satan is "a symbolic personal savior." *See also* Satanism.

General: Melton, *Encyclopedia*, pp. 663-64.
Occult: Larson, pp. 140-42.

Church of Satanic Brotherhood
Formed in 1973 by former members of the Church of Satan: Harry L. Booth, John DeHaven, Joseph M. Daniels, and Ronald E. Lanting. It lasted only a few years. DeHaven reportedly converted to Christianity. *See* Satanism.

Church of Scientology
Official cult name. *See* Scientology.

"Church of Spiritual Healing"
Typical name for a New Age church. *See* New Age Movement.

"Church of the Earth Nation"
Typical name for a New Age church. *See* New Age Movement.

Church of the Eternal Source
Witchcraft group in Burbank, California. Majors on the occultism of ancient Egypt. *See* Witchcraft.

Church of the First Born of the Fulness of Times
Fundamentalist spinoff. *See* Mormonism.

Church of the Living Word
Also known as The Walk. Founded by the late John Robert Stevens in 1954. Headquarters is in Los Angeles. Background is the occult, gnosticism, and Eastern religions.

Man can become God and can become perfect in this life by good works. The Bible is outdated; it must be supplemented by the revelations of Stevens. Great emphasis is placed on the supernatural gifts of the Holy Spirit. This is the only church that is in God's will; God has rejected all other churches.

Publishes *Living Word for . . .* (a collection of Stevens's utterances), *To Every Man That Asketh*, and *The First Principles*. Owns Living Word Publishers and Impact Industries, a paint roller factory in California.

General: Larson, *New Book*, pp. 176-79; Martin, *New Cults*, p. 269; Tucker, *Another Gospel*, pp. 360-62.

Church of the Lukumi Babalu Aye
Related group. *See* Santeria.

Church of the New Jerusalem
Also known as Swedenborgianism. Originated in 1787 in London by Emmanuel Swedenborg, son of a Lutheran bishop. Brought to America in 1792. Background is Spiritualism.

Denies the Trinity. God is one person: the Father. Salvation is purely subjective: "Christ's redemptive work does not consist in his bearing our sins upon the tree, or making satisfaction to the justice of God for our offenses." "The Lord forgives every man his sin."

Parts of the Old and New Testaments are accepted as "books of the Word," those that have "the internal sense." Only the four gospels and the Revelation are accepted from the New Testament.

Headquarters of the General Convention of the New Jerusalem in the U.S.A. is in Newton, Massachusetts; the other more conservative branch, General Church of the New Jerusalem, is based in Bryn Athyn, Pennsylvania. In the 1930s an even more conservative group, Lord's New Church Which Is Nova Hieroslyma, broke away from the General Church under the leadership of H. D. G. Groeneveld.

Swedenborg's writings include: *Arcana Coelestia, Conjugal Love, The Divine Providence, The Four Doctrines, Heaven and Hell, Miscellaneous Theological Works,* and *The True Christian Religion.* The Swedenborg Foundation in New York distributes Swedenborg's books. The Church publishes a journal, *Chrysalis.* Helen Keller, author of *My Religion,* and Johnny Appleseed (John Chapman) were adherents.

General: Larson, *New Book,* pp. 409-10; Martin, *Kingdom,* pp. 513-25; Melton, *Encyclopedia,* pp. 531-33; Robertson, pp. 164-67; Tucker, *Another Gospel,* pp. 381-82.

Church of the Sacred Alpha

Based in Southern California. Uses electroencephalograms to help a person learn how to mentally control his own body. (Angus Hall, *Strange Cults* [Garden City, N.J.: Doubleday, 1976], pp. 20-21.)

Church of the Universal Design

Founded by Annie C. Bill after she broke away from the Mother Church of Christian Science to establish her own Parent Church. She later wrote *Science and Reality.*

General: Rice, p. 89.

"Church of Truth"

Typical name for a New Age church. *See* New Age Movement.

Church of Universal Brotherhood

Background is Egyptian mysticism and the occult. Members are taught how to custom design dreams so that they automatically come true. They learn the "seven spells for supreme success." The aim is to build a "World of Universal Brotherhood Through SELF Improving Humanhood" (with help from the friendly stars). There are three laws: (1) Love yourSELF, (2) love your brothers and sisters as yourSELF, and (3) take charge of your own head and do as you will.

A person can be ordained as a minister in the Church and receive the doctor of divinity degree for $25, which comes complete with a "Manual of Church Operations." Michael Valentine Zamoro is president. Based in Hollywood, California. (From a packet of material from the Church.)

General: Melton, *Encyclopedia*, p. 476.

Church of World Messianity

Also known as Johrei, or Sekai Kyusei Kyo. Features "johrei" (prayer in action), the act of channeling the Direct Light of God by using a focal point (the palm of the hand) to concentrate the energy in order to "develop greater spiritual awareness."

Homes where groups meet are called Johrei Centers. Promotes natural farming, using no chemicals. Looks for the coming of Maitreya, the Buddha of the future.

Started in Japan in 1935 by the late Mokichi Okada, called by his followers "Enlightened Lord." Brought to America in 1954; chartered in Los Angeles. Part of the New Age movement.

General: Melton, *Encyclopedia*, p. 776.

Eastern Mysticism: Ellwood, pp. 111-46.

Church Universal and Triumphant (CUT)

Founded in 1958 by Mark L. Prophet (d. 1973) as the Summit Lighthouse. Background is Catholicism and ancient wisdom teachings of Theosophy.

The major authoritative text is *Climb the Highest Mountain*, by the Prophets. The Trinity is the threefold light of power, wisdom, and love. God is impersonal, dwells in his creation, is "Father-Mother." "Christ" refers to a principle or consciousness. The Holy Spirit is the "energy man uses either to expand Good or to expand an energy veil [evil]."

Man is basically good; salvation is realizing that self is God. "I am that I am" is its affirmation of self-deity. Its teachings have come from the Great White Brotherhood; those who follow these teachings "will have their souls purified by

63

the Violet Consuming Flame so that they may achieve Christ-consciousness."

Elizabeth Clare Wulf Prophet (also called Guru Ma or World Mother) is the current spokesman. She is now married to Edward Francis, vice-president of the Church. Clare Prophet claims to have talked with Jesus, who gave her His true teachings, which she wrote down in the three-volume series *The Lost Teachings of Jesus*. She has also talked with Christopher Columbus, Shakespeare, Merlin, Hercules, the archangel Gabriel, the Virgin Mary, and the late Pope John XXIII. She claims to have lived previously as St. Catherine of Siena, a fourteenth-century mystic, and as Marie Antoinette.

Pearls of Wisdom, a weekly publication, serves as a voice for the latest teachings of the Ascended Masters. *Heart* is a magazine. Summit Lighthouse is the publisher for their materials and sponsoring agency for the Montessori International schools.

Operates Summit University, where intense training in occultic practice is offered in twelve-week quarters. The Church owns a 12,000-acre ranch in Park County, Montana, near Yellowstone National Park. CUT is building underground shelters to protect members from "imminent nuclear war." Has been ordered to halt construction because of a major fuel leak that has damaged the environment. The Cosmic Honor Guard forms Prophet's bodyguard. This group is aligned with the New Age movement. Located in Colorado Springs, Colorado, and Malibu, California.

General: Larson, *New Book*, pp. 180-84; Martin, *New Cults*, p. 214; Tucker, *Another Gospel*, pp. 362-64.

Churches' Fellowship for Psychic and Spiritual Studies

Background is Spiritualism. Advocates the use of mediums.

Occult: Koch, p. 212.

Circle Network News

Newsletter published by the Church of Circle Wicca in Mt. Horeb, Wisconsin. *See* Witchcraft.

Citizens Emergency Defense System

Private militia prepared to be activated in the event that the governments of North America fall. *See* Christian Conservative Churches of America.

City of Immortals
Planned community in Austin, Texas, designed to provide "a crime-free, anxiety-free lifestyle" for the occupants of up to two hundred homes. *See* Transcendental Meditation.

"City of Joseph"
Pageant presented annually by the Mormons in Nauvoo, Illinois, depicting the history of the Church of Jesus Christ of Latter-day Saints. *See* Mormonism.

Clairaudience
"Hearing at a distance" while alert or in meditation. One of the forms of extrasensory perception. *See* Spiritualism.

Clairvoyance
"Seeing at a distance" while alert or in meditation. One of the forms of extrasensory perception. *See* Spiritualism.

Clarke, Arthur C.
Science fiction writer revered by New Agers. His *2001: A Space Odyssey* and *2010: Odyssey Two* depict evolution, contact with extraterrestrials, and a New Age millennial concept. The latter also expresses devotion to Lucifer, the Light Bearer. *See* New Age Movement.

ClearMind Trainings
Offers New Age training programs. *See* Ken Keyes Center.

Climb the Highest Mountain
Written in 1973 by Mark and Elizabeth Clare Prophet. *See* Church Universal and Triumphant.

Cloven Hoof
Regular publication of the Church of Satan. *See* Satanism.

Club of Rome
Globalistic group seeking to achieve international economic cooperation. Promotes population control. *See* New Age Movement.

Clymer, Emerson M.
Cult leader and Grand Master. *See* Fraternitas Rosae Crucis.

Clymer, Reuben Swinburne
Former cult leader and Grand Master. *See* Fraternitas Rosae Crucis.

Cobb, C. E.
Cofounder of The Body of Christ. *See* The Body of Christ.

COBU
Cult acronym. *See* Church of Bible Understanding.

Cognition
Consciousness of events past, present, and future. One of the forms of extrasensory perception. *See* Spiritualism.

Cole, Donna
Coauthor of a popular ritual book, *A Book of Pagan Rituals*. *See* Witchcraft.

Cole-Whittaker, Terry
Cult founder. Motivational speaker for the New Age movement. Author of *How to Have More in a Have-Not World*, *The Inner Path from Where You Are to Where You Want to Be*, and *Prosperity, Your Divine Right*. *See* Science of Mind Church International.

Coll, Francisco
Founder of the Inner Peace Movement. *See* Inner Peace Movement.

Collegians International Church
Founded by LaVedi Lafferty, coauthor of *The Eternal Dance*, published by Llewellyn Publishing. Based in Fairbanks, Alaska. Offers full-moon meditation, karmic recall, and esoteric healing.
New Age: Khalsa, p. 50.

Collegiate Association for the Research of Principles (CARP)
Evangelistic front group that recruits members from college areas. Raises money to support "international efforts," which allegedly goes into the leaders' coffers. Members sell items like roses on street corners and in malls, hoping to reach their daily quotas before the van picks them up. If they don't, they are ridiculed. *See* Unification Church.

Color Therapy
Use of color to heal. A patient sits under a certain color light or holds a colored object to heal a specific disease. Also called chromotherapy. *See* Holistic Health.

The Coming of the Cosmic Christ
Written in 1988 by Matthew Fox, a Dominican priest. Describes his "Creation Spirituality." *See* New Age Movement.

The Coming World Order
Written by Alice A. Bailey in 1942. *See* New Age Movement.

Community Chapel

Founded by Donald Lee Barnett in Seattle. *See* Fundamentalist Fringe Movements.

Community of Islam in the West

Also called Black Muslims and Bilalians. Sacred writing is the *Koran*. Originally held that God is actually Prophet Wallace D. Fard, who taught that blacks are by nature divine and good. Whites are sinful; "the white man is a devil." Christianity is the white man's religion.

It has now shed its anti-white doctrines and has been recognized by American Islam. Members observe physical cleanliness and morality.

Headquarters is in Detroit. Founded by Timothy Drew in 1913. Many of his teachings came from *The Aquarian Gospel*, by Levi Dowling. When Drew died, Wallace D. Fard claimed to be his reincarnation. When Fard disappeared in 1930, Elijah Muhammad assumed the leadership. When Elijah died in 1975, his son, Wallace Muhammad, took over. Fard later founded his own group, the Nation of Islam, now known as American Muslim Mission.

Bilalian News is a regular publication. Owns sixty-nine temples and other real estate holdings. One famous adherent is Muhammad Ali (Cassius Clay).

General: Larson, *New Book*, pp. 99-102; Rice, p. 168.

Community Unity Church

Original cult name. *See* Peoples' Temple Christian Church.

The Compleat Witch

Written in 1970 by Anton Szandor LaVey, Satanic church founder. *See* Church of Satan.

The Complete Art of Witchcraft

Written in 1973 by Sybil Leek, self-proclaimed witch. *See* Witchcraft.

Confluent Education

Developed by the late Beverly Galyean. Teaches students that they are God and are perfect. *See* New Age Movement.

Confucianism

Teaches ancestor worship, supreme respect for elders, and a strict code of ethics. It has more to do with human relationships than a relationship with a supernatural being. Man is basically good. Seeks to perfect people within the world.

Founded by Confucius about 500 B.C. in China. He was a wise teacher to whom many people were attracted. After his death he was deified by his followers.

Confucius (551-479 B.C.) collected and edited four ancient books and one of his own into an anthology and called them *The Five Classics*, described as follows: *The Book of Changes* (*I Ching*) is used in divination; *The Book of Annals* described how the superior man should behave; *The Book of Poetry* would help a man become virtuous; *The Book of Ceremonies* taught how to act the right or traditional way; and *The Annals of Spring and Autumn* by Confucius gave commentary on current events of his day.

Four books by his disciples contain his teachings: *The Analects*; *The Great Learning*; *The Doctrine of the Mean*; and *The Book of Mencius*. Mencius, who lived two centuries later, systematically developed and spread Confucius's teachings.

General: Boa, pp. 37-40; McDowell, pp. 325-38.

Confucius

Chinese teacher; founder of a major world religion. *See* Confucianism.

Conjugal Love

Written by Emanuel Swedenborg in 1898. *See* Church of the New Jerusalem.

Conservative Judaism

One of the three main Jewish branches. Focuses on preserving the Jewish race. *See* Judaism.

Cooper, Irving Steiger

First Regionary Bishop of the Liberal Catholic Church and author of *Ceremonies of the Liberal Catholic Rite*. *See* Theosophy.

Cooperative Spiritual Living Program

Offers training in how to maintain a daily program of meditation and yoga. *See* Ananda.

Copeland, Kenneth

Church leader, televangelist based in Fort Worth, Texas. *See* Positive Confession.

Coptic Fellowship of America

Ancient wisdom group founded by Hamid Bey in Wyoming, Michigan, in 1927. Based on the teachings of the White Brotherhood of Moses and the Essenes. Envisions the spiritual unity of nations. Offers Self-mastery Training Seminars.

General: Melton, *Encyclopedia*, pp. 575-76.
New Age: Khalsa, p. 51.

Cosmic Honor Guard
Bodyguard for Elizabeth Clare Prophet. *See* Church Universal and Triumphant.

Cosmic Masters
Publication. *See* UFO Cults.

Cosmic Philosophy
Written by George Adamski. *See* George Adamski Foundation.

Cosmic Study Center
Located in Potomac, Maryland. Based on the textbook *True Art of Creation. See* UFO Cults.

Cosmic Voice
UFO cult periodical. *See* Aetherius Society.

Council for Unified Research and Education
Cult front group. *See* Unification Church.

The Counseling Program
Trained counselors use meditation techniques to diagnose spiritual problems and give advice to individuals. *See* Inner Peace Movement.

A Course in Miracles
Three-volume New Age course published in 1975 by the Foundation for Inner Peace and distributed by Miracle Distribution Center in Fullerton, California, which offers workshops. It is one of the most widely used teaching tools among New Agers and some churches. A Christianized form of occultism that denies many basic Christian doctrines, it was dictated to Helen Schucman over a period of seven years by an inner voice claiming to be Jesus. The messages came daily, sometimes several times a day. "The Course aims to correct what it says are errors of Christianity that overemphasize suffering, sacrifice, and sacrament." Teaches that "sin is the illusion that separates us from our own innate divinity, our own godhood." *See* New Age Movement.

Cousins, Norman
Former editor of *Saturday Review*; author of *The Healing Heart* and *Anatomy of an Illness*. Cofounder of Planetary Citizens, a political action group. A well-known New Age speaker. *See* Planetary Citizens.

69

Coven of Arianhu
Associated with the national Church and School of Wicca. *See* Witchcraft.

Covenant of the Goddess
Second largest national witchcraft organization. Headed by Miriam Starhawk, a self-described witch, in Berkeley, California. "The Goddess . . . is the world. Manifest in each of us, she can be known by every individual, in all her magnificent diversity." Others active include Zsuanna Budapest, Margot Adler (author of *Drawing Down the Moon*), Allison Harlow, and Deborah Bender. Shares ideology with the New Age movement. *See* Witchcraft.

Covenant of Unitarian Universalist Pagans
Located in Cambridge, Massachusetts. A blend of witchcraft (goddess religion) with Unitarian teachings. *See* Unitarian Universalist Association.

The Covenant, the Sword, the Arm of the Lord
Militant Identity Movement group founded by Jim Ellison in 1976. Headquarters is the survivalist commune called Zarephath-Horeb near the Arkansas-Missouri border. In 1985 Ellison was arrested and convicted on racketeering charges and was sentenced to twenty years in prison.
Teaches that God will soon judge America and will use CSA to bring it about. Publishes the *CSA Journal*. *See* Identity Movement.

The Craft
Alternate name. *See* Witchcraft.

Cramer, Malina E.
Cult cofounder. *See* Divine Science Federation International.

"Creation Spirituality"
Developed by Matthew Fox, a controversial Dominican priest. Teaches New Age philosophy with a Catholic Christian covering, blending mysticism, pantheism, environmentalism, and feminism. *See* New Age Movement.

Creative Community Project
Public relations front group. *See* Unification Church.

Creme, Benjamin
Former Scottish painter. One of the leaders of the New Age movement. Founder of the Tara Center. Wrote *The Reap-*

pearance of Christ and the Masters of Wisdom. *See* New Age Movement.

Crossroads Church of Christ
Church in Gainesville, Florida, where the Discipling Movement was begun by Charles H. Lucas. *See* Discipling Movement.

Crouch, Paul
President of Trinity Broadcasting Network. *See* Positive Confession.

Crowley, Aleister
Master of ritual occult magic, "a homosexual, murderer, and practitioner of black sex magic," who was attracted to sadism. Claimed to be the "Beast 666" of the Revelation. Others called him "the wickedest man in the world."
The basic tenet of his teachings was "Do what thou will shall be the whole of the law." These teachings still influence such groups as Ancient Mystical Order Rosae Crucis, Ordo Templi Orientis in New York City, the Society of Ordo Templi Orientis in America in Nashville, Tennessee, and Ordo Templi Astarte in Pasadena, California. *See* Magick.

Crystal Gazing
Also called Mirror Mantic. Spiritualist practice of divination by the use of crystal balls, mirrors, colored glass, or pools of ink or water. *See* Divination.

Crystal Therapy
Use of quartz crystals to heal or bring success. Crystals are believed to be conveyors of cosmic energy. Some New Agers sleep with them, wear them as pendants, or suspend them over their chairs or beds. Used in holistic health practices. *See* Holistic Health *and* Spiritualism.

CSA Journal
Sect publication. *See* The Covenant, the Sword, the Arm of the Lord.

CSA Press
Sect publisher. *See* Center for Spiritual Awareness.

A Cult with No Name
Sometimes called "The Garbage Eaters." Founded by Brother Evangelist, alias Jimmie T. Roberts, in 1969. It is a nomadic group. Does not believe in using doctors.
Members dress in long robes, seldom wash, and pray fervently. They leave behind them broken homes and battered

women and children. They sort through restaurant trash bins looking for food. Members hypnotically obey everything Brother Evangelist says. (James C. Hefley, *The Youthnappers* [Wheaton: Victor, 1977], p. 160.)

Cultural Center
    Home of Way Productions in New Bremen, Ohio. *See* The Way International.

CUT
    Cult acronym. *See* Church Universal and Triumphant.

Cymry Wicca
    Witchcraft group in Athens, Georgia, founded by Rhuddlwm Gawr in 1967. Organized on seven levels of initiation instead of the usual three. *See* Witchcraft.

D

D. C. Striders Track Club
Front group. *See* Unification Church.

Daily Word
Magazine. *See* Unity School of Christianity.

Dallas Northtown Church
Body of Christ group in Dallas, Texas. *See* The Body of Christ.

Dancing in the Light
Written by Shirley MacLaine in 1985. *See* Spiritualism.

Daniels, Joseph M.
Cofounder of the now defunct Church of Satanic Brotherhood and Ordo Templi Satanas. *See* Satanism.

Dass, Baba Ram
Sect founder and founder of the Seva Foundation. Author of *The Only Dance There Is*. *See* Ram Dass.

Daughters of the Nile
Masonic organization for wives of members of the Ancient, Arabic Order of Nobles of the Mystic Shrine. *See* Freemasonry.

Davidson, Gordon
Cofounder of Sirius Community and coauthor of *Builders of the Dawn*. *See* Sirius Community.

Davies, Ann
Former occultic group leader. *See* Builders of the Adytum.

Davis, Andrew Jackson
Clairvoyant and author respected by Spiritualists. Wrote *The Great Harmonia* and *The Principles of Nature*. *See* Spiritualism.

Davis, Ray Eugene
Sect president and director. *See* Center for Spiritual Awareness.

Dawn Bible Students Association
Splinter group. *See* Jehovah's Witnesses.

Dawn Horse Press
Publishing division. *See* Johannine Daist Communion.

Dawn Horse Society
Communal group. *See* Johannine Daist Communion.

Day of Atonement (Yom Kippur)
Jews' most solemn day, observed ten days after Rosh Hashanah. *See* Judaism.

de Chardin, Pierre Teilhard
Jesuit paleontologist and philosopher whose writings are highly regarded by New Agers. *See* New Age Movement.

The Decoded New Testament
Authoritative text. Revised in 1983 as *The Millennium Edition of the Decoded New Testament*. *See* International Community of Christ.

Dederich, Chuck
Cult founder. *See* Synanon Foundation.

Deep Self: Profound Relaxation and the Tank Isolation Technique
Written by John Lilly in 1977 to describe the use of sensory deprivation devices. *See* New Age Movement.

de Grimston, Robert
Author of *As It Is*. Cult founder. *See* Process Church of the Final Judgment.

DeHaven, John
Cofounder of the now defunct Church of Satanic Brotherhood. He reportedly converted to Christianity. *See* Satanism.

DeMolay
Alternate name for the Order of DeMolay, a Masonic organization for boys. *See* Freemasonry.

Denning, Melita
Spiritualist cult leader. *See* Order Aurum Solis.

Denver, John
 Folk singer, New Age leader. Founder of Windstar Foundation near Aspen, Colorado, which publishes the *Windstar Journal*. Was a member of the advisory board for est. *See* est *and* New Age Movement.

de Peyer, Christopher
 Cult leader known as Father Lucius. *See* Foundation Faith of God.

Deseret News Press
 Publishing house in Salt Lake City. *See* Mormonism.

The Desire of Ages
 Written by Ellen Gould White in 1898. *See* Seventh-day Adventism.

Devi, India
 Sect leader. *See* SAI Foundation.

Dharma Publishing
 Publishing house. *See* Nyingma Institute.

Dharmadatus
 Local teaching center. *See* Vajradhatu.

Dianetics: The Modern Science of Mental Health
 Science fiction story written by L. Ron Hubbard; later expanded into a book. Authoritative text. Dianetics is also an alternate name for Hubbard's cult. *See* Scientology.

Diary of a Witch
 Book by Sybil Leek, self-proclaimed witch. *See* Witchcraft.

Dimensions of Evolvement (DOE)
 Founded and directed by Genevieve Paulson in Melbourne, Arkansas. Offers workshops on auras, dreams, herbs, kundalini, meditation, and T'ai Chi Ch'uan.
 New Age: Khalsa, 53.

Diocese of Manasseh
 Area composed of the United States. *See* Church of Israel.

Discernment: A Study in Ecstasy and Evil
 New Age book written by a Christian, Morton Kelsey, in 1978. *See* New Age Movement.

Discipling Movement
 Also called Crossroadsism since the concept was first used by Charles H. Lucas in the Crossroads Church of Christ

in Gainesville, Florida. The leading group now is the Boston Church of Christ led by Kip McKean. It directs the work of twenty-four "pillar" churches, seven of which are in the United States: Atlanta, Georgia; Chicago, Illinois; Denver, Colorado; New York City; Providence, Rhode Island; and San Diego and San Francisco, California. Each pillar church also directs the work of churches it has established.

Discipling as practiced by this movement is a system of "intense training and close personal supervision" in a one-on-one situation. Disciples adopt Christians to disciple. The student is required to submit to the discipler, obey him, imitate him, and confess his sins to him. This confession brings rebuke, correction, and prayer. In some cases the discipler may ask direct questions to draw out a confession. There is a certain degree of psychological manipulation involved that can result in "unnatural and unhealthy personality changes."

Disciplers are viewed as superior to untrained Christians. After a person has been discipled he is expected to disciple others, resulting in a multi-level marketing-type hierarchy. Members are required to attend Sunday morning corporate worship, Wednesday night home meetings, and one Bible Talk session each week. They are expected to obey man-made religious laws. They are taught that the pillar churches are "the faithful remnant," the only true churches. (Bill Kellogg, "Confronting the Church of Christ," *SCP Newsletter* 15, no. 2: 11-13.)

Miscellaneous: Yeakley.

Discourses
Teachings of Meher Baba. *See* Sufism Reoriented, Inc.

Discovery
Periodical. *See* Theosophy.

Divination
Occultic practice of obtaining information about the future by using various props as aids. Also called fortune telling.

Divining practices include aeromancy (reading ripples on water), arithmancy (divining by numbers), astrology (reading the stars and planets), augury (reading the flight of birds), capnomancy (smoke reading), cartomancy (card reading), cartouche (Egyptian form of fortune telling), chirognomy (reading the shape of the hands), chiromancy (palm reading), geomancy (special map reading), graphology (reading handwriting), I Ching (using I Ching sticks or coins), metoposcopy (reading lines on the forehead), mirror mantic (crystal balls, mirrors, still water, etc.), and moleosophy (reading moles on the face).

Also includes numerology (reading numbers combined with astrology), Ouija board (a special board with letters and numbers), phrenology (reading bumps on the head), physiognomy (reading the shape of the face), psychometry (using an object worn by a person), pyromancy (fire reading), rhabdomancy (dowsing or water witching), rhapsodamancy (reading a line in a sacred book), runes (using the Rune alphabet), Tarot cards, and tasseography (tea leaf reading).

All divination leads persons away from faith in God. For more information, see the separate entry on each item. *See also* Spiritualism.

General: McDowell, pp. 161, 186, 190, 207.

Divine Light Mission

Formerly known as E'lan Vital. Founded in India by Guru Paran Sant Satgurudev Shri Hans Maharaj Ji in 1931. Headed by his son, Guru Maharaj Ji (Perfect Master), since 1966; he brought the cult to the United States in 1971. Background is Hinduism and Tantra.

The young Maharaj Ji is "Lord of the Universe." Jesus was only a man, a Perfect Master for His age. Sin is forgiven by meditation since sin is in the mind. Respects all holy books. Practices communal living in ashrams, and mind control is evidenced. "Nothing you do has value unless it is related to the Guru and the Ultimate Purpose."

Four yogic techniques are taught to reveal to followers how to experience the divine light, sound, word, and nectar: (1) divine light—place knuckles on your eyeballs, (2) divine sound—plug your ears with your fingers, (3) divine word—concentrate on your own breathing, and (4) divine nectar—curl your tongue back and hold it there for a while.

Divine Times is the newspaper; *And It Is Divine* is the monthly magazine. Owns or has owned 480 ashrams in thirty-eight countries, a film company, a recording studio, a publishing house, an airline, a travel agency, an electronics firm, a theater chain, a janitorial service, Divine Sales (second-hand shops), a vegetarian restaurant in New York, a $400,000 estate in Malibu, California, and an $80,000 house in Denver. Some of these holdings have had to be released in recent years.

Headquarters is in Miami Beach, Florida. Aligned with the New Age movement.

General: Appel; Boa, pp. 188-95; Larson, *New Book*, pp. 200-206; Melton, *Encyclopedia*, p. 738; Robertson, pp. 115-17; Tucker, *Another Gospel*, pp. 364-65.

Divine, Major Jealous
Born George Baker. Cult founder known as Father Divine. *See* Peace Mission Movement.

Divine Principle
"The completed testament," by Sun Myung Moon. Sacred cult text. *See* Unification Church.

The Divine Providence
Written by Emanuel Swedenborg in 1764. *See* Church of the New Jerusalem.

Divine Sales
Second-hand shops. *See* Divine Light Mission.

Divine Science Church
Original cult name. *See* Divine Science Federation International.

Divine Science College
School in Denver, Colorado. *See* Divine Science Federation International.

Divine Science Federation International
Teaches (1) the fatherhood of God; (2) the brotherhood of man; (3) the unity of all life; (4) the higher thought in science, philosophy, and religion; (5) the awareness of man's relation to God as expressed in each man's inheritance of health, abundance, peace, and power; and (6) the transcendence and immanence of God seen in all created things.

Headquarters is in Denver. Emma Curtiss Hopkins split off from the Mother Church of Christian Science and founded Christian Science Theological Seminary. Three sisters in Denver developed principles similar to Christian Science: Alethea Brooks Small, Fannie Brooks James, and Nona Lovell Brooks. Mrs. Hopkins, along with the three sisters and Mrs. Malina E. Cramer of San Francisco, formed Divine Science Church in 1898 and incorporated Divine Science College.

In 1957 the separate congregations and college organized the Divine Science Federation. Prints the daily devotion magazine *Aspire*.

General: Melton, *Biographical Dictionary*, pp. 43-44; Melton, *Encyclopedia*, pp. 520-21; Rice, p. 90.

Comparative Religions: Mead, pp. 107-8.
Miscellaneous: Harm.
Occult: Koch, p. 212.

The Divine Spectrum
Sect publication. *See* Followers of Jesus.

Divine Times
Sect newspaper. *See* Divine Light Mission.

Divine Wisdom
Alternate cult name. *See* Theosophy.

Dixon, Jeane
Modern-day prophetess who has made quite a reputation out of foretelling events, many of which have come true. She claims that her gift comes from God, though she consults a crystal ball, cards, and astrology. Her story is told in *A Gift of Prophecy* by Ruth Montgomery, New Age author. *See* Spiritualism.

Doctrine and Covenants
One of the scriptural authorities of Mormonism written by Joseph Smith, Jr. Published in 1835. *See* Mormonism.

The Doctrine of the Mean
One of the books by disciples of Confucius. Contains his teachings. *See* Confucianism.

Dodd, C. O.
Sect founder. *See* Assemblies of Yahweh.

DOE
Cult acronym. *See* Dimensions of Evolvement.

Do'in
Method similar to acupuncture that seeks to open the flow of "universal energy" in the body by using massage. *See* Holistic Health.

Dolphins
Thought by many New Agers to be mentally superior to humans. Barbara Rollinson-Huss and others believe they can channel the spiritually important messages the dolphins have for us. *See* Channeling.

Domnitz, Linda Deer
Channeler of John Lennon. Her encounters have been published in the book *John Lennon Conversations*. *See* Channeling.

Don't Fall Off the Mountain
Written by Shirley MacLaine in 1987. *See* Spiritualism.

Dowd, Freeman B.
Late cult leader. *See* Fraternitas Rosae Crucis.

Dowsing
Spiritualist art of locating water, lost articles, treasure, human bodies, and archaeological sites by means of a forked rod. Also called rhabdomancy or water witching. A related method using a pendulum is called radiesthesia. *See* Divination.

Dr. Peebles
Spirit entity channeled by William Rainan and Thomas Jacobson, a former pupil. Dr. Peebles says he was a Scottish physician in the nineteenth century. Using a shrill but cheerful voice he dispenses medical and spiritual guidance. *See* Channeling.

DragonQuest®
Fantasy role-playing game similar to Dungeons and Dragons® that teaches occultic practices. *See* Occult.

Drawing Down the Moon: Witches, Druids, Goddess-Worshipers, and Other Pagans in America Today
Important book for witches by Margot Adler. Revised in 1987. *See* Witchcraft.

Dream Work
New Age practice of intentional dreaming to cause a certain thing to happen. Teaches that by controlling his dreams, a person can manipulate real life. *See* New Age Movement.

Dreams: A Way to Listen to God
New Age book written by a Christian, Morton Kelsey, in 1978. *See* New Age Movement.

Drew, Timothy
Muslim sect founder. *See* Community of Islam in the West.

Dungeons and Dragons®
Fantasy role-playing game that teaches occultic practices. It has been called "a catechism of the occult." *See* Occult.

E

Eagle Society
Splinter group. *See* Jehovah's Witnesses.

Earth at Omega: Passage to Planetization
Written by Donald Keys in 1982 to explain the political and spiritual agenda of Planetary Citizens and the New Age movement. Says that humanity is ready to take a giant evolutionary step toward global civilization. *See* New Age Movement.

East/West Journal
Monthly magazine concerned with the quality of life, holistic health, and medical alternatives. *See* New Age Movement.

Eastern Star
Common name for the Order of the Eastern Star, a masonic organization for female relatives of Master Masons. *See* Freemasonry.

Ebon, Martin
Popular lecturer on parapsychology and the occult. *See* Spiritual Frontiers Fellowship.

ECK
Alternate sect name. *See* ECKANKAR.

ECKANKAR (ECK)
Also known as the Ancient Science of Soul Travel. Background is Hinduism and Scientology. *Shariyat-Ki-Sugmad* is the sacred text.
God is the Evil Power that rules this world and keeps souls imprisoned. He is detached and unconcerned. Soul trav-

el is taught; it allows the soul to soar free and reach higher states of consciousness. The soul can choose to be reincarnated. Service to fellow man is "one of God's greatest traps."

Founded in 1965 by Sri Paul Twitchell, the "971st Living ECK Master." Was succeeded by Sri Darwin Gross. Headed by Sri Harold Kemp since 1981 in Menlo Park, California.

Twitchell wrote *ECKANKAR: The Key to Secret Worlds.* Gross wrote *Your Right to Know.* Kemp wrote *The Winds of Change,* his autobiography.

Offers "Spiritual Workshops" in cities around the country. Aligned with the New Age movement.

General: Ellwood, pp. 220-24; Larson, *New Book*, pp. 207-11; Melton, *Encyclopedia*, pp. 739-40; Tucker, *Another Gospel*, pp. 365-67.

ECKANKAR: The Key to Secret Worlds
Book written by Paul Twitchell, late ECK Master, in 1969. *See* ECKANKAR.

Ecosophical Research Association
Subsidiary organization. *See* Church of All Worlds.

Eddy, Mary Baker
Cult founder. Author of *Science and Health with Key to the Scriptures* and *Retrospection and Introspection. See* Christian Science.

Eden Springs
Amusement park in Benton Harbor, Michigan. *See* Israelite House of David.

The Edgar Cayce Reader
Collection of Edgar Cayce's "readings" compiled by his son, Hugh Lynn Cayce, in 1974. *See* Association for Research and Enlightenment.

Edgar Cayce: The Sleeping Prophet
Biography of Edgar Cayce written by Jess Stearn in 1966. *See* Association for Research and Enlightenment.

Effective Learning Systems, Inc.
"Pioneers in developing Human Potential." Producer of the Love Tapes, instructional audio cassette tapes on New Age themes. *See* New Age Movement.

Effendi, Shoghi
Former Baha'i leader in America. His writings are considered sacred. *See* Baha'i World Faith.

Egyptian Museum
Established by Harvey Spencer Lewis in San Jose, California. *See* Ancient Mystical Order Rosae Crucis.

Eighth to Thirteenth Books of Moses
Popular occult magic spell book. *See* Magick.

E'lan Vital
Alternate sect name. *See* Divine Light Mission.

Elijah Voice Movement
Splinter group. *See* Jehovah's Witnesses.

Ellison, Jim
Founder of The Covenant, the Sword, the Arm of the Lord, a militant group based at a survivalist commune called Zarephath-Horeb near the Arkansas-Missouri border. *See* Identity Movement.

Elpis-Israel—An Exposition of the Kingdom of God
Classic views of John Thomas published in 1851. *See* Christadelphians.

Emanuel
Spirit entity channeled by Pat Rodegast. *See* Channeling.

Emergence: The Rebirth of the Sacred
Written by David Spangler, a New Age prophet. *See* New Age Movement.

Emerson, Ralph Waldo
Transcendental poet, many of whose works were influenced by East Indian mysticism. *See* Unitarianism *and* Vedanta Society.

Emissaries of the Divine Light
Spiritualist-psychic group. *See* Spiritualism.

Emphatic Diaglot
Interlinear version of the Bible used alongside the *New World Translation of the Holy Scriptures*. *See* Jehovah's Witnesses.

Enchanted Words of Black Forest
Popular occult magic spell book. *See* Magick.

End Time Books
Materials distributor. *See* Alamo Christian Foundation.

End Time Ministry
Alternate sect name. *See* The Body of Christ.

Enid
Nineteenth-century "earthy" Irish woman channeled by Iris Belhayes. *See* Channeling.

Enlightened Masters
Disembodied spirits who have reached the highest level of spiritual consciousness and now guide the spiritual evolution of mankind. Also called ascended masters, Great White Brotherhood, and Universal Brotherhood. *See* New Age Movement *and* Spiritualism.

Enlightenment of the Whole Body
Sacred text written by Da Free John in 1978. *See* Johannine Daist Communion.

Ephemeris
Reference book showing the position of the planets in the astrological signs. Used to chart a person's horoscope. Published annually by the Rosicrucian Fellowship. *See* Astrology *and* Rosicrucian Fellowship.

ERAWS
Acronym for Education, Relief, and Welfare Section. Volunteers assist in meditation programs, food cooperatives, adult literacy programs, and drug and alcohol rehabilitation. *See* Ananda Márga Yoga Society.

Erdmann, Paul
Cult founder known as Love Israel. *See* Church of Armageddon.

Erhard Seminars Training
Original cult name. *See* est.

Erhard, Werner
Founder of est. Birth name is John Paul Rosenberg. *See* est.

Esalen Institute
New Age think tank founded in 1962 by Michael Murphy and Richard Price. Promotes the "human potential" ideals of the New Age movement. Background is Eastern mysticism. Offers seminars for body, mind, and soul at its Big Sur, California, headquarters.

Members "wander naked through its groves and give vent to whatever suppressed feelings haunt their psyches." In some sessions, members stare at white squares until they see visions.

General: Larson, *New Book*, pp. 212-13.
New Age: Larson, pp. 27-29.

Esoteric

Knowledge that is possessed or understood by just a few. Esoteric Christianity is the mystical belief that Christianity's "core truth" is the same as the "core truth" of all other religions. This core truth is "man is divine." *See* New Age Movement.

Esoteric Christianity

Written by Annie Besant in 1901. *See* New Age Movement *and* Theosophy.

Esoteric Seminary and College

Cult textbook. *See* International Church of Ageless Wisdom.

ESP

Acronym for the ability to perceive beyond the five senses. *See* Extrasensory Perception.

ESPress, Inc.

Publishing division. *See* National Spiritual Science Center.

The Essaei Document: Secrets of an Eternal Race

Authoritative text. Revised in 1983 as *The Millennial Edition of the Essaei Document. See* International Community of Christ.

Essenes

Communal, esoteric sect of Judaism from the second century B.C. to about A.D. 135. Most noted for their preservation of Jewish Scriptures, especially the Dead Sea Scrolls. *See* Coptic Fellowship of America.

est

Originally known as Erhard Seminars Training; sometimes referred to by the name of its training seminar, The Forum. Launched in 1971 by Werner Erhard, alias John Paul Rosenberg. Renamed The Forum in 1985 to be more appealing to corporations. Considered a part of the New Age movement. Background is Zen Buddhism, pseudopsychology, Scientology, and Silva Mind Control.

Erhard is the final word, totally powerful. Adherents are trained in a sixty-hour traumatic seminar similar to LifeSpring that "challenges and threatens participants and everything in their world." It "rips from the mind all values implanted by parents, school, church, and society and implants the idea that only what is experienced personally can be true and worthwhile.''

Everyone wills his own fate. Self-satisfaction, self-fulfillment, and self-survival are the ultimate good. Vulgarity is used in the sessions because "it makes you see where you're at and be more open.'' Recruitment includes repeated "high pressure phone calls.'' The cost of the training is about $525 per person.

Transformational Technologies (Trans Tech) trains Fortune 500 corporation executives in positive thinking, hypnosis, visualization, and yoga.

The Hunger Project, whose goal has been to raise consciousness about the problem of world hunger instead of providing food, has fallen into disrepute because of the small percentage of donations (about 3 percent) that is actually used for feeding needy people.

John Dean of Watergate fame was known to be involved with this cult. John Denver sits on the advisory board (as of 1980). Other celebrity graduates are Cher, John Davidson, Valerie Harper, Cloris Leachman, Norman Lear, Yoko Ono, Diana Ross, and Richard Roundtree.

General: Larson, *New Book*, pp. 214-18, 224-27; Martin, *New Cults*, p. 105; McDowell, pp. 90-93; Tucker, *Another Gospel*, pp. 367-69.

Miscellaneous: Weldon.

New Age: Brooke, pp. 93-95; Larson, pp. 22-23; Newport, pp. 106-17.

The Eternal Dance

Written by LaVedi Lafferty in 1984. *See* Collegians International Church.

Ethiopianism

Alternate cult name. *See* Rastafarianism.

Eureka

Commentary on Revelation written by John Thomas in 1861. *See* Christadelphians.

Eurythmy

Art of movement to speech and music. *See* Anthroposophical Society.

Expression

Monthly magazine. *See* Inner Peace Movement.

The Externalisation of the Hierarchy
Written by Alice A. Bailey. Her most powerful revelation containing the New Age "Plan." *See* New Age Movement.

Extrasensory Perception (ESP)
Ability to perceive beyond the normal capacity of the five senses. Includes clairvoyance ("seeing at a distance" while alert or in meditation), clairaudience ("hearing at a distance" while alert or in meditation), mental telepathy (transference of thought from one mind to another), and cognition (consciousness of events past, present, or future). *See* Spiritualism.

F

The Faith
Magazine published by the Assembly of Yahweh (Michigan). *See* Assemblies of Yahweh.

Faith Assembly
This fundamentalist fringe group, located in northern Indiana and other Midwestern states, teaches that members should avoid doctors, discard eyeglasses and hearing aids, shun birth control, and cancel insurance policies. "There is a punishment for those who disobey." This "powerful punishment" can take the form of exposure by other members, ridicule in front of the congregation, and excommunication. Only members of Faith Assembly are saved. Founded by the late Hobart Freeman in Fort Wayne, Indiana, in the early 1970s.
General: Tucker, *Another Gospel*, p. 19.

Faith Bible and Tract Society
Literature publisher of the Assembly of Yahweh in Holt, Michigan. *See* Assemblies of Yahweh.

Family of Love
Alternate cult name. *See* Children of God.

Fard, Wallace D.
Early sect leader considered to be an incarnation of Timothy Drew. *See* American Muslim Mission.

The Farm
Begun in 1971 by Stephen Gaskin on a 1,700-acre site near Summertown, Tennessee, this cult has as its background Buddhism, the drug culture, and the occult. Gaskin openly claims to be God. Mystical religious experiences include ritu-

alistic sex and the use of drugs. Jesus and Buddha were incarnations of God for their age. Sin is a doctrine that is "no longer necessary."

The Farm operates a school, a health clinic, and an ambulance service; owns a recording studio and a typesetting service; and operates Plenty, a relief organization providing aid to Third World countries. Fits in the mainstream of the New Age movement.

General: Larson, *New Book*, pp. 219-20; Melton, *Encyclopedia*, pp. 506-7.

Farollones Institute
Scientific community in California, related to the New Age movement.
New Age: Khalsa.

Farrakhan, Louis
Sect leader. *See* American Muslim Mission.

Father Andre
Ascended master channeled by Karen Glueck. *See* Channeling.

Father David
Another name for Moses Berg, cult founder. *See* Children of God.

Father Divine
Cult founder. *See* Peace Mission Movement.

Feast of Lights (Hannukah)
Jewish commemoration of the rededication of the Temple in 167 B.C. *See* Judaism.

Feast of Tabernacles (Sukkoth)
Jewish celebration of the harvest. *See* Judaism.

Feldenkrais Method
Alternate name for Functional Integration, a holistic health method using one thousand physical and meditative exercises related to yoga. Developed by Israeli scientist Moshe Feldenkrais. Also called Awareness Through Movement, and Western Yoga. *See* Holistic Health.

Feldenkrais, Moshe
Israeli scientist who developed a holistic health practice called Functional Integration, using one thousand physical and meditative exercises related to yoga. Also called Awareness Through Movement, Feldenkrais Method, and Western Yoga. *See* Holistic Health.

Fellowship of Friends

Offshoot of the Gurdjieff Foundation. Worship of material things and beauty enhance the quality of life. A person can realize a higher consciousness by surrounding himself with beauty and comfort. Founder Robert Burton claims he may be Christ returned. His followers do whatever he says. Based on a north California ranch.

General: Larson, *New Book*, pp. 402-3.

Feraferia

Background is the occult. Holds that religious life should be a part of a person's interaction with nature and with erotic awareness. Worships the divine maiden of the Greeks, Kore. Nudity is practiced. Publishes a monthly magazine, *Korythalia*. Incorporated in 1967 by Frederick M. Adams in Los Angeles. Now based in Eagle Rock, California.

General: Ellwood, pp. 194-200; Melton, *Encyclopedia*, p. 649.

Ferguson, Marilyn

Wrote *The Aquarian Conspiracy*, an important New Age resource. Publishes the *Mind/Brain Bulletin*. *See* New Age Movement.

Ferraby, John

Author of *All Things Made New*. *See* Baha'i World Faith.

Fife, Sam

Sect cofounder and author. *See* The Body of Christ.

Fillmore, Charles R.

Current cult president. *See* Unity School of Christianity.

Fillmore, Charles Rickert

Former cult president. *See* Unity School of Christianity.

Fillmore, Charles Sherlock and Myrtle

Cult founders. Charles wrote *Christian Healing* and *Jesus Christ Heals*. *See* Unity School of Christianity.

Findhorn Community

Prototype learning center and think tank located in northern Scotland, founded by Peter and Eileen Caddy. Offers an ongoing educational program in New Age principles. *See* New Age Movement.

Fire Walking

Practice of walking barefoot across a bed of hot coals or stones without injury to the feet. This is done to achieve spiritual purification and demonstrate one's confidence in the protection of the gods. Actually, this is most often merely spiritualistic fakery. Fire walkers may undergo neurolinguistic programming to prepare for this feat. *See* Spiritualism.

First Community Church of America
Founded by Robert Taylor. *See* Fundamentalist Fringe Movements.

First Earth Battalion
Also called the Natural Guard. Projected to be the New Age militia of soldier-monks trained in conflict-resolution methods such as martial arts, yoga, and meditation. *See* New Age Movement.

The First Principles
Written by John Robert Stevens, late cult leader. *See* Church of the Living Word.

Fitch, Ed
Coauthor of a popular book, *A Book of Pagan Rituals*, used by witches. *See* Witchcraft.

The Five Classics
Anthology collected and edited by Confucius. *See* Confucianism.

Flaming Ball of Fire
Book by Benjamin Purnell. *See* Israelite House of David.

Fliess, Wilhelm
Developer of biorhythms in which physical, emotional, and intellectual cycles are plotted on a chart to warn of critical days when caution should be exercised. *See* Spiritualism.

The Flight of the Eagle
Written by Jiddu Krishnamurti in 1973. *See* Krishnamurti Foundation of America.

"Flirty Fishing"
What Moses Berg calls prostitution for the purpose of fund-raising. *See* Children of God.

Flotation Tank
Also called isolation tank or sensory deprivation device. The practitioner floats in a special salt water solution in a closed tank, completely shut off from the world. Used in psychic research and for meditation. *See* New Age Movement.

Flying Saucers Farewell
Written by George Adamski in 1961. *See* George Adamski Foundation.

Flying Saucers Have Landed
Written by George Adamski in 1953. *See* George Adamski Foundation.

Flying Saucers International
Magazine of the Amalgamated Flying Saucer Clubs of America, founded by Gabriel Green. *See* UFO Cults.

Focusing Institute
Teaches the New Age technique of focusing in psychotherapy, psychosomatic healing, stress reduction, creative writing, and education. Sponsors "Weekend Training in Focusing." Founded by Eugene T. Gendlin in Chicago, Illinois. New Age: Khalsa, p. 58.

Followers of Jesus
"We worship God and God the Father but not Christ. God the Son and the Holy Spirit are manifestations of God. We are all sons of God." Jesus was "a Master, perfect natural man." The Old Testament is disregarded. Members claim they can't be hurt. Also claim to have visions.

Founded by Dom Mark Ryan in 1963 and headquartered in New York. Background is Catholicism. Publications are *The Divine Spectrum* and *Poems of a Believer*.

For Sinners Only
Written by Arthur James Russell in 1932. *See* Moral Rearmament.

Ford, Arthur
Spiritualist cult cofounder. *See* Spiritual Frontiers Fellowship.

Forever Family
Alternate cult name. *See* Church of Bible Understanding.

Forever Forests
Subsidiary organization. *See* Church of All Worlds.

The Forum
Human potential seminar, and alternate cult name. *See* est.

Foundation Faith of God
Formerly called the Process Church of the Final Judgement and Foundation Faith of the Millennium. Background is

Satanism and Scientology. God is manifested through four gods or symbols: Jehovah, Lucifer, Satan, and Christ. Since Christ "loves" Satan, Processians love and worship Satan. Evil and good are reconciled. The Christian church is blamed for creating guilt and shame. Fear is beneficial. Services feature healing, dramatics, meditation, chanting, and forums. The Christian cross and the satanic goat symbol adorn the altar. Psychic powers are taught.

The clergy conducts "angel listenings" for a donation, in which they hear what an angel is telling the client and write it down for him. Reincarnation is taught.

The Process was founded by Robert de Grimston in England in 1963 and came to America in the late sixties. Centers are located in large cities. Publications are *So Be It* and *The Processians*, its magazine.

In 1974 de Grimston was ousted by members who were tired of the black clothing, somber theology, and satanic symbolism. He continued to practice under the Process Church name. The disenchanted members changed their group's name to Foundation Faith of the Millennium. Occultic practices persist, but ceremonies like the Jewish Sabbath were added. Present leaders are Christopher de Peyer (Father Lucius) and Peter McCormick (Father Malachi). Headquarters is in New York.

General: Larson, *New Book*, pp. 228-31; Melton, *Encyclopedia*, p. 578.

Foundation Faith of the Millennium
Former cult name. *See* Foundation Faith of God.

Foundation for Inner Peace
Headed by parapsychological investigators Robert and Judy Skutch. Publisher of *A Course in Miracles*. *See* New Age Movement.

Foundation for Mind Research
Codirected by Jean Houston and her husband, Robert Masters. *See* New Age Movement.

Foundation of Human Understanding
Founded by Roy Masters in 1961. Masters's words are elevated to the level of spiritual truth; the Bible is not the final authority. Dedicated to helping "a person thread his way back to a state of consciousness (innocence) that existed before the shock, trauma, upset, or corruption."

Background is Eastern mysticism, gnosticism, yoga, and hypnotism. God is both personal and impersonal; referred to as Principle, the Ultimate Stillness, and Reality. Jesus is rarely mentioned in publications and then usually in a negative context. The Holy Spirit is never mentioned; we are to rely on ourselves, made all-powerful by successful meditation. Man is inherently good, not guilty of sin, and has the capability to perfect himself through meditation. Salvation comes through self-effort alone.

Headquarters is in Los Angeles. Foundation Press has published *How Your Mind Can Keep You Well* (the primary textbook by masters), *Be Still and Know, Hypnosis of Dying and Death, The Secret of Life and Death, The God Game, Sex: the Substitute Love,* and *Hypno-Christianity.*

General: Larson, *New Book,* pp. 232-35; Martin, *New Cults,* pp. 297.

Foundation Press

Publishing house. *See* Foundation of Human Understanding.

The Fountainhead

Novel written in 1943 by Ayn Rand, which propagated capitalism as God. *See* Ayn Rand.

The Four Doctrines

Written by Emanuel Swedenborg, cult founder, in 1918. *See* Church of the New Jerusalem.

The Fourth Way

Alternate cult name. *See* Gurdjieff Foundation.

Fox, Leah, Kate, and Margaret

Three sisters to whom modern-day Spiritualism traces its origins in 1848. *See* Spiritualism.

Fox, Matthew

Controversial Dominican priest whose "Creation Spirituality" blends New Age mysticism, pantheism, environmentalism, and feminism. Author of *The Coming of the Cosmic Christ. See* New Age Movement.

Franz, Frederick William

Cult president. *See* Jehovah's Witnesses.

Fraternitas Rosae Crucis

Oldest Rosicrucian body in America. The Church of Illumination is the outer court for the Fraternity. Teaches the Divine Law and seeks to bring the two natures (masculine and feminine) into a state of equilibrium. Members of the Fraternity learn the secret teaching by correspondence; they can progress until they are ordained into the Council of Initiated Priests.

Founded by Pascal Beverly Randolph in 1858 after he was named the Supreme Master for the Western World. He was succeeded by Freeman B. Dowd, then Edward H. Brown, and Reuben Swinburne Clymer. The current Grand Master is Emerson M. Clymer. Headquartered at Beverly Hall in Quakertown, Pennsylvania. The Philosophical Publishing Company was begun by Reuben Clymer. *See* Rosicrucianism.

Free Communion Church
Related to Rosicrucianism. *See* Johannine Daist Communion.

Free Community Order
Organization led by Da Free John. *See* Johannine Daist Communion.

Free Primitive Church of Divine Communion
Former cult name. *See* Johannine Daist Communion.

Freed Men of New Jerusalem
Alternate cult name. *See* The Christ Family.

Freedom
Magazine. *See* Scientology.

Freedom Leadership Foundation.
Anti-Communist front group. *See* Unification Church.

Freeman, Hobart
Founder of a fundamentalist fringe movement. *See* Faith Assembly.

Freeman Institute
Has been called "the Moral Majority of Mormons." *See* Mormonism.

Freemasonry
Also known as Masons and Masonic Lodge. Freemasonry is not a cult in the truest sense, but as R. A. Torrey said, "a man can be a Christian and a Free Mason, but he cannot be an intelligent Christian and an intelligent Mason at the same time."

Teaches that all religions are one and that there are many gods who are considered equal to Jesus. Masonic literature denies that Jesus is the only savior of the world and rejects Christ's death on the cross as God's sole remedy for sin. Salvation depends on works, not faith in God. The sacred books of many religions are regarded equally as revelations from God.

In the seventeenth century, craftsmen who were masons traveled in Europe helping build cathedrals. They built "lodges" near their temporary homes, where they could spend leisure time together. The first Grand Lodge was founded in England in 1717. There is a link between Freemasonry and Rosicrucianism, the former deriving the names and meanings of several ritual degrees from the latter.

According to *Morals and Dogma* by Albert Pike, "Masonry is a search after light. That search leads us directly back, as you see, to the Kabbalah (Jewish book of occult knowledge) [see Kabbalah]. In that ancient and little understood medley of absurdity and philosophy, the Initiate will find the source of many doctrines: and may in time come to understand the Hermetic Philosophors [sic], the alchemists, all the thinkers of the middle ages, and Emanuel Swedenbourg [sic; *See* Church of the New Jerusalem]" (p. 741).

Other authoritative texts are *Revised Encyclopedia of Freemasonry*, *The Manual of the Lodge*, and *The Masonic Ritualist*, by Albert G. Mackey, and *A Text Book of Masonic Jurisprudence*.

Associated groups include Ancient Arabic Order of Nobles of the Mystic Shrine, for Masons who are at least 32d degree; Daughters of the Nile, for wives of Shrine members; International Order of Job's Daughters, for girls twelve to twenty years old and related to a Mason; International Order of the Rainbow, for girls who are twelve to twenty; Order of Amaranth; Order of DeMolay for young men fourteen to twenty-one; Order of the Builders; and Order of the Eastern Star, for female relatives of Master Masons.

General: Larson, *New Book*, pp. 236-39.

Miscellaneous: Ankerberg; Shaw.

Froom, L. E.

Highly respected author. *See* Seventh-day Adventism.

Frost, Gavin and Yvonne

Founders of the Church and School of Wicca in New Bern, North Carolina, in 1972. Wrote *Astral Travel: Your Guide to the Secrets of Out-of-the-Body Experience*. *See* Witchcraft.

Fry, Daniel

Author of *White Sands Incident* and UFO cult founder. *See* Understanding, Inc.

Fuller, Buckminster
Futurist. One of the New Age "significant thinkers."
See New Age Movement.

Functional Integration
Also called Western Yoga, the Feldenkrais Method, and Awareness Through Movement. Method of holistic health using one thousand physical and meditative exercises related to yoga. Developed by Israeli scientist Moshe Feldenkrais. *See* Holistic Health.

Fundamentalist Army
Founded by R. L. Hymers. Based in Los Angeles. *See* Fundamentalist Fringe Movements.

Fundamentalist Fringe Movements
Generally orthodox Christian groups that take on cultic characteristics in their methodology. Led by authoritarian leaders who strictly control the personal lives of their followers.

Includes such groups as Community Chapel, Faith Assembly, First Community Church of America, Fundamentalist Army, Maranatha Campus Ministries, Maranatha Christian Church, Northeast Kingdom Community Church, and University Bible Fellowship.

General: Tucker, *Another Gospel*, pp. 17-19.

G

Gaia

New Age name for the living planet Earth, which is worshiped as being one with us. *See* New Age Movement.

Galyean, Beverly

Late developer of "Confluent Education," designed to teach students that they are God and are perfect. *See* New Age Movement.

Gandhi, Mahatma

Born Mohandas Karamchand Gandhi. "Peaceful revolutionary" for India's independence from Britain and a Hindu reformer. *See* Self-revelation Church of Absolute Monism.

Gandhi Memorial Center

Built in Washington, D.C., to honor Mahatma Gandhi. *See* Self-revelation Church of Absolute Monism.

Garbage and the Goddess

Published by Da Free John. *See* Johannine Daist Communion.

Garbage Eaters

Alternate cult name. *See* A Cult with No Name.

Gardner, Gerald Brousseau

Credited with reviving the ancient art of witchcraft. Author of *The Meaning of Witchcraft* and *Witchcraft Today*. *See* Witchcraft.

Gardnerian Wicca

One of the major national witchcraft organizations. Based in Wheeling, Illinois. *See* Witchcraft.

Garuda
Buddhist sect periodical. *See* Vajradhatu.

Garvey, Marcus
Cult founder. *See* Rastafarianism.

Gaskin, Stephen
Cult founder. *See* The Farm.

Gautama, Siddhartha
Known as Buddha, founder of one of the major world religions. *See* Buddhism.

Gawr, Rhuddlwm
Founder of Cymry Wicca. *See* Witchcraft.

Gayman, Daniel
Sect leader. *See* Church of Israel.

GCI
Sect acronym. *See* Great Commission International.

GEA
Acronym for Global Education Associates. *See* New Age Movement.

Gendlin, Eugene T.
Cult founder. *See* Focusing Institute.

General Church of the New Jerusalem
Conservative cult branch based in Bryn Athyn, Pennsylvania. *See* Church of the New Jerusalem.

General Convention of the New Jerusalem in the U.S.A.
Cult branch based in Cambridge, Massachusetts. *See* Church of the New Jerusalem.

Genesis Group
"Separate but equal" black branch of Mormonism. *See* Mormonism.

Genesis Reflections
Company in Simi Valley, California, that produces Subliminal Motivation Tapes for children. *See* New Age Movement.

The Genuine Fiery Dragon
Popular occult magic spell book. *See* Magick.

Geomancy
Spiritualist method of divination using a map or globe with twelve divisions in which geomancy symbols are placed in conjunction with the planets. *See* Divination.

George Adamski Foundation
Founded in 1965 by Alice Wells, daughter of George Adamski, to carry on his work with UFOs and publish his books: *Cosmic Philosophy, Flying Saucers Farewell, Flying Saucers Have Landed, Inside the Space Ships,* and *Questions and Answers by the Royal Order of Tibet.*
Adamski became interested in UFOs in the 1940s. He claimed to be the first to meet and converse with a UFO inhabitant, a Venusian, in November 1952. After his death, a former secretary Charlotte Blob founded the UFO Education Center in Valley Center, California. *See also* UFO Cults.
General: Melton, *Biographical Dictionary*, pp. 2-4.

Georgian Church
Witchcraft group in Bakersfield, California. *See* Witchcraft.

Gerling, Helene
Spiritualist cult founder. *See* Universal Harmony Foundation.

Giant Rock Space Convention
UFO convention held annually near Yucca Valley, California. *See* UFO Cults.

A Gift of Prophecy
The story of Jeane Dixon, modern-day prophetess, written by Ruth Montgomery in 1965. Describes how she uses a worn deck of cards to see the future. *See* Spiritualism.

Global Congress of the World's Religions
Front organization. *See* Unification Church.

Global Education Associates (GEA)
Particularly significant New Age group that provides speakers for schools, religious organizations, and civic groups. Teaches a "planetary perspective." *See* New Age Movement.

Global Family
Founded and directed by Barbara Marx Hubbard, New Age futurist and activist. *See* New Age Movement.

Globalism
New Agers' reference to the transformation of Earth from nation-state divisions to a one-world community. *See* New Age Movement.

Glueck, Karen
Channeler of Father Andre, an ascended master. *See* Channeling.

Gnosticism
Began in the first century A.D. Teaches a sharply divided duality: spirit and body. The spirit is divine and good; the body is earthly and evil. Salvation is a product of a person's gaining the "secret knowledge" (gnosis) of his spiritual nature.

Jesus could not have been God in the flesh. He was a human who had gained a superior knowledge of His divinity (the Christ Principle within) and offered salvation to others through this knowledge. Satan did Adam and Eve a favor in bringing them to the Tree of the Knowledge of Good and Evil.

The Mandaeans of Iraq and Iran are the only surviving remnant of the ancient Gnostics, though their beliefs pervade numerous cults and sects.

Comparative Religions: Beaver, p. 110.

G-O
Alternate sect name. *See* Gurdjieff Foundation.

The God Game
Published by Foundation Press. *See* Foundation of Human Understanding.

God Speaks
Sacred scripture. *See* Sufism Reoriented, Inc.

God's Valley
Founded in 1966 near Williams, Indiana. Teaches New Age life-style, holistic health, and self-sufficiency.

New Age: Khalsa, p. 59.

Gohozon
Sacred scroll. *See* Nichiren Shoshu of America.

Going Within
"Guide for inner transformation," by Shirley MacLaine in 1989. *See* Spiritualism.

The Golden Book of the Theosophical Society
Important theosophical text. *See* Theosophy.

Golden Lotus Temple
Worship center and headquarters in Washington, D.C. *See* Self-revelation Church of Absolute Monism.

101

Golden Temple

Symbol of the Sikh religion in Amritsar, India. *See* Sikhism.

Gonzales, Laycher

Founder of the Assembly of YHWHOSANA sect. *See* Assemblies of Yahweh.

Good Business

Periodical for working people. *See* Unity School of Christianity.

Good News

Periodical. *See* Worldwide Church of God.

Gosho

Writings of Nichiren Daishonin. *See* Nichiren Shoshu of America.

Gospel Temple

Church in Hopkins, Minnesota. *See* Identity Movement.

Gould, Sylvester C.

Original occultic group leader. *See* Societas Rosicruciana in America.

Graceland College

School in Lamoni, Iowa. *See* Reorganized Church of Jesus Christ of Latter-day Saints.

Granth Sahib

Sacred scriptures. *See* Sikhism.

Graphology

Spiritualist practice of divination by reading a person's character and future from his handwriting. *See* Divination.

Great Among the Nations

Based in Colorado. Leader is Benjamin Altschul. Members are expected to turn all their money over to the group and to cut ties with their families. Anyone outside the group is considered evil. Mind control and brainwashing techniques are allegedly used. (*The Cult Observer*, American Family Foundation [July/August 1989].)

Great Commission International (GCI)

Street preachers invite people to fellowship Bible studies, then gradually pressure them into spending more and more time working for the group. They don't mention that the individual's independence will be slowly taken away. Considered a destructive cult because of its use of deception, manipulation, and coercion.

Members report being told that their parents would die soon if they quit the group. They are prevented from forming close relationships with other members so that their dependence on the group's leaders will grow. (Denny Golick, "Destructive Cults Eliminate Freedom of Thought," *The Diamondback*, U. of Maryland, April 18, 1988.)

The Great Controversy
Written by Ellen Gould White in 1858. Now titled *America in Prophecy*. *See* Seventh-day Adventism.

The Great Harmonia
Written in 1855 by Andrew Jackson Davis, a leader in the Spiritualist movement. *See* Spiritualism.

"The Great Invocation"
New Age prayer written by Alice A. Bailey in 1937. Circulated by her students, hoping that worldwide utterance of this prayer will bring the New Age of enlightenment into being. *See* New Age Movement.

Great Lakes Fellowship
Splinter group cofounded by Paul Rawlins in 1988. *See* The Way International.

The Great Learning
One of the four books by disciples of Confucius. Contains his teachings. *See* Confucianism.

Great White Brotherhood
Ascended masters (spiritual teachers of the past) who enlighten and guide. Also called Enlightened Masters, and Universal Brotherhood. *See* Church Universal and Triumphant.

Green Egg
Neopagan cult magazine. *See* Church of All Worlds.

Green, Gabriel
Founded the Amalgamated Flying Saucer Clubs of America in 1956 after he received contacts from the planet Clarion. *See* UFO Cults.

The Green Party
Growing political party intent on challenging traditional politics through an emphasis on ecology, feminism, and disarmament. *See* New Age Movement.

Greenpeace U.S.A.
Worldwide environmentalist group that seeks to bring a "planetary consciousness" to the world. *See* New Age Movement.

Grimoire
Manual of occult magic rituals and spells. Some of the more widely used grimoires are *The Black Raven, Eighth to Thirteenth Books of Moses, Enchanted Words of Black Forest, The Genuine Fiery Dragon, The Key of Solomon, The Lesser Key of Solomon, The Little Book of Romanus, The Necronomicon, Saint's Blessing, The Sixth and Seventh Books of Moses, The Spring Book, The Spiritual Shield*, and *The Testament of Solomon*. See Magick.

Grist for the Mill
Written by Baba Ram Dass. The latest edition was published in 1987. *See* Ram Dass.

Groeneveld, H. D. G.
Led ultraconservatives to break away from the General Church of the New Jerusalem in the 1930s. *See* Lord's New Church Which Is Nova Hieroslyma.

Gross, Sri Darwin
Former "Living ECK Master." Author of *Your Right to Know. See* ECKANKAR.

Guardian Angels
New Age related group. *See* New Age Movement.

Guided Imagery
Also called visualization. Involves relaxation techniques, self-hypnosis, and meditation. The person concentrates on an image in his mind in an effort to make something happen. The image may be suggested by a therapist. *See* New Age Movement.

Guided Opportunities for Affective Learning (Project GOAL)
Originally developed to help handicapped children in Irvine, California. Has also been used with nonhandicapped elementary children. Introduces them to the Inner Self, which can guide them in decision-making and in determining right and wrong. *See* New Age Movement.

Gurdjieff Foundation
Also known as G-O and The Fourth Way. Background is Buddhism and Kabbalah. Founded in Russia by Georgei Ivanovitch Gurdjieff. There is no sacred writing. There is no need for God. To know oneself is all important; a person can evolve to spiritual understanding when he becomes aware of his own imperfections.

Based in San Francisco. Has published *In Search of the Miraculous*, *All and Everything*, and *Meetings with Remarkable Men*, an autobiography. Owns thirty acres in Westchester County, New York. Peter D. Ouspensky was a mathematician and mystical philosopher who did much to spread Gurdjieff's teachings until they separated. Frank Lloyd Wright and Katherine Mansfield were adherents. An offshoot of this cult is the Fellowship of Friends led by Robert Burton.

General: Ellwood, pp. 135-40; Larson, *New Book*, pp. 401-4; Melton, *Encyclopedia*, pp. 687-88.

New Age: Newport, pp. 72-73.

Gurdjieff, Georgei Ivanovitch
Cult founder whose writings are used in the New Age movement, including *All and Everything*, *In Search of the Miraculous*, and *Meetings with Remarkable Men*. *See* Gurdjieff Foundation.

Guru
Religious teacher who gives personal instruction. Common in Hindu sects. *See* Hinduism.

Guru Bawa Fellowship
Headquarters is in Philadelphia. Background is Islam (Sufism).

Guru Ma
Another name for Elizabeth Clare Prophet, cult cofounder. *See* Church Universal and Triumphant.

H

Hagin, Kenneth
Church leader, televangelist, based in Broken Arrow, Oklahoma. *See* Positive Confession.

Hallucinogens and Shamanism
Edited by Michael Harner. Published in 1973. *See* Shamanism.

Hanafi Muslim Movement
Begun in 1968 by Hamaas Abdul Khaalis, a Black Muslim who broke away because he felt they were not orthodox. Background is Sunni Islam. Based in Washington, D.C. Basketball star Kareem Abdul-Jabbar is an adherent.
General: Melton, *Encyclopedia*, pp. 696-97; Rice, p. 186.

Hand, Beth R.
"Archbishop Primate" and cult leader. *See* International Church of Ageless Wisdom.

Handbook to Higher Consciousness
Book by Ken Keyes, revised in 1975. *See* New Age Movement.

Hanley, John
Human potential seminar cooriginator. *See* Lifespring.

Hanukkah (Feast of Lights)
Jewish commemoration of the victory over Syrian oppressors and the rededication of the Temple in 167 B.C. *See* Judaism.

Hanuman Foundation
Recognizes the Hindu monkey-god. *See* Ram Dass.

Haoma

Hallucinogenic drink used in worship. *See* Zoroastrianism.

Hare Krishna (ISKCON)

Official name is International Society for Krishna Consciousness. A Hindu Bhakti sect. Sacred writing is the *Bhagavad Gita* as interpreted by Prabhupada in a book called *Srimad Bhagavatam*. All holy scriptures must be harmonized with the *Gita*. *Back to Godhead* is a regular publication. Bhaktivedanta Book Trust in Los Angeles is the publishing house.

There are three gods: Brahma, Vishnu, and Shiva. Krishna is the eighth incarnation of Vishnu and is superior to Jesus. Salvation is achieved by chanting, "Hare Krishna, Hare Rama." Other religions are complementary. Teaches reincarnation and that troubles in this life are the result of bad karma in a former life.

Teaches vegetarianism because they do not kill animals (animals have souls). Idolatry is practiced. Teaches that the material world is superficial and unreal. "We accept the Lord Jesus Christ as the son of God. We believe if one really follows his teachings they can develop the love of God. But we have not seen anyone following his teachings yet." Jesus was just a good man.

Founded in India by Caitanya Mahaprabu in the sixteenth century. Formerly headed in the United States by A. C. Bhaktivedanta Swami Prabhupada, who brought it to America in 1965. Based in Los Angeles. Presently led by a group of eleven men, who rule over spiritual matters, and a board of directors, who take care of administrative matters.

This sect was ordered in 1983 to pay $32 million damages in the year-long abduction of a teenager who claimed she had been brainwashed and convinced that her parents were of the devil. She had been deprived of sleep and food and was forced to chant for hours.

The Beatles made Krishna popular, and George Harrison later sang about him in "My Sweet Lord" and the album "Living in the Material World." Krishna followers manufacture candles, incense, and other products sold under the "Spiritual Sky" label. Owns vegetarian restaurants around the country. Members live in communes and farming communities such as New Vrindaban near Moundsville, West Virginia. *See also* Eastern Mysticism.

General: Boa, pp. 178-87; Larson, *New Book*, pp. 259-67; Martin, *Kingdom*, pp. 361-62; *New Cults*, pp. 88-91; Mc-

Dowell, pp. 41-43; Passantino, pp. 139-58; Robertson, pp. 118-21; Tucker, *Another Gospel*, pp. 267-84, 397-98.

New Age: Newport, pp. 30-40.

Harlow, Allison
Feminist activist. Member of the Covenant of the Goddess, second largest national witchcraft organization. *See* Witchcraft.

Harman, Willis
Futurist and New Age group member. *See* Planetary Citizens.

Harmonic Convergence
Gathering of meditators at places all over the world at the same astrological time for the purpose of ushering in "world peace." *See* New Age Movement.

Harner, Michael
Professor of anthropology at Oxford who wrote *The Way of the Shaman*, which teaches shamanistic techniques, and *Hallucinogens and Shamanism*. Teaches seminars on how to become a shaman. *See* Shamanism.

Harrell, John R.
Sect founder. *See* Christian Conservative Churches of America.

Hasidim
Ultra-orthodox Jews. *See* Judaism.

The Healing Gifts of the Spirit
Written in 1984 by Agnes Sanford, a Christian author who explores New Age themes such as past-life regression. *See* New Age Movement.

Healing Haven
One of five divisions. *See* Mark-Age.

The Healing Heart
Book by Norman Cousins in 1984. Presents healing from a New Age standpoint. *See* New Age Movement.

Health and Happiness
Written by Ellen Gould White. *See* Seventh-day Adventism.

Healthy, Happy, Holy Organization
Also called 3HO and Sikh Dharma. Background is Sikhism. Teaches Kundalini Yoga and "the use of breath and the

mental and verbal use of sound current, or a mantra, to attune the individual consciousness to the vibration of infinity." Stresses communal living and vegetarianism.

Founded in 1968; presently headed by Yogi Bhajan, the "only Living Master of tantrism" and "Supreme Religious and Administrative Authority of the Sikh Religion in the Western Hemisphere." Owns ashrams in 150 cities and a forty-acre ranch near Espanola, New Mexico. Controls the Kundalini Research Foundation in Pomona, California.

General: Larson, *New Book*, pp. 377-78; Melton, *Encyclopedia*, pp. 737-38.

Heart
Magazine. *See* Church Universal and Triumphant.

Heart
Bimonthly periodical. *See* The Way International.

Heaven and Hell
Written in 1950 by Emanuel Swedenborg, cult founder. *See* Church of the New Jerusalem.

Heaven's Magic
Alternate cult name. *See* Children of God.

Heavy Metal Music
Type of hard rock music. Its lyrics and the actions of the performers on stage promote occultic practices, drug use, sexual abuse, murder, and suicide.

Some of the groups that have been labeled "heavy metal" or "black metal" are AC/DC, Anarchy, Anthrax, The Beastie Boys, Black Roses, Black Sabbath, Bon Jovi, Celtic Frost, The Cult, Danzig, Dead Kennedys, Dio, Exodus, Grim Reaper, Guns 'n' Roses, Helloween, Iron Maiden, Judas Priest, King Diamond, Kingdom Come, KISS, Megadeth, Metal Church, Metallica, Motley Crue, Ozzy Ozbourne, Possessed, Psychic TV, Raven, Sam Hain, Satan, Santana, Slayer, Sodom, Suicidal Tendencies, Twisted Sister, Venom, Wasp, and Whitesnake, to name just a few. *See* Occult.

Heiau
Sacred shrines. *See* Polynesian Religions.

Heindel, Max
Born Carl Louis Von Grasshoff. Occult group founder and teacher. Author of *The Rosicrucian Cosmo-Conception*, the basic textbook. *See* Rosicrucian Fellowship.

Henderson, Hazel
Futurist; New Age activist. *See* New Age Movement.
Hensley, Kirby J.
Cult founder. *See* Universal Life Church.
Herald Publishing House
Located in Independence, Missouri. *See* Reorganized Church of Jesus Christ of Latter-day Saints.
Here and Hereafter
Written by Ruth Montgomery in 1985. *See* New Age Movement.
Hewitt, William
Author of *Beyond Hypnosis,* a program for developing one's psychic and healing power. *See* New Age Movement.
The Hidden Path
Periodical published by Gardnerian Wicca, in Wheeling, Illinois. *See* Witchcraft.
Hidden Treasures
Book by Ellen Gould White. *See* Seventh-day Adventism.
High Watch
Inner circle of trained students. *See* The Prosperos.
Higher Self Potential
Human potential seminar taught by Dick Sutphen, New Age author. *See* New Age Movement.
Himalayan International Institute
Established by Swami Rama in Honesdale, Pennsylvania. Teaches Raja Yoga to students who flock to the Institute to learn how to "exhale all problems" and "inhale energy." Formerly a monk of the Shankaracharya Order, Rama is dedicated to "creating a bridge between East and West." Publishes the *Himalayan News* bimonthly.
General: Larson, *New Book,* pp. 240-41; Melton, *Encyclopedia,* pp. 714-15.
Himalayan News
Bimonthly periodical. *See* Himalayan International Institute.
Hinduism
One of the major world religions; a composite of religious, social, and philosophical doctrines indigenous to India. The various expressions of Hinduism emphasize these ideas to some degree: pantheism (the belief that God is one with cre-

ation); either reincarnation or transmigration (the successive rebirth of a soul into this life); karma (the debt accumulated against a soul); and nirvana (bliss, or final spiritual fulfillment).

Hindu scriptures include the *Vedas* (collection of wisdom books), the *Upanishads* (collection of speculative treatises), *Ramayana* and *Mahabharata* (two epic tales of India), the *Puranas* (legends of gods and goddesses), and *Bhagavad Gita* (the most sacred book).

There are three ways by which salvation or liberation from the cycle of rebirth can be achieved: (1) By works, religious duty. By doing these a person can add favorable karma to affect the bad karma, thus increasing his chances of liberation. (2) By knowledge. Human suffering is caused by ignorance. A person must learn all about his oneness with Brahman (Ultimate Reality, essence of the universe). When he attains this knowledge through a life of self-discipline and meditation, he is freed from the cycle. (3) By devotion. A person shows perfect devotion to a deity through public and private worship, which is carried over into human relationships. He will then be freed from the cycle.

Hindus do not all worship the same god. They may worship Brahma, Shiva, Vishnu (or one of his incarnations such as Krishna or Rama), or one of the goddesses such as Kali. Some believe in one god but worship the many manifestations of him. Cows are worshiped as having great power; they are allowed to roam freely and are treated with respect.

Hinduism gave birth to Buddhism, Jainism, and Sikhism. Many cults and sects in America, including New Age philosophy, are based on Hindu doctrines.

General: Boa, pp. 12-17; Larson, *New Book*, pp. 61-71; McDowell, pp. 283-95.

Comparative Religions: Beaver, pp. 170-96.

Hinkins, Roger Delano
Real name of John-Roger, sect founder. *See* Movement of Spiritual Inner Awareness.

Holiness Tabernacle Church
Congregation in Dyer, Arkansas. *See* Alamo Christian Foundation.

Holism
New Age belief that all reality is organically one. *See* New Age Movement.

Holistic Health
    Could also be called metaphysical health or New Age medicine. Generally refers to health care that involves the whole person. Health is viewed as more than the absence of disease. Individuals are held responsible for their own health or sickness and are referred to as clients. People are viewed more as energy than as matter.
    Natural forms of healing are promoted rather than drugs and surgery; there is a disdain for conventional medicine. Tools and practices include acupressure, acupuncture, applied kinesiology, aromatherapy, Ayurveda, bioenergetic analysis, biofeedback, body-work therapies, channeling, chromotherapy, crystal therapy, do'in, functional integration, guided imagery, homeopathy, iridology, macrobiotics, mandala drawing, nutritional therapy, orgonomy, polarity therapy, psychic healing, reflexology, Reiki, rolfing, shiatsu, Therapeutic Touch, Transcendental Meditation, visualization, yoga, and zone therapy.
    Some chiropractics and osteopaths (though certainly not all) provide some of these alternative therapies, including acupressure, nutrition therapy, or reflexology. The Academy of Parapsychology and Medicine and the Association for Research and Enlightenment promote research in psychic healing. *See also* New Age Movement.
    New Age: Hoyt, pp. 55-73; Larson, pp. 79-100; Reisser.

Holistic Medical Center
    Practices holistic health. *See* National Spiritual Science Center.

Holloway, Gilbert N., and June
    Cult founders. *See* Christ Light Community.

Holmes, Ernest Shurtleff
    Gnostic cult founder. Author of *Science of Mind. See* Church of Religious Science.

The Holy Bible from Ancient Eastern Manuscripts
    Written in 1959 by George M. Lamsa, Aramaic teacher. *See* The Way International.

The Holy Feedback Church
    Uses electroencephalograms to help a person learn how to mentally control his own body. Based in Southern California. (Angus Hall, *Strange Cults* [Garden City, N.J.: Doubleday, 1976], pp. 20-21.)

The Holy Name Bible
Translation of the Bible by A. B. Traina, published by the Scripture Research Association. *See* Assemblies of Yahweh.

Holy Order of MANS
MANS is an acronym for *mysterion* (mystery), *agape* (love), *nous* (knowledge), and *sophia* (wisdom). It is "deliberately designed to put a Christian gloss on a non-Christian movement." Jesus was a great human teacher or avatar who achieved "Christ-consciousness." Alchemy, tarot cards, astrology, kabbalah, psychic power, and parapsychology are used. Background is Hinduism and the occult. Reincarnation is taught. Part of the New Age movement.
Founded in 1965 by Paul W. Blighton. Headquarters is in San Francisco. Operates three seminaries and 100 missionary centers.
General: Larson, *New Book*, pp. 248-50; Melton, *Encyclopedia*, pp. 599-600.
New Age: Newport, p. 147

Holy Order of Mother Earth (HOME)
Subsidiary organization. *See* Church of All Worlds.

Holy Orthodox Church
Founded by George Winslow Plummer. *See* Societas Rosicruciana in America.

Holy Spirit Association for the Unification of World Christianity.
Official cult name. *See* Unification Church.

Holy Sutra, Nectarean Shower of Holy Doctrine
Revered scripture. *See* Seicho-no-Ie.

HOME
Acronym for Holy Order of Mother Earth, a subsidiary organization. *See* Church of All Worlds.

Homeopathy
Practice of healing the body naturally, treating the patient with the same thing that made him sick. *See* Holistic Health.

Hopkins, Emma Curtis
Cult cofounder. *See* Divine Science Federation International.

Horoscope

Chart that is made up to determine a person's destiny based on the positions of the stars and planets. *See* Astrology.

Hoskins, Cyril

Tuesday Lobsang Rampa, a Tibetan monk-doctor-pilot, at the time of his death supposedly left his body and persuaded Cyril, an Englishman, to let him take over his body. As Rampa he founded a Buddhist sect. *See* T. Lobsang Rampa.

House of Miracles

Name for communal houses. *See* Christ Communal Organization.

House of Prayer for All People

Founded by William Lester Blessing in 1941 in Denver, Colorado. Doctrines are stated in the "First Principles." Emphasizes the name of God as Yahveh. The name of his wife is Khaveh, who is our heavenly mother and the Holy Ghost. The name of their son is Yashua. All the sons of Yahveh (all believers) are the Elohim (gods). Publishes the *Showers of Blessing* newsletter.

General: Melton, *Encyclopedia,* pp. 463-64.

Houston, Jean

Codirector with her husband, Robert Masters, of the Foundation for Mind Research in New York. Has written ten books on subjects of altered states of consciousness, self-healing, and other New Age themes. She is called "the Master Evocateur of our times." *See* New Age Movement.

How to Have More in a Have-Not World

Written by Terry Cole-Whittaker in 1983. *See* Science of Mind Church International.

How Your Mind Can Keep You Well

Written by Roy Masters in 1976. *See* Foundation of Human Understanding.

Hubbard, Barbara Marx

Futurist. Cofounder and director of the Global Family. New Age activist. *See* New Age Movement.

Hubbard, Lafayette Ron

Cult founder. Wrote *Dianetics: The Modern Science of Mental Health, Purification: An Illustrated Answer to Drugs,* and *The Way to Happiness. See* Scientology.

Human Potential Movement

Developed by Abraham Maslow, founder of the Association of Humanistic Psychology. Stresses man's essential goodness and unlimited potential. *See* New Age Movement.

Humanism

Sometimes called secular humanism, it is a man-centered religion that is a "cousin" to New Age thought. *The Humanist Manifesto II* (1973) states, "As non-theists, we begin with humans, not God, nature, not deity. . . . no deity will save us: We must save ourselves."

All matter and energy have been arranged by chance. The universe is self-existent. Man is an evolved animal whose problem is superstition and ignorance. The answer to this problem is human reason and technology.

Jesus was a moral teacher. Death is the end of existence.

General: McDowell, pp. 459-78.

New Age: Groothuis, *Unmasking*, pp. 52-55, 167; Larson, p. 217.

The Hundredth Monkey

New Age classic by Ken Keyes in 1982. *See* New Age Movement.

Hunger Project

Program designed to raise consciousness of the hunger problem. *See* est.

Hymers, R. L.

Founder of the Fundamentalist Army in Los Angeles. *See* Fundamentalist Fringe Movements.

Hypno-Christianity

Published by Foundation Press. *See* Foundation of Human Understanding.

Hypnosis of Dying and Death

Published by Foundation Press. *See* Foundation of Human Understanding.

I

I AM Movement

Pantheistic concept of God. Background is Theosophy and gnosticism. Jesus was but one of many "ascended masters." The Movement focuses 80 percent of its worship and praise toward St. Germain, an occultist in France in the eighteenth century. Anyone who dies without grasping the truth of the Law of Life must reincarnate and try again. Part of the New Age movement.

Founded by Guy W. and Edna Ballard in 1930 after a visit from a divine messenger named St. Germain, who revealed the Truth and gave them the gift of healing. Guy Ballard wrote *Unveiled Mysteries*, chronicling his encounter with St. Germain, and also *The Magic Presence*, both under the pen name Godfré Ray King. *Life and Teachings of the Masters of the Far East*, by Baird T. Spalding, contains many of the beliefs central to modern I AM cults. Consists of many metaphysical "churches" and secret societies or "mystery schools" such as the Mighty I AM group. Incorporated under the name St. Germain Foundation.

General: Appel, p. 175; Larson, *New Book*, pp. 120-23; Martin, *New Cults*, p. 203; Robertson, pp. 162-63; Tucker, *Another Gospel*, pp. 369-70.

I Ching (Book of Changes)

One of the five classics of Chinese literature collected and edited by Confucius into *The Five Classics*. Gives instructions for an occultic form of divination. *See* Confucianism, Divination, *and* Martial Arts.

116

Ichazo, Oscar
New Age cult founder. *See* Arica Institute.

ICSA
Cult acronym. *See* Intercosmic Center of Spiritual Awareness.

ICUS
Acronym for International Conference on the Unity of the Sciences, a front group. *See* Unification Church.

Identity Movement
Background is Anglo-Israelism. Does not believe in the Trinity. Great emphasis is placed on the belief that Anglo-Saxon, Celtic, Scandinavian, and Germanic peoples are descendants of the ten lost tribes of Israel. Made up of several independent groups that are built around their own prominent leaders. They share literature. The Worldwide Church of God is the only one that has built up a denominational structure.

The Anglo-Saxon Federation of America was founded in 1928 by Howard B. Rand in Haverhill, Massachusetts. Christian Conservative Churches of America was founded in 1959 by John R. Harrell in Louisville, Illinois, to blend Christianity and patriotism. The Church of Israel in Schell City, Missouri, led by Daniel Gayman was formed in 1972 as a split from a Mormon splinter group. The Church of Jesus Christ Christian, Aryan Nations was founded by Wesley A. Swift as a "white racial theopolitical movement."

The Covenant, the Sword, the Arm of the Lord is a militant group founded by Jim Ellison in 1976 and is based at Zarephath-Horeb, a survivalist commune near the Arkansas-Missouri border. The Ministry of Christ Church was established by William P. Gale in 1964 in Mariposa, California. The New Christian Crusade Church was founded in 1971 by James K. Warner, based in Metairie, Louisiana, and is closely associated with the Ku Klux Klan.

Some of the smaller groups that publish literature and broadcast radio programs are the Church of Jesus Christ in Bass, Arkansas; the Gospel Temple in Hopkins, Minnesota; the Lord's Covenant Church in Phoenix, Arizona; the Mountain Church in Cohoctah, Michigan; New Beginnings in Waynesville, North Carolina; and Your Heritage in San Diego, California.

Many members of this movement also belong to Posse Comitatus, a populist organization that leads members to protest the income tax system.

General: Melton, *Encyclopedia*, p. 83.

Ikeda, Daisaku

International president of Soka Gakkai. *See* Nichiren Shoshu of America.

Impact Industries

Paint roller factory in California. *See* Church of the Living Word.

In Search of the Miraculous

Sect publication. *See* Gurdjieff Foundation.

Independence Sanitarium and Hospital

Institution in Independence, Missouri. *See* Reorganized Church of Jesus Christ of Latter-day Saints.

Injil (Gospel of Jesus Christ)

One of four sacred books for Muslims. *See* Islam.

Inner Light Foundation

Background is Spiritualism. The aim is "to develop among all people a conscious awareness of God through a knowledge and use of the extrasensory faculties possessed by each person." Headed by Betty Bethards, a psychic. Founded in 1967 in Novato, California. Bethards's teachings are channeled. She has written *The Sacred Sword* and *Sex and Psychic Energy*. She and her husband, Greg, give private readings.

General: Melton, *Encyclopedia*, pp. 582-83.

Inner Peace Movement (IPM)

Offers programs to help a person attain success by developing his self-confidence and skills and by programming his mind with IPM's formula for success. Background is Eastern mysticism and Theosophy. Founded in 1964 by Francisco Coll, a successful executive. The administrative office is in Washington, D.C.; national headquarters is in Osceola, Iowa.

Related organizations and programs include Americana Leadership College, Astro-Soul, Brotherhood of Spiritual Movements, The Counseling Program, Operation Action, and Peace Community Church. Publishes *Expression*, a monthly magazine.

General: Melton, *Encyclopedia*, p. 583.
Occult: Koch, p. 212.

Inside the Space Ships
    Written by George Adamski in 1955. *See* George Adamski Foundation.

Insight Transformational Seminars (ITS)
    Teaches that one can get rid of guilt and resentment and can develop a process for forgiveness within oneself. All the answers are within. Founded in 1978 by John-Roger, who heads the Movement of Spiritual Inner Awareness. Offers three "human potential" seminars that teach the New Age philosophy of individual self-reliance: Awakening Heart Seminar for $450, Opening Heart Seminar for $775, and Centering in the Heart Seminar for $775. *See* Movement of Spiritual Inner Awareness *and* New Age Movement.

Institute for World Order
    Elite group representing the New Age ideology. *See* New Age Movement.

Institute of Divine Metaphysical Research
    Founded by Henry Clifford Kinley in 1931 after a "face-to-face conversation with God." *See* Assemblies of Yahweh.

Institute of Human Development
    Produces metaphysical and self-improvement tapes providing guidance in meditation, visualization, and positive reprogramming. Tapes teach Kabbalah, awakening kundalini energy, ESP, hypnosis by mental telepathy, automatic writing, talking with animals, and becoming a Christ Master. *See* New Age Movement.

Institute of Noetic Science
    Sponsors five research projects at leading universities and research centers: (1) medical—to study life energies as they relate to health; (2) psychological—to develop new therapies and ways to help people realize their human potential; (3) physical—to measure psychic phenomena and apply it to solutions of planetary problems; (4) theoretical—to evoke a holistic scientific paradigm; and (5) religious/mystical—to study the nature of man's relationship to the cosmos. Founded in 1973 by former astronaut Edgar Mitchell to study human consciousness. (From a promotional brochure published by the Institute.) *See* New Age Movement.

Institute of Religious Science
    Original cult name. *See* Church of Religious Science.

Institute of Structural Integration

School in Boulder, Colorado, that trains rolf therapists. Rolfing is "massage with a vengeance," since rolfers administer painful pressure to the body with their hands and elbows to relieve energy blockages caused by previous traumatic experiences. Also called structural integration. *See* Holistic Health.

Institute of Transpersonal Psychology

Ph.D. program in Stanford, California, that offers courses in Aikido, Arica, astrology, Feldenkrais, Hatha Yoga, healing and hypnosis, Hinduism, parapsychology, sensory awareness, T'ai Chi Ch'uan, and Zen meditation. Daily one-hour sessions are offered for practicing yoga.

New Age: Larson, p. 27.

Integral Yoga Institute

"The body, the emotions, and the intellect can be developed to a level in which they can function healthfully and in perfect harmony with each other." "Evil also is God; evil is only the absence of good." Background is Eastern mysticism. Headed by Swami Satchidananda. Begun in America in 1966. Headquarters is in Pomfret Center, Connecticut. (James C. Hefley, *The Youthnappers* [Wheaton: Victor, 1977], p. 90.)

Intercosmic Center of Spiritual Awareness (ICSA)

"To experience one's self as the cosmic center of vibration" is the aim. Teaches how to recognize the unity of everything in all aspects of life. Practices Kundalini and Raja Yoga. Founded by Shri Ramamurti Mishra, a medical doctor. Headquartered at Ananda Ashram in Monroe, New York.

General: Hefley, p. 92; Melton, *Encyclopedia*, pp. 716-17.

New Age: Khalsa, pp. 65-66.

International Bible Students

Original cult name. *See* Jehovah's Witnesses.

International Church of Ageless Wisdom

The "oldest, largest Metaphysical/Spiritual Church in America teaching the Ancient Wisdoms and Truths taught by great spiritual teachers from ancient as well as modern religions." Studies offered in *Esoteric Seminary and College*, *Pathways to Truth*, and past issues of *Aquarian Lights* magazine. Sponsors the Radiant Heart World Healing Ministry. Founded by the late Archbishop Primate Beth R. Hand in Wyalusing, Pennsylvania.

General: Melton, *Encyclopedia*, pp. 537-38.
New Age: Khalsa, p. 66.

International Community of Christ

Also known as Jamilians. Founded in 1972 by Eugene Douglas Savoy, in Bellingham, Washington. Savoy claims to have had visions since age six that helped convince him that Jesus was merely an "inspired man of God" whose more important teachings were not included in the New Testament. He "discovered" that Jesus used a secret closed system of communication that is cryptically revealed in the gospels. "Christ is a universal force to be experienced" (instead of one to be worshiped as deity).

Practices include pyramidology, dream analysis, altered states of consciousness, biorhythms, auras, the study of light and color, and other occultic practices. Important texts are *The Decoded New Testament*, *The Essaei Document*, *Jamil: The Child Christ*, *The Jamilians*, and *The Lost Gospel of Jesus*. Presently based in Reno, Nevada.

General: Larson, *New Book*, pp. 256-58.

International Conference on the Unity of the Sciences (ICUS)

Front organization. *See* Unification Church.

International Cultural Foundation (ICF)

Cultural front group. *See* Unification Church.

International General Assembly of Spiritualists

Spiritualist denomination. *See* Spiritualism.

International Meditation Society

Alternate sect name. *See* Transcendental Meditation.

The International News

Monthly newspaper. *See* Church of God International.

International Order of Job's Daughters

Masonic organization for girls who are twelve to twenty years old and related to Masons. *See* Freemasonry.

International Order of the Rainbow for Girls

Masonic organization for girls ages twelve to twenty. Commonly called Rainbow Girls. *See* Freemasonry.

International Relief Friendship Foundation

Charitable program. *See* Unification Church.

International Religious Foundation

Sponsors academic seminars. *See* Unification Church.

International Society for Krishna Consciousness
Official sect name. *See* Hare Krishna.

International Training and Retreat Center
Located in Clearwater, Florida. *See* Scientology.

Irani, Merwan Sheriar (Meher Baba)
Sect founder. *See* Sufism Reoriented, Inc.

Iridology
Practice of studying the color and texture of the iris of the eye to diagnose illness. *See* Holistic Health.

Isis Unveiled
Book by Helena Petrovna Blavatsky. Published in 1877. Central document; an 800-page attack on Christianity. *See* Theosophy.

ISKCON
Acronym for International Society for Krishna Consciousness, official sect name. *See* Hare Krishna.

Islam
In A.D. 610, when he was forty years old, Muhammad had a vision in Mecca, Saudi Arabia, and recorded the revelations in the *Koran (Qur'an)*. In 622 he fled opposition; Muslims mark this as their beginning. When Jews and Christians rejected his teachings he returned to Mecca. He denounced the idols that surrounded the famous black stone, the Kaaba Stone, and declared that it represented the one true God, Allah.

There are four sacred books: the *Torah* of Moses, *Psalms of David (Zabin)*, *Gospel of Jesus Christ (Injil)*, and the *Koran*, which supercedes the others. Islam teaches the existence of angels. The six great prophets were Adam, Noah, Abraham, Moses, Jesus, and Muhammad, who was the last and greatest. Those who obey Allah and Muhammad will go to Paradise; those who oppose them will be tormented in hell. All good or evil comes by divine will.

There are "Five Pillars of Faith," things each Muslim must do: repeat the creed constantly; pray five times a day, kneeling toward Mecca; give one-fortieth of his income to the destitute; fast during the month of Ramadan; and go on a pilgrimage to Mecca at least once in his life.

Today the main branch of Islam is the Sunnis (approximately 90 percent, the traditional Muslims). The secondary branch is the militant Shia, or Shiites, who are predominant in Iran. The Wahhabi is the most strict and puritanical group. The mystical sect known as the Sufi Order is best known by the Dervish Orders with their "whirling dervish" dance. A number of cults and sects in America have their roots in one of these Muslim branches.

Islam is strongly missionary-minded, willing to exert financial pressure (such as the oil embargo), holy war (jihad), or whatever it takes to bring unbelievers under their authority. Muslims who go to war are promised immediate transition to Paradise if they die fighting for the cause.

General: Boa, pp. 49-56; Larson, *New Book*, pp. 89-102; McDowell, pp. 377-99.

Comparative Religions: Beaver, pp. 307-34.

Island Pond

Alternate name for the Northeast Kingdom Community Church in Island Pond, Vermont. *See* Fundamentalist Fringe Movements.

Isolation Tank

Also called a flotation tank or a sensory deprivation device. The practitioner floats in a special salt water solution in a closed tank, completely shut off from the world. Used in psychic research and for meditation. *See* New Age Movement.

Israelite House of David

Teaches that we are living in the last 6,000 years of God's time. Claims that automobiles, telephones, radios, and movies are signs of the end of Satan's kingdom. Founded by Benjamin Purnell in Benton Harbor, Michigan, in 1903. Members are "Israelites," direct descendants of the lost tribes of Israel. They turn over their worldly possessions to Purnell, called King Benjamin. Male members wear beards and don't cut their hair. Women must cover their heads at all times. They are vegetarian. The group owns an amusement park called Eden Springs, a vegetarian restaurant, and a cold storage plant. Publishes *Shiloh's Messenger of Wisdom*, a monthly newsletter. Prints King Benjamin's books including *The Book of Enoch*, *Flaming Ball of Fire*, and *Rolling Ball of Fire*.

General: Melton, *Encyclopedia,* pp. 457-59; Rice, pp.192-94.

It's All in the Playing

Written by Shirley MacLaine in 1988. *See* Spiritualism.

J

Jacobson, Thomas
Channeler for Dr. Peebles, a nineteenth-century Scottish physician. *See* Channeling.

Jainism
First faction to spring from Hinduism as an heretical movement. Founded in the sixth century B.C. by Mahavira, who denied that gods existed to be worshiped. Teaches self-denial and nonviolence. Adherents practice the "Five Great Vows" (renunciation of five sins: killing living things, lying, greed, sexual pleasure, and worldly attachments). Teaches reincarnation and vegetarianism.
General: Boa, pp. 18-21; McDowell, pp. 296-303.
Comparative Religions: Beaver, pp. 207-16.

James, Fannie Brooks
Cult cofounder. *See* Divine Science Federation International.

Jamil: The Child Christ
Written by Eugene Douglas Savoy in 1976. *See* International Community of Christ.

Jamilians
Cult text and alternate cult name. *See* International Community of Christ.

Jarmin, Gary
Former cult official who was cofounder of American Freedom Coalition. *See* Unification Church.

Jehovah's Witnesses

Its purpose is to usher in the kingdom age of the Millennium and join Jehovah's forces, who will be victorious at Armageddon. The Trinity is a creation of Satan. "How . . . Satan . . . succeeded in fostering the Trinity upon the Lord's people . . . is a real mystery." Jehovah is one God, not a Trinity. Jesus was the first and greatest creation of Jehovah. Denies Jesus' bodily resurrection.

There is no hell. If a person is one of the 144,000, he will go to heaven. If someone is a faithful witness but not one of the elect, he will live forever in paradise on earth. If a person is not a Jehovah's Witness, he will be instantly annihilated. Background is gnosticism.

Members are forbidden certain practices: to give or take a blood transfusion or an organ transplant; to vote, sing the national anthem, serve on a jury or in the military, or salute a flag; to celebrate any holiday or birthday, especially Christmas and Easter; to smoke or chew tobacco; to cook in aluminum pots; to attend another church, even a funeral or wedding; or to take Communion or worship Jesus. A Witness is saved by works, including knocking on doors and selling Watchtower material.

Founded by Charles Taze Russell in 1879. Originally known as International Bible Students. In 1884 he officially organized the movement as Zion's Watch Tower and Tract Society. After Russell's death many of his "Bible students" left the Society and began groups of their own, such as the Dawn Bible Students Association, the Eagle Society, the Elijah Voice Movement, the Layman's Home Missionary Movement, the Pastoral Bible Institute of Brooklyn, and the Standfast Movement.

Russell was succeeded by Joseph F. "Judge" Rutherford who led in the adopting of the present name in 1931. He was succeeded by Nathan Knorr. Headed by Frederick W. Franz since 1977. Headquartered at the Watchtower Bible and Tract Society in Brooklyn, New York. Meeting places are called Kingdom Halls.

Russell was influenced by pyramidology and wrote *Plan of the Ages as Shown in the Great Pyramid.* He also wrote a seven-volume theology called *The Millennial Dawn,* later titled *Studies in the Scriptures.* This cult uses its own version of the Bible called the *New World Translation of the Holy Scriptures.* The *Emphatic Diaglot* is an interlinear version that is used with its Bible. *Truth That Leads to Eternal Life* is used in recruiting new members. Periodicals include *The Watchtower* and *AWAKE!* All publishing is done by the Watchtower Bible and Tract Society.

General: Larson, *New Book*, pp. 268-73; Martin, *Kingdom*, pp. 38-125; McDowell, pp. 44-63; Passantino, pp. 47-86; Robertson, pp. 56-73; Starkes, pp. 33-43; Tucker, *Another Gospel*, pp. 117-48, 392-93.

Jehovah's Witnesses: Martin.

Jesus Christ Heals
Written in 1939 by Charles S. Fillmore. *See* Unity School of Christianity.

Jesus Christ Is Not God
Written by Victor Paul Wierwille in 1975. *See* The Way International.

Jesus Christ Our Passover
Written by Victor Paul Wierwille in 1980. *See* The Way International.

Job's Daughters
Alternate name for the International Order of Job's Daughters, a Masonic organization for girls who are twelve to twenty years old and related to Masons. *See* Freemasonry.

Jodosa, C. Jinara
Cult leader. *See* Theosophy.

Johannine Daist Communion
Founded by Da Free John, formerly known as Franklin Jones. Background is Hinduism.

John claims to be an avatar, the "Reality, the Self, and Nature and Support of all things and all beings." Seekers are required to have a steady job, tithe 10 percent to the group, eat a lactovegetarian diet, confine sex to marriage, and study Da Free John's teachings daily. The goal is to abandon reliance on reality, which doesn't exist, and become absorbed into Da Free John (God).

Headquarters is in Clearlake Highlands, California. John has published *Garbage and the Goddess*, *The Knee of Listening*, *The Method of Siddhas*, and *No Remedy*. The sacred text is John's *Enlightenment of the Whole Body*. Other organizations led by John are the Free Community Order and the Laughing Man Institute. The Dawn Horse Press publishes materials.

Various communal groups revere Da Free John and loosely fall in this category: Dawn Horse Society, Free Communion Church, Surrey Community, and Vision Mound.

General: Larson, *New Book*, pp. 196-99.

John

Member of the Essene community at the time of Jesus. John is now channeled by Kevin Ryerson. *See* Ryerson, Kevin.

John, Da Free

Formerly known as Franklin Jones. Cult founder. Author of *Enlightenment of the Whole Body*, *Garbage and the Goddess*, *The Knee of Listening*, *The Method of Siddhas*, and *No Remedy*. *See* Johannine Daist Communion.

John Lennon Conversations

Book by Linda Deer Domnitz in 1984 describing her channeling experiences with the late music star John Lennon. *See* Channeling.

John-Roger

Founder of the Movement of Spiritual Inner Awareness and its Insight Transformational Seminars. Was born Roger Delano Hinkins in Utah. Claims to be the embodiment of the divine Mystical Traveler Consciousness. *See* Movement of Spiritual Inner Awareness.

Johrei

Alternate sect name. *See* Church of World Messianity.

Johrei Center

Home where meetings are held. *See* Church of World Messianity.

Jonah

Spirit entity channeled by Laura Camaron-Fraser, the first woman Episcopal priest in the Pacific Northwest. Was forced to resign after she admitted that a spirit named Jonah spoke through her. *See* Channeling.

Jonathan Livingston Seagull

Early introduction to New Age thought. Reportedly dictated to author Richard Bach in 1970 by a spirit being in the form of a seagull. *See* New Age Movement.

Jones, James Warren "Jim"

Cult founder. *See* Peoples' Temple Christian Church.

Journey to Inner Space: Finding God-in-Us

Written in 1984 by Rodney R. Romney, pastor of the First Baptist Church, Seattle, Washington. Espouses the New

Age philosophy of "realizing one's own godhood." *See* New Age Movement.

Journey to Ixtlan

Written by Carlos Castaneda in 1983, teaching that man can talk with animals and trees. *See* Occult.

Judaism

One of the major world religions. Began with Abraham and his call by God to leave Ur of the Chaldees and go to Canaan, the Promised Land. Worships the one true God, Yahweh of the Old Testament. Most of the Old Testament is accepted, particularly the *Torah*, the first five books.

Saturday is observed as the Sabbath, a day of rest and worship. Jesus is acknowledged as a prophet but not the still-awaited Messiah. Several feasts are observed throughout the year: Passover, Shavuot (Pentecost), Rosh Hashanah (Jewish New Year), Yom Kippur (Day of Atonement), Sukkoth (Feast of Tabernacles), Purim, and Hanukkah (Feast of Lights).

There are three main branches of Judaism: Orthodox, Reform, and Conservative. Orthodox Jews observe the traditional dietary and ceremonial laws and regard themselves as the only true Jews. The Hasidim are the ultra-orthodox Jews who live isolated from the Gentile world, obey the law strictly, and wear black coats and ear locks.

Reform Jews are liberal, believing that the *Torah* cannot be accepted as factual and binding. Dietary laws are not kept. Prayers are spoken in the language of the people. Some worship on Sunday. Neglects the spiritual and religious side of Jewish life.

Conservative Jews are the "happy medium." They reject most of the liberal views of Reform Jews, instead focusing on preserving the Jewish race. A lesser known branch is Reconstructionism, which regards religion, culture, and ethics equally.

General: Boa, pp. 57-62; McDowell, pp. 364-76.
Comparative Religions: Beaver, pp. 272-306.

Judge, William Quan

Cofounder of the Theosophical Society. *See* Theosophy.

Judith, Ms. Anodea

Cult priestess and president. Founder of LIFEWAYS. Author of *Wheels of Life*. *See* Church of All Worlds.

Judo

Type of jujitsu. *See* Martial Arts.

Jujitsu

One of the variations of kung fu. *See* Martial Arts.

The Just Law of Compensation

Written by S. R. Parchment. *See* Rosicrucian Anthroposophical League.

K

Kaaba Stone

Black stone resting in the center of the Muslim shrine in Mecca, Saudi Arabia, that represents the one true God, Allah. *See* Islam.

The Kabbalah

Mystical sect of Judaism, highly complex and shrouded in secrecy. It probably began in the third century B.C. Rabbis tried to decipher esoteric meanings in Scripture by assigning numerical values to Hebrew letters and words. The "Tree of Life" they developed shows God's ten creative emanations, which correspond to man's ten levels of consciousness.

God is present in all that He has caused. "White" occult magic is practiced, invoking the esoteric names of God and the angels. Chiromancy, astrology, and Tarot cards are used for divination. The name is spelled in a variety of ways: cabbalah, cabala, kabala, kabalah, kabbla, qabala, and qabalah.

A game by this name is on the market. It resembles a Ouija board in design and function.

General: Boa, pp. 136-42.
New Age: Larson, p. 34.

Kahl, Gordon

Former cult leader. *See* Posse Comitatus.

Kahlil, Phez

Sect cofounder. *See* The Prosperos.

Kahuna

Ancient religious rituals practiced in Hawaii and associated with the occult. *See* Polynesian Religions.

Kairos Foundation
Operates a human potential seminar. *See* Life Training.

Kali
Female counterpart of the Hindu deity, Shiva. *See* Hinduism.

Kamala, Srimati
Current sect swami. *See* Self-revelation Church of Absolute Monism.

Kanaloa
Sea and death god. *See* Polynesian Religions.

Kane
Creator god. *See* Polynesian Religions.

Kapu
Prohibitions that protect the power in a certain place or person. *See* Polynesian Religions.

Karate
One of the variations of kung fu. *See* Martial Arts.

Karma
Means "action." Refers to the debt accumulated against a soul because of his actions during his lives. *See* Hinduism.

Kelsey, Morton
Writes Christian books with New Age themes: *Afterlife: The Other Side of Dying*; *The Christian and the Supernatural*; *Christopsychology*; *Discernment: A Study in Ecstasy and Evil*; and *Dreams: A Way to Listen to God*. *See* New Age Movement.

Kemp, Harold
Current "Living ECK Master." Author of *The Winds of Change*, his autobiography. *See* ECKANKAR.

Ken Keyes Center
New Age retreat center at Coos Bay, Oregon. Offers a human potential program called the Science of Happiness, giving instruction in the "Living Love Methods" found in the *Handbook to Higher Consciousness*, by Ken Keyes. Also offers training programs through ClearMind Trainings. *See* New Age Movement.

The Key of Solomon
One of the best-known grimoires, or occult magic spell books. *See* Magick.

Keyes, Ken
   Leader of the Ken Keyes Center at Coos Bay, Oregon. Author of *Handbook to Higher Consciousness* and *The Hundredth Monkey. See* New Age Movement.

Keys, Donald
   Cofounder of Planetary Citizens, New Age political action group. Author of *Earth at Omega. See* Planetary Citizens.

Khaalis, Hamaas Abdul
   Sect founder. *See* Hanafi Muslim Movement.

Khan, Pir Hazrat Inayat
   Sufi leader responsible for bringing the sect to America. *See* Sufi Order.

Khan, Pir Vilayat Inayat
   Contemporary sect leader. *See* Sufi Order.

Khual, Djwal
   Ascended master whose teaching inspired Alice A. Bailey. *See* New Age Movement.

King Benjamin
   Cult founder whose real name is Benjamin Purnell. *See* Israelite House of David.

King, George
   UFO cult founder. *See* Aetherius Society.

King, Godfré Ray
   Pen name of Guy W. Ballard. *See* I AM Movement.

Kingdom Hall
   Local meeting place. *See* Jehovah's Witnesses.

Kinley, Henry Clifford
   Founded the Institute of Divine Metaphysical Research in 1931 after a "face-to-face conversation with God." *See* Assemblies of Yahweh.

Kirlian Photography
   Used to capture a person's aura on a photographic plate. Claimed to be proof of a universal energy that emanates from all living things. *See* Aura *and* New Age Movement.

Kirpal Light Satsang, Inc.
   Background is Hinduism. Claims to be a worldwide spiritual and service organization. Surate Shabd Yoga meditation is practiced three hours a day in order to attain God-realization. Members must become vegetarians, be ethical, and be

totally devoted to their master. Participation in politics is forbidden.

Founded by Sant Thakar Singh in 1974. U.S. headquarters is in Kensington, California. Monthly magazine is *SAT*. Plans to build Lighthouse School near Umpqua, Oregon. Peacehaven near Deer, Arkansas, is a retreat center offering seminars on the unity of man based on the teachings of Singh.

General: Larson, *New Book*, pp. 274-79; Melton, *Encyclopedia*, p. 740.

Kirpan

Ceremonial dagger carried by Khalsa Sikhs, including children. *See* Sikhism.

Klanwatch

Publication. *See* Ku Klux Klan.

The Knee of Listening

Published by Da Free John. *See* Johannine Daist Communion.

Knight, J. Z.

Real name is Judy Hampton. New Age channeler of Ramtha, a 35,000 year old warrior. *See* Channeling *and* Ramtha.

Knorr, Nathan

Former cult president. *See* Jehovah's Witnesses.

Koan

Nonsensical statement or sound used to "nudge the mind into perception of truth." *See* Zen Buddhism.

Koinonia

Educational "community" in Maryland. *See* New Age Movement.

Koran (Qur'an)

Sacred writing of Islam. *See* Community of Islam in the West, Islam, *and* Sufism.

Korean Folk Ballet

Cultural front group. *See* Unification Church.

Korean Little Angels Choir

Cultural front group. *See* Unification Church.

Korean National Folk Dance Company

Cultural front group. *See* Unification Church.

Korythalia

Monthly occultic magazine. *See* Feraferia.

Kou Ch'ien Institute

Offers what it calls "creative meetings." (Peter Rowley, *New Gods in America* [New York: David McKay, 1971], p. 85.)

Krishna

One of ten incarnations of the Hindu deity Vishnu. *See* Hare Krishna *and* Hinduism.

Krishnamurti Foundation of America

Started by followers of the late "nonguru" Jiddu Krishnamurti. Theosophists believed he was God, and preparations were made to announce him to the world. But in 1929 he let it be known he wasn't interested in being worshiped. He declared, "Discard all theologies and all beliefs," teaching instead that mankind's problems are due to psychological problems and that everything one needs to know can be found within oneself. He was called the "World Teacher," his trips usually sponsored by New Age groups.

Operates elementary and secondary schools in Canada, England, India, and the United States.

General: Larson, *New Book*, pp. 280-81.

New Age: Khalsa, pp. 84-85.

See also Occult.

Krishnamurti, Jiddhu

Former World Teacher. Author of *The Awakening Intelligence*, *The Flight of the Eagle*, *Life Ahead*, and *You Are the World*. *See* Krishnamurti Foundation of America.

Krivé, Taryn

Channeler of Bell Bell, a "giggly six-year old from the legendary lost civilization of Atlantis." *See* Channeling.

Kriyananda, Swami

Born J. Donald Walters, he was vice-president of the Self-realization Fellowship Foundation until he decided to start his own commune. Wrote *Songs of Joy*, used in worship, and *The Path: A Spiritual Autobiography*. *See* Ananda.

Krone, Charles

Human potential training developer. *See* Krone Training.

Krone Training

Human potential motivational training sessions developed by Charles Krone referred to as "leadership development." Some say the training is based on the occult teachings of Georgei Gurdjieff. *See* Gurdjieff Foundation *and* New Age Movement.

Ku

God who helps in strenuous activities. *See* Polynesian Religions.

Ku Klux Klan

Founded by Confederate General Nathan Bedford Forrest. Not generally regarded as a cult, it bears some of the marks of cults. Arising in the aftermath of the Civil War, the movement didn't receive widespread support until after the release of the 1915 film *The Birth of a Nation*, which romanticized the Klan.

The Klan has used violence (lynchings, murders, and bombings) to achieve its goal of preserving the white race and ensuring voluntary separation of the races. Klan groups attempt to Christianize their prejudices by appealing to Scripture. But their interpretations are clearly erroneous. They have been labeled "white- or Aryan-supremacist, neo-Nazi, and anti-Semitic."

In 1984 it was estimated that about twenty-five different Klan groups still operate, the three largest being located in Tuscaloosa and Tuscumbia, Alabama, and Denham Springs, Louisiana. *Klanwatch* is a regular publication. (Verne Becker, "The Counterfeit Christianity of the Ku Klux Klan," *Christianity Today*, April 20, 1984, pp. 30-35.) *See also* Identity Movement.

General: Larson, *New Book*, pp. 282-85.

Kübler-Ross, Elisabeth

Death-and-dying researcher, hospice pioneer. Author of *On Death and Dying*. Often invited to speak at holistic health conferences. New Age spokesperson who has admitted consulting spirit guides. Founder of the Shanti Nilaya teaching and healing center where Spiritualism is practiced. *See* New Age Movement.

Kum Nye Relaxation

Meditation technique. *See* Nyingma Institute.

Kundalini Research Foundation

Yoga research center in Pomona, California. *See* Healthy, Happy, Holy Organization.

Kundalini Yoga

Meditation technique used by numerous cults and sects. *See* Chakras.

Kung Fu

Original of the Martial Arts. *See* Martial Arts.

L

Lafferty, LaVedi
Occultic group founder. Author of *The Eternal Dance.* *See* Collegians International Church.

Lama Foundation
New Age commune and cult headquarters in Taos, New Mexico. *See* Ram Dass.

Lamb-Lion Institute
Teaches that human relationships, daily work, and international politics "must conform to the same universal laws of order." New Age group in Salt Lake City, Utah.
New Age: Khalsa, p. 85

Lamsa, George M.
Aramaic teacher and author of *The Holy Bible from Ancient Eastern Manuscripts.* *See* The Way International.

Lanting, Ronald E.
Cofounder of the now defunct Church of Satanic Brotherhood. *See* Satanism.

Lao-tzu, or Lao-tse
Legendary founder of Taoism in China in the mid sixth century B.C. *See* Taoism.

A Lasting Peace
Collection of the addresses of Daisaku Ikeda. *See* Nichiren Shoshu of America.

Latari, Indira
Nineteenth-century Hindu woman channeled by Verna Yater. *The Butterfly Rises*, by Kit Tremaine, includes dia-

logues with Indira as well as other spirit entities. *See* Channeling.

Latihan
Worship services that feature shouting, weeping, leaping, speaking in tongues, chanting, whatever the worshipers want to do. *See* Subud.

Laughing Man Institute
Founded in 1975. Offers the teaching of the "God-Realized Adept Da Free John who magnifies the God-Realized disposition in those who respond to him wholeheartedly." *See also* Johannine Daist Communion.
New Age: Khalsa, p. 86.

LaVey, Anton Szandor
Satanic high priest. Author of *The Satanic Bible*, *The Satanic Rituals*, and *The Compleat Witch*. *See* Church of Satan.

Layman's Home Missionary Movement
Splinter group. *See* Jehovah's Witnesses.

Lazaris
Ascended master channeled by Jach Pursel. Sharon Gless of the "Cagney and Lacey" television series has been known to consult Lazaris. She thanked him when she won an Emmy award, saying "Lazaris—it is magic." He teaches how to use crystals and meditation. He wrote *The Sacred Journey: You and Your Higher Self. See also* Channeling.
General: Tucker, *Another Gospel*, pp. 327-28.
New Age: Larson, p. 105; Miller, pp. 152-53.

LDS
Acronym for Latter-day Saints. *See* Mormonism.

Lead Outdoor Academy
School in Tinnie, New Mexico. *See* The Way International.

Leadbeater, Charles Webster
Second presiding Bishop of the Liberal Catholic Church. Wrote *The Life After Death and How Theosophy Unveils It. See* Theosophy.

League for Spiritual Discovery
Founded by Timothy Leary. Uses the drug LSD as a sacrament, capable of causing "a mystical union of the universe with the self."
New Age: Brooke, pp. 31-35.

Leah

Venusian woman channeled by Jamie Sims. *See* Channeling.

Leary, Timothy

Cult founder and advocate of the drug LSD. *See* League for Spiritual Discovery.

Lectorium Rosicrucianism

Thinks of itself as a new instrument for the Great White Brotherhood. Founded in Holland in 1971 by a former member of the Rosicrucian Fellowship. Led by J. Van Rijckenborgh. Headquarters is in Bakersfield, California. *See* Rosicrucianism.

Lee, Mother Ann

Cult leader and "the Christ second-come." *See* Shakers.

Leek, Sybil

Leader of witchcraft in England and America. Author of *The Complete Art of Witchcraft* and *Diary of a Witch. See* Witchcraft.

Lemuria

Mythical island in the Pacific or Indian Ocean similar to Atlantis, whose former inhabitants serve mankind as ascended masters who want to impart ancient wisdom to us. Also called Mu. *See* Spiritualism.

Lemuria: the Lost Continent of the Pacific

Written by Wishar S. Cerve. Last published in 1982. Used as a textbook. *See* Rosicrucian Fellowship.

Lennon, John

Late member of the Beatles, now channeled by Linda Deer Domnitz. Her encounters have been published in the book *John Lennon Conversations. See* Channeling.

Lenz, Frederick

Former name of New Age guru Zen Master Rama. *See* New Age Movement.

The Lesser Key of Solomon

One of the best-known grimoires, or occult magic spell books. *See* Magick.

Levitation

Spiritualist practice of raising tables, persons, or objects by the power of the spirits. *See* Spiritualism.

Lewis, Harvey Spencer
Credited with starting a Rosicrucian revival in the United States in 1915. *See* Ancient Mystical Order Rosae Crucis.

Liberal Catholic Church
Spin-off theosophical group that interprets Christianity in the light of Theosophy. Irving Steiger Cooper was its first Regionary Bishop and author of *Ceremonies of the Liberal Catholic Rite*. C. W. Leadbeater was the second presiding Bishop and author of *The Life After Death and How Theosophy Unveils It*. *See* Theosophy.

The Life After Death and How Theosophy Unveils It
Book by C. W. Leadbeater. Published by the Theosophical Publishing House. *See* Theosophy.

Life After Life
Written by Raymond A. Moody, Jr., in 1976. Examines near-death experiences. *See* New Age Movement.

Life Ahead
Written by Jiddu Krishnamurti in 1975; published by the Theosophical Publishing House. *See* Krishnamurti Foundation of America.

Life and Teachings of the Masters of the Far East
Five-volume series by Baird T. Spalding. Contains many of the beliefs central to modern I AM cults. *See* I AM Movement.

Life Training
Human potential seminar founded by two Episcopal priests, W. Roy Whitten and K. Bradford Brown, in the late 1970s. Background is est. Training centers are located in Los Gatos, California; Atlanta, Georgia; and Dallas and Houston, Texas.

Following the suggestions given eliminates the need for a savior. Self-awakening leads to God-realization. Man creates his own universe. Sin is ignored. Sacred texts of all major religions are viewed as important as the Bible. Part of the New Age Movement.

Sessions last for two weekends, seventeen hours per day. They are operated by the Kairos Foundation and are available for a donation of between $350 and $1,000. Participants are told where to sit and when to talk. They may not chew gum, wear watches, or bring in any outside reading material.

General: Larson, *New Book*, pp. 286-89.
New Age: Larson, pp. 25-26.

Lifespring
Human potential seminar originated by John Hanley and Randy Revell. Teaches that man is perfect and that self-love is the greatest love one can experience. The purpose is to help people deal with problems and discover themselves. Some graduates, though, begin to withdraw from reality. The cult has been accused of using brainwashing and voodoo techniques. It has been said that it is a "destructive force in the mental health field" and "irresponsible, unethical."

Participants in the sessions are paired into "diads" and are taught that "people cause most of their own problems —mental and physical." They are pressured not to leave the sessions. "If you don't return after a break, they come looking for you." Trainers have no professional training. The one thing a participant fears most is his "holy grail"—he must confront it. "If you're a good person, you get your grail." Trainees become worn down and disoriented. There is "considerable potential for emotional harm."

Based in Portland, Oregon, and in thirteen other major cities. Similar to "The Forum." Basic training fee is $400; follow-up session fee is $750. Grosses more than $20 million a year. Considered part of the New Age movement.

General: Larson, *New Book*, pp. 290-91.
New Age: Larson, pp. 23-25.

LIFEWAYS
School for the study of consciousness and the healing arts. *See* Church of All Worlds.

Light Center
Meeting place for MSIA in major cities. *See* Movement of Spiritual Inner Awareness.

Light Traveler
Guiding force in a person's life. *See* Movement of Spiritual Inner Awareness.

Lighthouse School
Moral education school to be built near Umpqua, Oregon. *See* Kirpal Light Satsang, Inc.

Lilly, John
Medical doctor who wrote *Deep Self: Profound Relaxation and the Tank Isolation Technique. See* New Age Movement.

Lindisfarne Association
New Age think tank. *See* New Age Movement.

Listen Humanity
Book published by the Baba Lovers. *See* Sufism Reoriented, Inc.

The Little Book of Romanus
Popular occult magic spell book. *See* Magick.

Living Word for . . .
Collection of John Robert Stevens's revelations. *See* Church of the Living Word.

Living Word Publishers
Publishing house. *See* Church of the Living Word.

Llewellyn News Times
Publishing house for cults associated with the New Age movement, such as Church of All Worlds and Order Aurum Solis. *See* New Age Movement.

Lono
Storm, rain, and fertility god. *See* Polynesian Religions.

Loomis, Jean
One of the current channelers for Seth. Lives in Connecticut. *See* Channeling.

Lord of the Second Advent
Title of the second Messiah, said to be Sun Myung Moon. *See* Unification Church.

Lord's Covenant Church
Small group in Phoenix, Arizona. *See* Identity Movement.

Lord's New Church Which Is Nova Hieroslyma
Very conservative group formed in 1937 by H. D. G. Groeneveld as a split. *See* The Church of the New Jerusalem.

Lorian Association
New Age think tank near Madison, Wisconsin. Current president is David Spangler. *See* New Age Movement.

The Lost Gospel of Jesus: The Hidden Teachings of Christ
Authoritative text by Eugene Douglas Savoy in 1984. *See* International Community of Christ.

The Lost Teachings of Jesus
Three-volume series by Mark and Elizabeth Clare Prophet, reportedly channeled by Jesus. *See* Church Universal and Triumphant.

Lotus Sutra

Sacred writing attributed to Buddha. *See* Nichiren Shoshu of America.

Love

Written by Paul Erdmann in 1971. *See* Church of Armageddon.

The Love Family

Alternate cult name. *See* Church of Armageddon.

Lovecraft, Howard Phillips

Author of the *Necronomicon*, an occult grimoire, or ritual manual. *See* Magick *and* Occult.

Lucas, Charles H.

Instrumental in beginning the Discipling Movement at the Crossroads Church of Christ in Gainesville, Florida. *See* Discipling Movement.

Lucis Publishing

Publisher of New Age movement materials. *See* New Age Movement.

Lucis Trust

Concentrates on translating and publishing the works of Alice A. Bailey. Also sponsor of the Arcane School, which trains people in New Age thought. *See* New Age Movement.

Lycanthropy

Occult belief that people can change into animals such as werewolves, bats, or frogs under the influence of certain occult magic spells. *See* Witchcraft.

M

Mackey, Albert

Masonic author whose books include *Mackey's Revised Encyclopedia of Freemasonry*, *The Manual of the Lodge*, and *The Masonic Ritualist*. *See* Freemasonry.

Mackey's Revised Encyclopedia of Freemasonry

Written by Albert Mackey; revised in 1966. A Masonic text. *See* Freemasonry.

Mackinac College

School in Michigan. *See* Moral Re-armament.

MacLaine, Shirley

Actress. One of the more public adherents of Spiritualism and a leading spokesperson for the New Age movement. Author of *Dancing in the Light*, *Don't Fall Off the Mountain*, *Going Within*, *It's All in the Playing*, *Out on a Limb*, and *You Can Get There from Here*. *See also* New Age Movement *and* Spiritualism.

New Age: Sire, *Shirley MacLaine*; Smith.

Macrobiotics

Way of life in which one is careful to control food selection, preparation, and consumption in order to prevent illness and cure disease. Usually practiced in connection with visualization. *See* Holistic Health.

Macumba

Spirit worship practiced in South America, primarily in Brazil. Also known as Umbanda or Candombl. *See* Voodoo.

Mafu

First-century leper in Pompeii channeled by Penny Torres. He claims to be a member of the "brotherhood of light" in the "seventh dimension." Almost identical to Ramtha in speech patterns, personality, and teachings. Was first brought to public attention by television star Joyce DeWitt of "Three's Company" fame. *See* Channeling.

Magi

Zoroastrian priests. *See* Zoroastrianism.

The Magic Presence

Written by Godfré Ray King (Guy W. Ballard) in 1935. *See* I AM Movement.

Magick (occult magic)

Conjuring spells in the exercise of power over someone or something. Some occult magicians classify "magick" in three types: (1) Black magick is used to hurt others. Satanists use black magick. (2) White magick is considered "good" and is used to help others. Witches call themselves white magicians. (3) Neutral magick is involved with neutral forces in nature, which can be used for good or evil purposes.

A manual of spells is called a grimoire. The best-known grimoires are *The Key of Solomon*, *The Lesser Key of Solomon*, *The Testament of Solomon*, *The Necronomicon*, and *The Sixth and Seventh Books of Moses*. Other popular magick spell books are *The Black Raven*, *Eighth to Thirteenth Books of Moses*, *Enchanted Words of Black Forest*, *The Genuine Fiery Dragon*, *The Little Book of Romanus*, *Saint's Blessing*, *The Spring Book*, and *The Spiritual Shield*.

A magick circle is used to call on spirits to do what the occultist wants. The occultist prepares for this ritual by following requirements described in the grimoire. Drugs, alcohol, or sex may be used to heighten powers just before the ritual. During the ceremony, the desired spirit is summoned by various incantations. The ritual must be precisely done so that the spirit will not get out of control.

Symbolism is extremely important in magick. Knots in a string symbolize strangling the life out of a victim. Sacred things that are backwards or broken have power. Salt and iron can be used to control demons. Copper, the color green, the dove, and the swan are used in love spells. Iron, the color red, and the number five are used in hate spells. Different colored candles have different meanings. One of the most notorious black magicians was Aleister Crowley.

NOTE: Occult magic is not the same as sleight-of-hand magic, or illusion, that is purely for entertainment. *See also* Occult.

General: McDowell, pp. 203-6.

Occult: Koch, pp. 126-40; Larson, pp. 149-59.

Mahabharata
One of two epic tales of India revered by Hindus. *See* Hinduism.

Mahaprabha, Chaitanya
Fifteenth-century sect founder. *See* Hare Krishna.

Maharaj, Acharya Sushil Kumarji
Sect founder. *See* Siddhachalam.

Maharaj Ji, Guru
Sect leader. *See* Divine Light Mission.

Maharishi International University (MIU)
Campus is in Fairfield, Iowa. *See* Transcendental Meditation.

Maharishi International University Press
Publishing division in Fairfield, Iowa. *See* Transcendental Meditation.

Mahavira
Religious sect founder. *See* Jainism.

Mahayana Buddhism
Liberal branch of Buddhism that spread outside India, primarily into China and Japan. *See* Buddhism.

MAIN
Acronym for an educational program, Mark-Age Inform-Nations, designed to "prepare mankind for Age of Aquarius and for spiritual government's plan for Earth to rejoin Federation of Planets (UFOs) of our solar system." *See* Mark-Age.

Maitreya, Lord
New Age messiah promoted by Benjamin Creme, who was supposed to appear in 1982. He will now reveal himself when mankind is ready and the press is willing to give him coverage. *See* New Age Movement.

Maitri Therapeutic Community
Treats neuroses with Buddhist practices. *See* Vajradhatu.

Makiguchi, Tsunesaburo
Buddhist sect founder. *See* Nichiren Shoshu of America.

MAM

Acronym for a weekly radio program, "Mark-Age Meditations," designed "to help raise mankind into fourth dimensional consciousness." *See* Mark-Age.

Mana

Power that exists in everything and can be transferred from one thing to another. *See* Polynesian Religions.

Mandala

Concentric geometric design that focuses attention on one point and aids in meditation. *See* New Age Movement.

Mandala Drawing

Used in holistic healing as a way of tapping the subconscious. *See* Holistic Health.

Manley, Michael

Current cult leader. *See* Rastafarianism.

Mantra

Sanskrit word or phrase that is chanted repetitively in meditation to clear the mind and help the chanter achieve "cosmic consciousness." *See* New Age Movement.

The Manual of the Lodge

Written by Albert Mackey in 1870. One of the texts used by the Masons. *See* Freemasonry.

Many Mansions: The Edgar Cayce Story on Reincarnation

Book published by A.R.E. *See* Association for Research and Enlightenment.

Maranatha Campus Ministries International

Ministry aimed at college students. *See* Maranatha Christian Church.

Maranatha Christian Church

Fundamentalist group founded by Robert Weiner in 1972. Operates Maranatha Campus Ministries International and Maranatha Christian Fellowship aimed at college students.

Alleged authoritarian group that expects obedience to the rules: read only approved magazines, don't date, give more than 10 percent of one's income to Maranatha, give Maranatha priority in one's life, and get Maranatha's permission to marry. (Tanya Gazdik, "Some Colleges Warn Students That Cult-Like Methods Are Being Used by Christian Fundamentalist Groups," *The Chronicle of Higher Education*, November 15, 1989.) *See also* Fundamentalist Fringe Movements.

Maranatha Christian Fellowship
College campus ministry. *See* Maranatha Christian Church.

Mark-Age
UFO cult founded in 1960 by El Morya-Mark and Nada-Yolanda. Based in Fort Lauderdale, Florida. An educational organization with five divisions: Centers of Light, Healing Haven, Mark-Age Inform-Nations (MAIN), Mark-Age Meditations radio program (MAM), and University of Life. *See also* UFO Cults.
General: Melton, *Encyclopedia*, pp. 563-64.
New Age: Khalsa, p. 89.

Mark-Age Inform-Nations (MAIN)
Offers an educational program to "prepare mankind for Age of Aquarius and for spiritual government's plan for Earth to rejoin Federation of Planets (UFOs) of our solar system." *See* Mark-Age.

Mark-Age Meditations (MAM)
Weekly radio program "to help raise mankind into fourth dimensional consciousness." *See* Mark-Age.

Marley, Bob
Late reggae musician. *See* Rastafarianism.

Martial Arts
When practiced to their fullest extent, these studies in self-defense are really studies in paranormal feats and psycho-kinetic phenomena that have their roots in ancient Eastern religion, including Zen Buddhism and Taoism. "They view the universe as an interplay of harmonizing opposites, the yin and yang." Teaches the use of "universal energy" for self-defense and spiritual development.

Kung fu is the original; the variations are known as karate, T'ai Chi Ch'uan, judo, jujitsu, aikido, ninjutsu, and Tae Kwon Do. Kung fu dates back to 2696 B.C. in an occultic form of divination called *I Ching*. The use of psychic powers is taught. Emphasis is given to using force to break objects. Tae Kwon Do is the Korean version.

Karate is the best known form of kung fu in the West. It is mostly used for self-defense and sport-fighting. The word means "empty hand." The Buddhist flavor is exhibited in the bowing, breathing exercises, seated meditation, and intense concentration and awareness.

T'ai Chi Ch'uan is "soft" kung fu. Practitioners "shadow box," concentrating on the body's psychic center. "The ultimate goal is to become an immortal . . . by placing the body in harmony with . . . nature." Slow movements are used with meditation to develop self-discipline and spiritual awareness.

Jujitsu is a blend of kung fu and Japanese martial arts emphasizing knowing an opponent's vulnerable parts and how to attack them. Judo is jujitsu without the killing aspects. Judo is more like wrestling.

Aikido is the most overtly religious of the martial arts. The name means "the road to a union with the universal spirit."

Ninjutsu is a Japanese martial art form banned in the 1600s for its occultic powers. Practitioners, called Ninjas, are mercenary agents hired for covert operations involving espionage, sabotage, and assassination. They employ mind control, hypnosis, yoga, occult rituals, and other New Age practices.

General: Larson, *New Book*, pp. 298-305.

Martindale, Craig
Current cult leader. *See* The Way International.

A Marvelous Work and a Wonder
Written by LeGrand Richards. Used as a public relations tool. *See* Mormomism.

Maslow, Abraham
Founder of the Association of Humanistic Psychology and father of the Human Potential Movement. Coined the New Age terms "peak-experience," "self-actualization," and "synergy." *See* Association of Humanistic Psychology *and* New Age Movement.

Masonic Lodge
Meeting place for Masons. *See* Freemasonry.

The Masonic Ritualist
Written by Albert Mackey in 1867. One of the texts used by Masons. *See* Freemasonry.

Masons
Common name for members of the Masonic lodge. *See* Freemasonry.

Master Speaks
Tapes and transcriptions of Sun Myung Moon's messages to his followers. *See* Unification Church.

Masters, Robert
Codirector of the Foundation for Mind Research. *See* New Age Movement.

Masters, Roy
Cult founder. Author of *How Your Mind Can Keep You Well* and *The Secret of Life and Death*. *See* Foundation of Human Understanding.

Matea
David Swetland channels this 35,000-year old "six-foot eight-inch black female spice trader." *See* Channeling.

McCormick, Peter
Cult leader known as Father Malachi. *See* Foundation Faith of God.

McHugh, Charles
Sect founder who calls himself "Jesus Christ Lightning Amen." *See* The Christ Family.

McKean, Kip
Pastor of the Boston Church of Christ, leading church in the Discipling Movement. *See* Discipling Movement.

McLaughlin, Corinne
Cofounder of the Sirius Community. Coauthor of *Builders of the Dawn*. *See* Sirius Community.

McLean, E. Blair
New Age cult founder and director. *See* Christ Truth Foundation.

McNallen, Stephen A.
Founder of a Norse neopagan group. *See* Asatru Free Assembly.

McPherson, Aimee Semple
Founder and messianic evangelist of the Four Square Gospel movement in the 1920s, who called herself Christ's Bride. She was a healer whose "miracle room" in her Los Angeles temple was filled with previously used wheelchairs and crutches.
General: Appel; Melton, *Biographical Dictionary*, pp. 168-70.

McPherson, Tom
Mischievous Irish spirit entity channeled by Kevin Ryerson. *See* Channeling.

The Meaning of Witchcraft
Written by Gerald B. Gardner in 1959. *See* Witchcraft.

149

Meetings with Remarkable Men
Autobiography by Georgei Ivanovitch Gurdjieff. *See* Gurdjieff Foundation.

Meffen, James
Cofounder of The Body of Christ. *See* The Body of Christ.

Megatrends
Best-seller written in 1982 by John Naisbitt, a New Age lecturer and founder of Bellweather foundation. Although it doesn't endorse New Age ideology per se, its ideas coincide with New Age thought. *See* New Age Movement.

Meher Baba Spiritual Center
Training center in Myrtle Beach, South Carolina. *See* Sufism Reoriented, Inc.

Mencius
Student of Confucius's teachings who systematically developed them. *See* Confucianism.

Mental Telepathy
Transference of thought from one mind to another. One of the forms of extrasensory perception. *See* Spiritualism.

Mercury Publishing Company
Founded by George Winslow Plummer. *See* Societas Rosicruciana in America.

Metamorphosis, Inc.
Headquartered in Lake Oswego, Oregon. Develops human technology companies. Offers a time and information tool, *Skill Builder,* which helps persons prioritize time and store information in a holistic way. Offers New Age training for corporations.
New Age: Khalsa, p. 92.

Metaphysical Bible Dictionary
Doctrinal glossary by Charles S. Fillmore in 1931. Redefines biblical terms. *See* Unity School of Christianity.

Metaphysical Health
Another name for health care that involves the whole person. *See* Holistic Health.

Method of Siddhas
Published by Da Free John. *See* Johannine Daist Communion.

Metoposcopy
Spiritualist practice of divination by interpreting the lines on the forehead. *See* Divination.

Meyer, Charles E.
Occultic group leader. *See* Societas Rosicruciana in Civitatibus Foederatis.

Meyer, Jacob O.
Radio preacher for the "Sacred Name Broadcast," based in Bethel, Pennsylvania. *See* Assemblies of Yahweh.

The Middle Path
Book by S. R. Parchment. *See* Rosicrucian Anthroposophical League.

Miki, Tokuchika
Buddhist sect founder. *See* Perfect Liberty.

Miki, Tokuhito
Successor to Tokuchika Miki; current Buddhist sect leader. *See* Perfect Liberty.

The Millennial Dawn
Original name of the seven-volume theology by Charles Taze Russell. Now titled *Studies in the Scriptures*. *See* Jehovah's Witnesses.

Miller, William
Brought Adventism to America. *See* Seventh-day Adventism.

Mind at Large
Written by Edgar Mitchell, former astronaut, as a study in paranormal events. *See* New Age Movement.

Mind/Brain Bulletin
Published by Marilyn Ferguson. *See* New Age Movement.

Mind Control Bookstore
Cult-related bookstore. *See* Silva Mind Control.

Mind Science
Religious philosophy created by Ernest Holmes, founder of the Church of Religious Science. Denies orthodox Christian doctrines. Teaches that everyone can experience "Christ-realization." Views are shared by such groups as Christian Science, Church of Religious Science, est, Science of Mind International, and Unity School of Christianity. Related to the New Age movement.
General: Larson, *New Book*, pp. 306-7.

Ministry of Christ Church

The kingdom Jesus preached was of a government. Jesus is a kinsman of the white race whose roots go back to Adam. The black and yellow races began thousands of years before Adam. The Bible was written for the "generations" of Adam and no one else. The government Jesus set up is now in the United States, the New Jerusalem.

Established in 1964 by William P. Gale. Headquarters is in Mariposa, California. Publishes *Identity. See* Identity Movement.

Miracle Distribution Center

Located in Fullerton, California. Distributes *A Course in Miracles* and offers workshops. *See* New Age Movement.

Mirror Mantic

Also called crystal gazing. Spiritualist method of divination using a crystal ball, mirror, colored glass, or a pool of ink. *See* Divination.

Miscellaneous Theological Works

Written in 1792 by Emanuel Swedenborg, cult founder. *See* Church of the New Jerusalem.

Mishael

New Age cult leader called "Enlightened World Teacher." Author of *Pools in Parched Ground. See* Universal Faith Church.

Mishra, Shri Ramamurti

Cult leader and medical doctor. *See* Intercosmic Center of Spiritual Awareness.

Mitchell, Edgar

Former astronaut who, in 1972, resigned from NASA and founded the Institute of Noetic Sciences to study human consciousness. He has written *Mind at Large*, supporting such New Age methods as mental telepathy, psychic healing, and other paranormal events. Member of Planetary Citizens, a political action group. *See* Planetary Citizens.

Mitchell, William Irwin

New Age political action group member. *See* Planetary Citizens.

MIU

Acronym for Maharishi International University, in Fairfield, Iowa. *See* Transcendental Meditation.

MO

Another name for Moses Berg, cult founder. *See* Children of God.

MO Letters

Periodical considered authoritative on matters of belief and practice. *See* Children of God.

Modern Thought

Early cult name. *See* Unity School of Christianity.

Mohammed

Alternate spelling of Muhammad, religious founder. *See* Islam.

Moleosophy

Spiritualist practice of divination by reading moles on the face. *See* Divination.

Monism

Belief that "all is One." All people and things in the universe are ultimately one reality. Hinduism and the New Age movement, for example, have monistic worldviews. *See* New Age Movement.

Montessori International Schools

Sponsored by Summit Lighthouse. *See* Church Universal and Triumphant.

Montgomery, Ruth

Psychic and writer of New Age material such as *Search for Truth* and *Here and Hereafter*, two of nine books transmitted to her by automatic writing. She also wrote *A Gift of Prophecy*, the story of Jeane Dixon. *See* New Age Movement.

Moody, Raymond A., Jr.

Medical doctor. Author of *Life After Life*, which stimulated interest in the meaning of near-death experiences. Often speaks at holistic health conferences. *See* New Age Movement.

Moon, Julie Hoon Sook

Prima ballerina of the Universal Ballet Company in Washington, D.C. Daughter of Bo Hi Pak, Sun Myung Moon's chief lieutenant. Daughter-in-law of Moon, having married his deceased son after his death. *See* Unification Church.

Moon, Sun Myung

Cult founder. Author of *Divine Principle*. *See* Unification Church.

Moonies

Cult nickname. *See* Unification Church.

Moral Re-armament

Also known as Buchmanism and, in England, the Oxford Group Movement. Its aim is to remake the world by restoring God to leadership as the directing force in the life of nations and working to strengthen morale and a healthful national life within a country.

The group is unwilling to state its doctrinal convictions, though members concentrate on cultivating the "Four Absolutes": honesty, purity, unselfishness, and love. Sins formerly committed are recounted at house parties. There is no mention of the saving blood of Christ; conversion is merely living a new life. The women do not use cosmetics.

Founded by Frank Nathan Daniel Buchman, a Lutheran minister, in Caux, Switzerland, in 1910. Current executive director is J. Blanton Belk, Jr. The United States corporate headquarters is in New York. The center for publication is in Los Angeles. Owns the Westminster Theatre in London, where it uses films and plays to convey its ideas. Publishes *For Sinners Only*, by Arthur James Russell.

Operates Mackinac College in Michigan to provide a strong academic education and training in moral and spiritual qualities needed by leaders in the modern age. Originally sponsored "Up with People," a singing group that travels all over the world building morale. Now this group is not related to any religious or political organization. (Jan Karel Van Baalen, *The Chaos of the Cults* [Grand Rapids: Eerdmans, 1962], pp. 277-91.)

General: Melton, *Biographical Dictionary*, pp. 47-49.

Morals and Dogma of the Ancient and Accepted Scottish Rite of Freemasonry

Written in 1906 by Albert Pike, an occult Luciferian. One of the texts of the Masons. Usually referred to simply as *Morals and Dogma*. *See* Freemasonry.

Morgan, Elizabeth and Ernest

School founders. *See* Arthur Morgan School.

Mormon Tabernacle Choir

Choir of 350 voices having a repertoire of 810 anthems. *See* Mormonism.

Mormonism (LDS)

Official name is Church of Jesus Christ of Latter-day Saints. Background is Spiritualism, Freemasonry, and fundamental Christianity. The *Book of Mormon*, *Doctrine and Covenants*, and *Pearl of Great Price* are its sources of spiritual authority that guide faith and practice. The Bible is "correct so far as it is correctly translated." The *Book of Mormon* is esteemed far more as God's word.

Mormonism's view of the Trinity is not the same as that of orthodox Christianity. God "was once as we are now and is an exalted man. The Father has a body of flesh and bone as tangible as man's." Every Mormon male can seek to become a god. This doctrine is clearly polytheism. Jesus is one god among many gods; the spirit brother of Lucifer; a polygamist. The Holy Spirit is personage of spirit.

About the doctrine of salvation Mormonism says, "The blood of Christ will never wipe out [sin]. Your own blood must atone for it." A person is saved by repentance, baptism, faith, and good works. It is not a finished transaction until death; a person can never really be sure of salvation.

The Mormon church is the "true" church. "There is no salvation outside the Church of Jesus Christ of Latter-day Saints." On the doctrine of the virgin birth, it teaches that "Jesus was not begotten of the Holy Ghost." Practices baptism for the dead so that non-Mormons who have died will have a chance in the spirit world. More than 100 million baptisms have been performed. Maintains the best collection of genealogical records available anywhere.

Founded by Joseph Smith, Jr., in New York State in 1830. By a gradual migration west, the group moved to the Great Salt Lake in Utah under the leadership of Brigham Young. The current president of the church is Ezra Taft Benson. Its Freeman Institute is called the "Moral Majority of Mormons." *A Marvelous Work and a Wonder*, by LeGrand Richards, is used as a public relations tool. The Deseret News Press is its publishing division.

The movie and television series *Battlestar Galactica* was a portrayal of Mormon theology and its ideas of how man came to earth. A pageant called "City of Joseph" is presented annually in Nauvoo, Illinois, depicting Mormonism in a favorable way to a largely non-Mormon audience. The LDS is also prominent in VISN, the Vision Inter-faith Satellite Network.

The Mormon Tabernacle Choir and the Osmond family are some of the more widely known people associated with this cult. The church owns temples and tabernacles all over the world and owns stock in many corporations. Has members in many positions of public office. Currently has more than 20,000 full-time missionaries around the world serving two-year terms. In 1978 a new revelation permitted blacks to be ordained to the priesthood. Since then, the Genesis Group, a "separate but equal" black branch of the church, has been formed with little success.

Other related groups are the Reorganized Church of Jesus Christ of Latter-day Saints and the Church of Christ, Temple Lot. Several fundamentalist groups (some practicing polygamy) have spun off: Apostolic United Brethren, the Church of Jesus Christ in Solemn Assembly, the Church of the First Born of the Fulness of Times, and United Order Effort.

General: Larson, *New Book*, pp. 308-17; Martin, *Kingdom*, pp. 166-226; McDowell, pp. 64-79; Passantino, pp. 87-120; Robertson, pp. 29-55; Starkes, pp. 17-32; Tucker, *Another Gospel*, pp. 49-92, 389-90.

Mormonism: Decker, *God Makers*; Martin; Tanner, *Mormonism*.

Morris Pratt Spiritualist Institute
Located in Whitewater, Wisconsin. Ordains ministers. *See* Spiritualism.

Morya-Mark, El
Cult cofounder. *See* Mark-Age.

Mother Divine
Contemporary cult leader. Wife of the late Father Divine. *See* Peace Mission Movement.

Mother Earth Church
Witchcraft organization. *See* Witchcraft.

Mother Serena
"Head of the church." *See* Societas Rosicruciana in America.

Mountain Church
Church in Cohoctah, Michigan. *See* Identity Movement.

The Movement
Alternate sect name. *See* The Body of Christ.

The Movement Newspaper
Periodical "dedicated to the light and the sound within all people everywhere." *See* Movement of Spiritual Inner Awareness.

Movement for a New Society
Political community in Philadelphia, Pennsylvania. *See* New Age Movement.

Movement of Spiritual Inner Awareness (MSIA)
Background is Hinduism and ECKANKAR. Teaches the brotherhood of man and Fatherhood of God. "Jesus the Christ" was the supreme master, the cosmic form, the head of the planet of His day. He was the extension of God "Itself."

One must ask the Mystical Traveler (Light Traveler, Spiritual Traveler) to become a guiding force in one's life. He is the pure force of Light who takes a person into the Higher Realms of existence by helping him get rid of his karma.

Founded by John-Roger, whose teachings come from a "very ancient Mystery School." Based in Los Angeles. MSIA Light Centers have been established in major cities. PRANA is the group's ashram in Los Angeles. Publishes *The Movement Newspaper*. Operates the Baraka Holistic Center for Therapy and Research. Sponsors Insight Transformational Seminars to large corporations to change the thinking and values of employees by helping them awaken higher states of consciousness within themselves. *See also* New Age Movement.

General: Melton, *Encyclopedia*, pp. 740-41.
New Age: Khalsa, pp. 93-94; Larson, p. 26.

MSIA
Cult acronym. Pronounced "mes-siah." *See* Movement of Spiritual Inner Awareness.

Mu
Another name for Lemuria, a mythical island in the Indian or Pacific Ocean. *See* Atlantis.

Muhammad
Religion founder. *See* Islam.

Muhammad, Warith Deen
Present cult leader. *See* Community of Islam in the West.

Muktananda, Paramahansa
Tantric cult founder. *See* Siddha Yoga Dham of America.

Muller, Robert
Former assistant secretary-general of the United Nations. Author of *The New Genesis*, a summation of the core New Age doctrine that portrays the United Nations as a catalyst of globalism and a friend of the New Age movement. *See* New Age Movement.

Murphy, Michael
Cult cofounder and member of Planetary Citizens. *See* Esalen Institute.

Music Square Church
Congregation in Tennessee. *See* Alamo Christian Foundation.

My Religion
Book by Helen Keller last published in 1972. *See* Church of the New Jerusalem.

"My Sweet Lord"
Song made popular by the Beatles that includes the chant "Hare Krishna, Hare Rama." *See* Hare Krishna.

Mystical Traveler
Guiding force in a person's life. *See* Movement of Spiritual Inner Awareness.

N

Nada-Yolanda

UFO cult cofounder. *See* Mark-Age.

Nagorka, Diane and Henry

New Age cult directors. *See* National Spiritual Science Center.

Naisbitt, John

Author of *Megatrends*; a New Age lecturer who teaches that mankind is shifting toward a global economy. Creator of Bellweather, a metaphysical foundation. *See* New Age Movement.

Nakayama, Miki Maegawa

Cult founder. *See* Tenri-kyo.

Nales, John

Current UFO cult president. *See* Urantia Brotherhood.

NAM

Acronym for New Age Media in Berkeley, California. Collects, files, and shares information related to the New Age movement. Publishes guidebooks and mailing lists. *See* New Age Movement.

Nanak, Guru

Religious founder. *See* Sikhism.

Narada Productions

Producer of New Age music. *See* New Age Movement.

Narconon International

Operates drug detoxification centers in several cities. Based on the teachings of L. Ron Hubbard expressed in the book *Purification: An Illustrated Answer to Drugs*. *See* Scientology.

Naropa Institute
New Age think tank in Boulder, Colorado. *See* Vajradhatu.

Nation of Islam
Original sect name. *See* American Muslim Mission.

National Council for the Church and Social Action
Charitable program. *See* Unification Church.

National Spiritual Alliance
Spiritualist denomination. *See* Spiritualism.

National Spiritual Science Center
Teaches metaphysical and New Age concepts. Founded in 1941 by Alice Tindall in Washington, D.C. Directed by Diane and Henry Nagorka. Offers the School of Spiritual Science and Holistic Medical Clinic. Publishes through ESPress, Inc.
New Age: Khalsa, p. 101.

National Spiritualist Association of Churches
Oldest and largest Spiritualist denomination. *See* Spiritualism.

Native American Church
Founded in 1918 by peyote-using Indians who had learned Christianity from Catholic and Protestant missionaries. Blends centuries-old Indian rites and Christianity. *See* Native American Religions.

Native American Religions
Most Native American tribes in North America have had their indigenous religious orders with unique rituals and beliefs, though all were based on spiritism and pantheism. Some tribes believed in a Great Spirit, or creator, and some believed in an afterlife. The Hopi taught a cyclical series of creations, whereas others refused to believe in creation at all. Many tribes established rites to appease the spirits and gain their favor in the hunt, harvest, or childbirth. The shaman (medicine man) was respected by nearly all Native Americans as their priest, prophet, and doctor.

The use of sacramental peyote in worship made its way north from Mexico after the American Civil War and has become a widespread practice. The peyote sacrament consists of hiking into the desert, chewing peyote buttons, and waiting for a vision.

In 1918, the Native American Church was founded by Native American peyote-users who had learned Christianity from Catholic and Protestant missionaries. The Peyote Way Church of God was founded by Immanuel Trujillo. Both use old worship methods that have been handed down for centuries. Carlos Castaneda's *The Teachings of Don Juan* popularized peyotism and Native American philosophy.

General: Larson, *New Book*, pp. 106-9.

Comparative Religions: Beaver, pp. 165-66.

Natural Guard

New Age militia. *See* First Earth Battalion.

Naturopathy

Practice of using herbs instead of drugs, usually prescribed by chiropractors and osteopaths. *See* New Age Movement.

Necromancy

Alternate name for Spiritualism. Occultic practice of making the dead appear. *See* Spiritualism.

Necronomicon

Book of occult magic spells and symbols by Howard Phillip Lovecraft. *See* Magick.

Nemeton

Subsidiary organization. *See* Church of All Worlds.

Neopaganism

Worship of gods and goddesses of this world (nature); usually connected with some form of witchcraft or magic. The term was reportedly coined by Tim Zell of the Church of All Worlds. *See* Witchcraft.

Neurolinguistic Programming

Developed by John Grider and Richard Bandler. The therapist is supposed to be able to help a client overcome his insecurities, fears, and learning disorders by observing his body language and word patterns. Sometimes hypnosis is used. Many fire walkers undergo this therapy. *See* Spiritualism.

"New Age Christian Sangreal Sacrament Mass"

Worship service outlined in *New Age Priesthood. See* Church of New World Religions.

New Age Church of Truth, Inc.

Parent corporation. *See* Christ Light Community.

New Age Journal
Prominent periodical. *See* New Age Movement.

New Age Media (NAM)
Collects, files, and shares information related to the New Age movement. Publishes guidebooks and mailing lists. In Berkeley, California. *See* New Age Movement.

New Age Movement
Not a cult but a system of thought that is rooted in Eastern/occult mysticism and pantheistic monism. Theosophy, transcendentalism, and Spiritualism were forerunners; the three have much in common. The New Age movement is an informal network of cults and other groups that share the common belief in a coming "New Age" of peace and enlightenment.

The foundational belief is that "all is One, and this One is God." This is the basis for "The Plan," the goal of which is a united world: one world government, one world religion, one world monetary system, one world language, etc. Harmonic convergence is supposed to create this shift of worldviews, referred to as the paradigm shift, a new way of considering old problems. Gaia, the living planet Earth, is worshiped.

All mankind are brothers. The 1980s song "We Are the World" supported this New Age idea. Lord Maitreya, thought by some to be the Anti-Christ, was supposed to appear as the leader of the world in 1982. He declined to appear because of insufficient press coverage. He now lives in London.

The movement is intent on "cleansing the negative elements" of religion; it is totally opposed to Christianity. Its propaganda drive to prepare the world for the new "Christ" includes the seven-point worldview shared by most New Agers: (1) all is one (monism), (2) all is God (pantheism), (3) "we are all divine," (4) we have lived and will live many lifetimes (reincarnation), (5) we create our own reality, decide our own truth, (6) all religions are true (universalism), and (7) a new world order is coming.

If all is one, there is no sin and death. Jesus' substitutionary death for our sins is meaningless. Jesus was no more God than anyone else. "Christ" is a divine principle within all people. Jesus recognized the Christ within when He finally purified Himself of "bad karma" after many reincarnations.

Holistic health techniques are encouraged: acupuncture, auras, body work, chakra cleansing, divination, "dream

162

work," homeopathy, macrobiotics, naturopathy, past-life regression, polarity therapy, psychic surgery, rebirthing, reflexology, sensory deprivation devices, and others. New Agers also use crystals, exotic herbal teas, and pyramids to achieve healing.

Astral projection, centering, channeling, mantras and yantras, meditation, self-hypnosis, and visualization lead to "altered states of consciousness," an interruption or halting of "one's normal patterns of conceptual thought." New Age music is largely instrumental and is designed to enhance meditation and visualization and to generate a peaceful, uplifting mood. It is produced by companies like Windam Hill and Narada Productions.

New Age thought permeates society, affecting all of us through motion pictures, television programming, educational methods, and seminars that promote "human potential" such as Applied Scholastics, the Forum, Insight Transformational Seminars, Krone Training, Life Training, Lifespring, Pacific Institute, Synetics, and Summit Workshop.

New Age ideas infiltrate the church in such forms as: "Creation Spirituality," developed by Matthew Fox, a Dominican priest; yoga; esoteric Christianity; "process theology"; *A Course in Miracles* and *Journey to Inner Space: Finding God-in-Us*, by Rodney R. Romney, pastor of the First Baptist Church in Seattle, Washington. Agnes Sanford and Morton Kelsey are two other Christians who write books with New Age themes.

Public education is the prime target for New Agers since through it they can influence more people at the most impressionable age. They have introduced such "right brain learning techniques" into the classroom as yoga, meditation, guided imagery, chanting, and fantasy role-playing games. Values clarification, confluent education, globalism, and human potential are major emphases that are introduced to our children through such curriculum as Project GOAL, Project Self-esteem (PSE), QUEST, and SOAR.

Lucis Trust and Llewellyn News Times are New Age publishers. The works of Alice A. Bailey (inspired by ascended master Djwal Khual) are translated and widely distributed, as are the writings of Helena Petrovna Blavatsky, Benjamin Creme, Pierre Teilhard de Chardin, Marilyn Ferguson, Georgei I. Gurdjieff, P. D. Ouspensky, and David Spangler. Walt Whitman's poetry, such as "Song of Myself," expresses New

Age beliefs. New Age Media publishes guidebooks to New Age related groups and events.

Other key people, past and present: Richard Alpert (*see* Ram Dass), Thomas Berry (Jesuit priest), Carlos Castaneda (occult author), Arthur C. Clarke (science fiction writer), Rev. Terry Cole-Whittaker, Norman Cousins (author), Werner Erhard (*see* The Forum), Buckminster Fuller (architect/inventor), Beverly Galyean (educator), Hazel Henderson (futurist), Jean Houston (psychologist), John Lilly (M.D.), Barbara Marx Hubbard (futurist), Ken Keyes (author, cult leader), Elisabeth Kübler-Ross.

Also Shirley MacLaine (actress; *see* Spiritualism), Margaret Mead (anthropologist), Edgar Mitchell (former astronaut), Ruth Montgomery (author), Raymond A. Moody, Jr. (M.D.), Robert Muller (former assistant secretary-general to the U.N.), John Naisbitt (author), M. Scott Peck (author), Zen Master Rama, Theodore Roszak (cultural historian), Jonas Salk (biologist), Mark Satin (author of *New Age Politics*), E. F. Schumaker (economist), Sun Bear (shaman), Dick Sutphen (author, seminar leader), William Irwin Thompson (social historian), Alvin Toffler (futurist), George Trevelyan (author/speaker), and Ken Wilber (consciousness researcher).

Some of the groups reportedly involved in the movement are Academy of Chinese Culture and Health Sciences, Amnesty International, Association for Humanistic Psychology, Association for Transpersonal Psychology, Bread for the World, Club of Rome, Esalen Institute, The Farm, First Earth Battalion, The Forum, Foundation for Mind Research, Global Education Association, Global Family, Green Party, Greenpeace U.S.A., Guardian Angels, Human Potential Movement, Institute for World Order, Lindisfarne Association, Lorian Association, Miracle Distribution Center.

Other organizations are New Group of World Servers, The New Spirituality, New Thought, Pacific Institute, People for the American Way, Planetary Citizens (founded by Norman Cousins, Donald Keys, and U. Thant), Planetary Initiative for the World We Choose, Quartus Foundation for Spiritual Research, Sirius Community, Tara Center (founded by Benjamin Creme), Third Force, Third Wave, Unity-in-Diversity Council (which publishes *Spectrum,* a quarterly newsletter), Windstar Foundation (founded by John Denver), World Goodwill, and Zero Population Growth.

The Findhorn Community in Scotland, founded by Peter and Eileen Caddy, is a prototype New Age learning center and think tank. Another is the Chinook Learning Center in Washington State. The Ken Keyes Center in Coos Bay, Oregon, offers a human potential program called the Science of Happiness. Perelandra is a learning center near Washington, D.C., which specializes in "nature research" and plant communication.

New Age communes include the Lama Foundation in Taos, New Mexico, the Renaissance Community in Massachusetts, the Stelle Community in Illinois, Sunburst Community, and Twin Oaks in Virginia.

Teaching tapes are produced by such companies as Effective Learning Systems, Genesis Reflections (children's tapes), Institute of Human Development, SyberVision, and Valley of the Sun Publishing. Many of the titles are offered in subliminal versions.

Jonathan Livingston Seagull, which introduced us to New Age concepts in 1970, was reportedly channeled to author Richard Bach by a being in the form of a seagull. *The New Genesis,* by Robert Muller, sums up the core doctrine —that a New Age is dawning. Marilyn Ferguson's *The Aquarian Conspiracy* has done more to promote New Age ideology on a popular level than any other book. Her *Mind/Brain Bulletin* is a continuing compendium on New Age thought. Fritjof Capra's *The Turning Point* is a manifesto of New Age ideology.

New Age groups publish many periodicals such as *East/West Journal, The Movement, New Age Journal, New Directions, New Realities, The Next Whole Earth Catalog, ReVision, Whole Life Times,* and *Yoga Journal.*

General: Larson, *New Book,* pp. 324-31; Tucker, *Another Gospel,* pp. 319-55.

New Age: Brooke; Cumbey; Hoyt; Kjos; Larson; Martin; Melton; Miller; Reisser.

New Age Politics
Written by Mark Satin in 1978. *See* New Age Movement.

New Age Priesthood
Contains the mass liturgy called "New Age Christian Sangreal Sacrament Mass." *See* Church of New World Religions.

New Beginnings
Church in Waynesville, North Carolina. *See* Identity Movement.

New Christian Crusade Church
Founded in 1971 by James K. Warner, a former member of the American Nazi Party. Based in Metairie, Louisiana. Closely associated with the Ku Klux Klan. Two related organizations are the Christian Defense League and Sons of Liberty publishing company. *See also* Identity Movement.
General: Melton, *Encyclopedia*, p. 464.

The New Day
Biweekly newspaper. *See* Peace Mission Movement.

The New England Network of Light Directory
New Age directory. *See* Sirius Community.

New Era
Front group of the Moonies, which sponsors dialogue meetings for philosophers, theologians, and scientists. *See* Unification Church.

The New Genesis: Shaping a Global Spirituality
Book by Robert Muller in 1982, which sums up the core doctrine of the New Age movement—that a New Age is dawning. Portrays the United Nations as a catalyst of globalism and a friend of the New Age movement. *See* New Age Movement.

New Group of World Servers
Front group. *See* New Age Movement.

New Hope Singers International
Public relations group. *See* Unification Church.

The New Nation News
Periodical. *See* Children of God.

New Realities
Bimonthly magazine promoting the unity of self, mind, and body. *See* New Age Movement.

The New Spiritualism
Group that shares New Age ideology. *See* New Age Movement.

New Testament Missionary Fellowship
Background is Spiritualism. Their aim is to "deprogram young people who have been given a Christian upbringing at home . . . to rid them of their Christian ideas" using brainwashing techniques and kidnapping.
Occult: Koch, p. 213.

New Thought

Mental healing movement in the late 1800s, which represented a wide variety of religious thinking and spawned several cults: Christian Science, Church of the Universal Design, Divine Science Federation International, and Unity School of Christianity.

Miscellaneous: Barron; McConnell.

New Vrindaban

Sect community in Marshall County near Moundsville, West Virginia. *See* Hare Krishna.

The New World Religion

Written by Alice A. Bailey in 1943. *See* New Age Movement.

New World Translation of the Holy Scriptures

Watchtower's version of the Bible. *See* Jehovah's Witnesses.

Newbrough, John Ballou

Author of *OAHSPE: A Sacred History of the Dominion of the Higher and Lower Heavens on the Earth for the Next Twenty-four Thousand Years. See* Spiritualism.

The Next Whole Earth Catalog

Publication. *See* New Age Movement.

Nichiren

Buddhist reformer. *See* Nichiren Shoshu of America.

Nichiren Shoshu of America (NSA)

Also called Value Creation Society. Sometimes known by the name of its lay organization, Soka Gakkai. A sect of Mahayana Buddhism, it was brought here by Japanese wives of GIs in the early 1960s. Sacred writings are the *Lotus Sutra* and *Gosho*. God is the creation (pantheism). Happiness, good luck, and world peace come by people's chanting the Daimoku in the worship of the *Gohonzon* (sacred scroll).

Founded in 1930 in Japan by Tsunesaburo Makiguchi; based on the teachings of Nichiren Daishonen. Daisaku Ikeda is the international president of Soka Gakkai. *A Lasting Peace* is a collection of his addresses. George M. Williams (Sadanaga) is the present head in Los Angeles.

NSA Quarterly and *Seikyo Times* are periodicals. Owns temples in Flushing, New York; Silver Spring, Maryland; Rancho Cucamonga, California; Chicago, Illinois; and Kaneohe, Hawaii, as well as worship centers in several major cities. Strong methods are used for recruiting.

General: Larson, *New Book*, pp. 332-34; Martin, *New Cults*, p. 321; McDowell, pp. 315-17.

Eastern Mysticism: Ellwood, pp. 69-110.

New Age: Newport, pp. 56-61.

Nichol, F. D.

Highly respected author. *See* Seventh-day Adventism.

Nineteen Day Feast

Observed on the first day of each month of the Baha'i calendar. *See* Baha'i World Faith.

Ninja

Practitioner of the occult martial art form called ninjutsu. *See* Martial Arts.

Ninjutsu

An occult martial art form. *See* Martial Arts.

Nirvana

Heaven, bliss, spiritual fulfillment, the final goal, the absence of physical desire and suffering. *See* Buddhism *and* Hinduism.

No Remedy

Published by Da Free John. *See* Johannine Daist Communion.

Northeast Kingdom Community Church

Also known as Island Pond. Based in Island Pond, Vermont. *See* Fundamentalist Fringe Movements.

Nostradamus

French astrologer and physician best known for his authorship of 1,000 prophetic quatrains called True Centuries. He claimed that these prophecies foretold the future up to the year 2,000. His writings are still popular today. *See* Spiritualism.

NSA

Buddhist sect acronym. *See* Nichiren Shoshu of America.

Numerology

Spiritualist practice of divination using numbers in a person's name and birth date. Based on the idea that numbers have sacred significance that can order life. Used in connection with astrology. *See* Divination.

Nutritional Therapy

Use of herbs, roots, and other natural foods to cure and prevent illness. *See* Holistic Health.

Nyingma Center

Background is Buddhism. Offers training in Kum Nye Relaxation, meditation, and the teaching of books offered by Dharma Publishing. Based in Berkeley, California.

New Age: Khalsa, p. 104; Larson, p. 32.

O

OAHSPE

Subtitled *A Sacred History of the Dominion of the Higher and Lower Heavens on the Earth for the Next Twenty-four Thousand Years*. Authoritative text by John B. Newbrough in 1881. *See* Spiritualism.

Objectivism

Philosophy that "through science and technology, man can produce a utopia here on earth." *See* Ayn Rand.

Occult

Means secret, hidden, concealed. It is a term that covers wide-ranging practices including astrology, other forms of divination, Spiritualism, magic, witchcraft, Satanism, and Hindu/occult ancient wisdom groups such as ECKANKAR, Theosophy, Rosicrucianism, UFO cults, self-styled prophets, and the New Age movement. Outside the U.S. the occult takes the form of voodoo and macumba. Gnosticism is behind all this—the desire to find hidden knowledge not available to the average person and to control life with this knowledge.

Although some of the "unexplained" phenomena in the occult is supernatural (demonic), much of it is fakery. Occultic influence pervades society in subtle ways. Children's cartoons and toys, particularly those that are fantasy-oriented, are laden with occultic imagery. "One of the greatest protective coverings of the occult is that people do not believe it exists" (W.A.T.C.H. Network).

Fantasy role-playing games offer children and young adults what amounts to a catechism of occultism. Gary North says, "These games are the most effective, most magnificently packaged, most profitably marketed, most thoroughly re-searched introduction to the occult in man's recorded history.'' These games include Dungeons and Dragons®, Arduin Grimoire®, Chivalry and Sorcery®, Dragonquest®, Powers and Perils®, RuneQuest®, Stormbringer®, Tunnels and Trolls®, Villains and Vigilantes®, Warhammer®, and Warlock of Firetop Mountain®.

Carlos Castaneda is the author of several books about Mexican Indian mythology; these books are occultic in nature.

General: McDowell, pp. 147-280.

Occult: Koch; Korem, *Fakers*; Larson; Leithart; Wedge.

Odinist Committee

Norse neopagan group in England. *See* Asatru Free Assembly.

Odinist Fellowship

Norse neopagan group. *See* Asatru Free Assembly.

Ofudesaki

Sacred writing. *See* Tenri-kyo.

Okada, Mokichi

Cult founder called ''Enlightened Lord.'' *See* Church of World Messianity.

Olcott, Henry Steel

Cult cofounder. *See* Theosophy.

On Death and Dying

Best-seller in 1970 by Elisabeth Kübler-Ross, a spokesperson for the New Age movement. *See* New Age Movement.

One World Crusade

International fund-raising activity. *See* Unification Church.

The Only Dance There Is

Written by Baba Ram Dass in 1973. *See* Ram Dass.

The Open Conspiracy: Blueprint for a World Revolution

Book by H. G. Wells. Last published in 1979. Inspired New Age thinking about a united world government. *See* New Age Movement.

Opening Heart Seminar

Human potential seminar. *See* Insight Transformational Seminars.

Operation Action

Program for children and teenagers to introduce them to Inner Peace Movement ideals. *See* Inner Peace Movement.

Operation Redemption

Written in 1986 by George Trevelyan, a popular New Age speaker. *See* New Age Movement.

Operative Masonry

Written by S. R. Parchment. *See* Rosicrucian Anthroposophical League.

The Oracle of Toth

Magazine published by the Ausar Auset Society, a black Rosicrucian order. *See* Rosicrucianism.

Order Aurum Solis

Background is Spiritualism. Founded in England in 1897. Melita Denning and Osborne Phillips, who wrote *Astral Projection*, are two leaders. Llewellyn News Times publishes their works.

Order of Amaranth

Masonic organization. *See* Freemasonry.

Order of DeMolay

Masonic organization for young men who are fourteen to twenty-one years old. Founded in 1919. Headquarters is in Kansas City, Missouri. *See* Freemasonry.

Order of the Builders

Masonic organization. *See* Freemasonry.

Order of the Eastern Star

Masonic organization for Master Masons and their wives, widows, mothers, sisters, and daughters. Founded in 1876. Headquarters is in Washington, D.C. *See* Freemasonry.

Order of the Templars of the East

Another name for Ordo Templi Orientis. *See* Ordo Templi Orientis.

Ordo Templi Astarte (OTA)

Background is the occult. Based in Pasadena, California. Specializes in ceremonial magic. Participants wear long, hooded robes and perform rites evoking Apollo or Astarte. *See also* Occult.

General: Ellwood, pp. 171-75; Melton, *Encyclopedia*, p. 637.

Ordo Templi Orientis (OTO)

Also called Order of the Templars of the East. Similar to Ordo Templi Astarte. Practices the ritual sex magic of Aleister Crowley, including physical sadism, homosexuality, and drugs. Satan is an angel in good standing, the dark side of the

God Jehovah. Headquarters is in New York City. Granted a charter to Ancient Mystical Order Rosae Crucis in 1921. Several lodges and camps publish their own newsletters.

General: Ellwood; Melton, *Encyclopedia*, pp. 637-38.
Occult: Wedge, pp. 61-62.

Ordo Templi Satanas

Founded by Clifford Amos and Joseph Daniels. Lasted only a few years. Published *True Grimoire*, a newsletter for the Order and the Church of Satanic Brotherhood. *See* Satanism.

Orgonomy

Belief that illness comes when the flow of "orgone" energy is inhibited in the body. It can be released by uninhibited sexual activity. *See* Holistic Health.

Orthodox Judaism

Traditionally one of the three main Jewish branches. *See* Judaism.

OTA

Cult acronym. *See* Ordo Templi Astarte.

OTO

Cult acronym. *See* Ordo Templi Orientis.

Ouija Board

Rectangular board imprinted with the words "yes," "no," and "goodbye," the letters of the alphabet, and the numbers 0-9. A small heart-shaped platform (planchette) is moved over the board, spelling out answers to questions and predicting the future. Dabbling in this seemingly harmless parlor game can lead to insanity and demonic control. *See* Divination.

Our Nation

Sect newsletter. *See* Church of Jesus Christ Christian, Aryan Nations.

Ouspensky, Peter D.

Mathematician and mystical philosopher who helped spread Georgei Gurdjieff's teachings until they separated. Writings are used in the New Age movement. *See* Gurdjieff Foundation.

Out on a Limb

Written in 1983 by Shirley MacLaine, indirectly inspired by someone she calls "the Mayan." A popular book in her five-volume memoirs; was made into a television miniseries in 1987, which has been called "a classic piece of New Age evangelism." *See* New Age Movement *and* Spiritualism.

Owl Management
Cult front group. *See* Scientology.

Oxford Group
Alternate cult name. *See* Moral Re-armament.

Oyashikiri
Principal form of prayer for a Buddhist sect. *See* Perfect Liberty.

P

Pacific Institute

Front group for the New Age movement that offers human potential seminars teaching self-actualization through visualization and affirmation. Many Fortune 500 companies are clients. *See* New Age Movement.

Pacific West Fellowship

Splinter group. *See* The Way International.

The Pagan

Occultic magazine. *See* Church of All Worlds.

Pak, Bo Hi

Chief Lieutenant for Sun Myung Moon. Chairman of Newsworld Communications, which publishes the *Washington Times*. Treasurer of Panda Motors Corporation in Vienna, Virginia. Founder of American Freedom Coalition. *See* Unification Church.

Palmistry

Spiritualist art of divination by reading lines and marks on the palms and fingers. Also called chiromancy. *See* Divination.

Palo Mayombe

Cult branch also called Palo Monte. *See* Santeria.

Panda Motors Corporation

Based in Vienna, Virginia. Has plans to build an automobile plant in China by 1991. *See* Unification Church.

Pantheism

Belief that the impersonal God is one in essence with his creation, that he inhabits every created thing. *See* Hinduism.

Papa

"Earth mother" goddess. *See* Polynesian Religions.

Paradigm Shift

Change in worldview; a shift in the way reality is perceived. New Agers hope to bring this about by replacing rationalism and Christian monotheism with mystical monism (all is one). *See* New Age Movement.

Paragon House

Publishing firm in New York. *See* Unification Church.

Parapsychology

Begun in 1882 when the English Society for Physical Research was formed. A laboratory for parapsychological research was set up at Duke University in 1934. It is a cross between the occult and psychology, the study primarily of extrasensory perception (ESP). One outcome of the study of parapsychology is the increasing lack of motivation for studying the Bible.

Spiritualists claim that paranormal manifestations are brought about by the help of friends on the "other side," called operators. *See* Spiritualism.

Parchment, S. R.

Cult founder. Author of *Astrology, Mundane and Spiritual; The Just Law of Compensation; The Middle Path; Operative Masonry;* and *Steps to Self Mastery. See* Rosicrucian Anthroposophical League.

Passover

Jewish feast celebrating the exodus of the Hebrews from Egypt after several centuries of slavery. *See* Judaism.

Past-Life Regression

Technique of uncovering one's previous incarnations. Teaches that phobias are rooted in traumatic events experienced in previous lives. By going back to the former life and dealing with the trauma, a person can be free from the related problems in this life. *See* New Age Movement.

Past-Life Therapy Professional Training

Human potential seminar taught by Dick Sutphen. *See* New Age Movement.

Pastoral Bible Institute of Brooklyn

Splinter group. *See* Jehovah's Witnesses.

The Path: A Spiritual Autobiography
Written by Swami Kriyananda (J. Donald Walters). Formerly titled *The Path: Autobiography of a Western Yogi.* *See* Ananda.

Pathways to Truth
Cult textbook. *See* International Church of Ageless Wisdom.

Paul Revere Club
Auxiliary group. *See* Christian Conservative Churches of America.

Paulk, Earl
Church leader. *See* Positive Confession.

Paulsen, Norman D.
Cult founder and author of *Christ Consciousness. See* The Builders.

Paulson, Genevieve
Cult founder. *See* Dimensions of Evolvement.

Peace Community Church
Church with no building that offers fellowships, healing services, marriages, baptisms, and ordinations. *See* Inner Peace Movement.

Peace Mission Movement
Founded by Rev. Major Jealous Divine (Father Divine), formerly George Baker, in the 1930s. Father Divine was God, Jesus, and the Holy Spirit; salvation came through him. His kingdom, God, Inc., was located in Harlem, New York, and operated twenty-five restaurants, ten butcher shops, two grocery stores, ten dry cleaners, three apartment houses, and thirty oyster wagons. The only unpardonable sin was independent thought.

Mother Divine (the second Mrs. Divine) now heads the Movement. Publishes a biweekly newspaper, *The New Day.*

General: Appel, p. 39.

New Age: Martin, pp. 48-53.

Peacehaven
Near Deer, Arkansas. Based on the teachings of Sant Thakar Singh. Offers seminars on the unity of man. Publishes a quarterly magazine. *See also* Kirpal Light Satsang, Inc.

New Age: Khalsa, pp. 113-14.

Peale, Norman Vincent
Religious leader, author of more than twenty-five books, speaker. *See* Positive/Possibility Thinking.

Pearl of Great Price
One of the scriptural authorities of Mormonism, by Joseph Smith, Jr. Published in 1851. *See* Mormonism.

Pearls of Wisdom
Weekly publication, a "voice for the ascended masters." *See* Church Universal and Triumphant.

Peck, M. Scott
New Age teacher. Author of *The Road Less Traveled*, which teaches how to grow toward godhood, and *Sex and Spirituality*. *See* New Age Movement.

Peditherapy
Also called reflexology. Spiritualist practice of massaging certain parts of the feet to produce healing of various diseases. *See* Holistic Health.

Penitentes
Also known as Brothers of Our Father Jesus. This secret community in southern Colorado and northern New Mexico practices self-flagellation and other torturous acts of penance, including actual crucifixion to achieve atonement. Adherents are mostly Hispanics. Founders were Spanish Catholic immigrants in the 1700s. A more open form of this is practiced in Brazil and the Philippines.
General: Larson, *New Book*, pp. 337-38.

Pentecost (Shavuot)
Jewish feast observed fifty days after Passover commemorating the giving of the law to Moses. *See* Judaism.

People for the American Way
New Age front group. *See* New Age Movement.

Peoples' Forum
Official publication. *See* Peoples' Temple Christian Church.

Peoples' Temple Christian Church
Founded in 1953 by the late James Warren "Jim" Jones in Indianapolis as the Community Unity Church. Was moved to Ukiah, California, in 1965 and later to San Francisco. Background is Unitarian Humanism, Father Divine, and Marxism. Publications are *The Temple Reporter* (newsletter) and *Peoples Forum* (official periodical). Jonestown, Guyana,

was established in 1977 as a "model socialist society, a place where all peoples of all races could live and work together in perfect harmony."

Jim Jones claimed to be God, Buddha, and Lenin; he denied the deity of Christ. He taught reincarnation. Beatings and catharsis sessions were common in the church. Jones's private army, called the Angels, kept people in order and punished rule-breakers.

November 18, 1978, four people were killed, including Congressman Leo Ryan, and ten others were injured when the group was boarding a plane at the Jonestown airstrip after investigating reports of physical abuse. Several in the group were there trying to talk relatives into coming home with them.

November 19, 1978, 811 members of this cult with their leader, Jim Jones, committed mass suicide by drinking poison in their Jonestown compound. Another 100 had been shot. The group had practiced brutality, child abuse, and welfare abuse. Adherents were mostly blacks.

General: Ellwood, pp. 297-302; Rice, 202-4; Tucker, *Another Gospel*, pp. 371-72.

Miscellaneous: Wooden.

Perelandra

Learning center near Washington, D.C., specializing in "nature research." Eighteen gardens offer residence for the spirits. Students are taught how to communicate with plants. The leader is Machaell Small Wright, who is directed by devas (spirits) in how to maintain the gardens. The name was borrowed from the title of a book by Christian author C. S. Lewis. *See* New Age Movement.

Perfect Liberty

Background is Buddhism. Believes that man is meant to enjoy life and that play is of great spiritual value. The principal form of prayer is the oyashikiri, which is slowly chanted. Founded in 1946 in Japan by Tokuchika Miki. His successor is Tokuhito Miki. The leader in the United States is Jiro Yano.

Eastern Mysticism: Ellwood, pp. 178-205.

Peterson, Marcia

Cult director. *See* Alive Polarity.

Peyote

Hallucinogenic cactus used by American Indians for religious purposes. In 1990 the U.S. Supreme Court, in *Oregon v. Smith*, declared that states could regulate the religious use of peyote. Its use is still illegal in Oregon. *See* Native American Religions.

Peyote Way Church of God
Combines centuries-old Indian rites with Christianity. Peyote use is a sacrament. Founded by Immanuel Trujillo. *See* Native American Religions.

PFAL
Short for an introductory course called "Power for Abundant Living." *See* The Way International.

Phillips, Osborne
Cult leader. *See* Order Aurum Solis.

Philosophical Publishing Company
Publisher. *See* Fraternitas Rosae Crucis.

Phrenology
Spiritualist method of divination by reading bumps on the head. *See* Divination.

Physiognomy
Spiritualist practice of divination by reading the shape of a person's face. *See* Divination.

The Plain Truth
Free monthly magazine. *See* Worldwide Church of God.

The Plan
New Age "conspiracy" designed to replace current religious, political, and economic systems with a merged one-world system given to us by ascended masters. Most effectively expressed in Alice A. Bailey's *The Externalisation of the Hierarchy*. *See* New Age Movement.

Plan of the Ages as Shown in the Great Pyramid
Book by Charles Taze Russell, cult founder. *See* Jehovah's Witnesses.

Planetary Citizens
Political action group founded in 1974 by Norman Cousins, Donald Keys, and U. Thant. Members include David Spangler, William Irwin Mitchell, Michael Murphy (of Esalen Institute), futurist Willis Harman, former astronaut Edgar Mitchell, and Isaac Asimov.
Humanity is evolving toward Omega (unification of consciousness and culture). Planetary Citizens is dedicated to transforming the world. Keys says the flagship for planetization is the United Nations. He has written *Earth at Omega*. In

1982 Planetary Citizens helped kick off a consciousness-raising project called "Planetary Initiative for the World We Choose." Part of the New Age movement.

New Age: Hoyt, p. 93; Khalsa, pp. 114-15; Martin, p. 65; Miller, pp. 124-25.

Planetary Initiative for the World We Choose
Consciousness-raising project. *See* Planetary Citizens.

Plant Communication
New Age belief that plants have feelings and intelligence that can be measured and nurtured. They are affected by prayer, ESP, and evil. The "nature elementals" can be worshiped by our nurture of plant life. *The Secret Life of Plants*, by Peter Tomkins and Christopher Bird, espouses these views, which are taught at learning centers such as Findhorn Community and Perelandra. *See* New Age Movement.

Plenty
Third World relief agency. *See* The Farm.

Plummer, George Winslow
Occultic group leader. *See* Societas Rosicruciana in America.

Poems of a Believer
Sect publication. *See* Followers of Jesus.

Polarity Therapy
"Natural system of health enhancement that stimulates a person's body's life energy" by balancing positive and negative polarities employing gentle massage, diet, and exercise. *See* Holistic Health.

Polynesian Religions
Wakea (sky father) and Papa (earth mother) were the source of everything, including the gods. There are four main gods: Kane (creator), Lono (storm, rain, fertility), Ku (helper in strenuous activities), and Kanaloa (sea, death).

Lesser gods include the shark god, canoe-building god, hula-dancing god, and (the most famous) Pele, goddess of the volcano. The names of the gods vary from one island nation to another.

Teaches that *mana* (power) exists in everything and can be transferred from one thing to another. The mana of gods can come into people or idols. Priests direct the *kahuna* (ritual) to direct mana by chanting. *Kapu* (prohibitions) protect the mana of a certain place or person. Shrines are known as *heiau*. (John F. Mulholland, *Hawaii's Religions* [Rutland, Vt.: Tuttle, 1970].)

Poole, Cecil A.
Present cult leader. *See* Rosicrucian Fellowship.

Pools in Parched Ground
Book by Mishael. *See* Universal Faith Church.

Popoff, Peter
Church leader. *See* Positive Confession.

Positive Confession
Background is gnosticism. Related to Positive/Possibility Thinking. Based largely on the esoteric, Swedenborgian, theosophical teachings of the late E. W. Kenyon. Also known as the "Name It and Claim It" gospel, the "Health and Wealth" gospel, and the Word of Faith Movement. Has been called "Christian Science in Christian garb."

Gives a supernatural approach to positive thinking. Prosperity, health, and success come with the supernatural realization that "everything God has belongs to you"; all one need do is name it and claim it by speaking a "word of faith." Based on the concept that people are divine. Primarily taught by several televangelists. The following comments are samples of what some of the movement leaders preach.

Kenneth Copeland, Fort Worth: "You don't have a god in you. You are one!" "Jesus is no longer the only begotten Son of God." "[Jesus] hadn't come to earth as God, He'd come as man." "Where [Jesus] says, 'I Am,' I say, 'Yes, I Am, too!'" "You are all-God."

Paul Crouch, president of Trinity Broadcasting Network: "I am a little god."

Kenneth E. Hagin: "I became a human-divine being!" The Christian "is as much an incarnation [of God] as is Jesus of Nazareth." "Sin is only what I think. There is a higher Knowledge."

Earl Paulk: "Just as dogs have puppies and cats have kittens, so God has little gods." "Man has no right to private interpretation of the Word of God apart from those whom God sets in the Church as spiritual teachers and elders." God "has given us the name of Jesus Christ like a blank check."

Peter Popoff: "Wash with the anointed sponge and send a monetary gift to the ministry to "unlock heaven's storehouse of blessings for you."

182

Fred Price: "I am no longer a sinner." "God made man a god."

Robert Tilton, pastor of Word of Faith church in Dallas: "Man was designed or created by God to be the god of this world." "You can actually tell God what you would like His part in the covenant to be!"

Casey Treat, pastor of Seattle's Christian Faith Center: "I'm an exact duplicate of God!"

Paul Yonggi Cho and Oral Roberts are also leaders in this movement.

Miscellaneous: Barron; Horton; McConnell.

New Age: Brooke, pp. 146-49.

Positive/Possibility Thinking

Related to Positive Confession. Background is gnosticism. "Believes in the power of the mind, the power of visualizing, the power of imagination, the power of faith. What one thinks, visualizes, imagines, or believes strongly enough will be realized." The greatest threats to this belief are "a bad self-image and an absence of self-love."

Emphasis on human sinfulness is a cardinal sin. All of our talk should be aimed at building up our self-esteem so that we can tap our vast inner resources and realize our incredible potential. Positive thinking concepts have inspired New Age ideas. Promoted by Norman Vincent Peale, Robert Schuller, and others.

General: Horton, pp. 70-71.

Posse Comitatus

Populist organization that leads its members to protest the income tax system. Many of the members are also members of the various Identity Movement groups. In 1983 the leader, Gordon Kahl, was killed in a shoot-out with federal marshals in Arkansas. *See* Identity Movement.

Power for Abundant Living

By Victor Paul Wierwille; his own personal study of the Bible. Also the introductory course to The Way (referred to as PFAL). *See* The Way International.

Powers and Perils®

Fantasy role-playing game that teaches occultic practices. *See* Occult.

Prabhupada, Abhay Charan De Bhaktivedanta Swami

Cult founder. *See* Hare Krishna.

Practical Spirituality

Written in 1985 by John Randolph Price, president of Quartus Foundation for Spiritual Research. *See* New Age Movement.

Practice of Joy

Seminar series teaching how to attain boundless energy and inward fulfillment. *See* Ananda.

PRANA

Ashram in Los Angeles. *See* Movement of Spiritual Inner Awareness.

Prana Theological Seminary

On the West Coast. Teaches Eastern mysticism. *See* Movement of Spiritual Inner Awareness.

Premananda, Swami

Cult founder. *See* Self-revelation Church of Absolute Monism.

Pretty Flower

Spirit channeled by Eileen Rota. *See* Channeling.

Price, Fred

Church leader. *See* Positive Confession.

Price, John Randolph

President of the Quartus Foundation for Spiritual Research, which researches the divinity of man. Author of *Practical Spirituality. See* New Age Movement.

Price, Richard

New Age cult cofounder. *See* Esalen Institute.

Prigmore, Rick and Jen-i

Cult founders. *See* Universal Brotherhood Movement.

Principle Life

Periodical for members only. *See* Unification Church.

The Principles of Nature

Written in 1847 by Andrew Jackson Davis, a leader in the Spiritualist movement. *See* Spiritualism.

Pristine Church of the Rose Cross

Incorporated by the Ancient Mystical Order Rosae Crucis. Founder Harvey Spencer Lewis served as its bishop until his death in 1939. It was later disincorporated. *See* Ancient Mystical Order Rosae Crucis.

Process Church of the Final Judgement

Teaches dualism, a "Unity of Christ and Satan" doctrine—the universe is dominated by opposing forces, neither better than the other. Satan is "loved" along with Christ. Involved in occultic practices. Celebrates in darkness lit by candles, burning incense before an altar with a crucifix and the "Goat of Mendes," symbol of Satan.

Founded by Robert de Grimston in 1963 in England. Brought to America in the late 1960s. Headquarters is in Boston with churches in New Orleans and New York. In 1974 most of his followers ousted de Grimston because of his heavy emphasis on Satan and changed the name of the cult to Foundation Faith of God. De Grimston wrote *As It Is* in 1967, spelling out the cult's philosophy. He continues to head up smaller groups under the original name. Charles Manson, the convicted murderer, was a member.

General: Larson, *New Book*, pp. 295-97; Rice, 205.

New Age: Newport, pp. 140-43.

Occult: Koch, pp. 172-74.

Process Theology

Propounded by some liberal Protestant theologians. Similar in many ways to New Age ideology. *See* New Age Movement.

The Processians

Occultic group magazine. *See* Foundation Faith of God.

Professors World Peace Academy

Cult front group. *See* Unification Church.

Project GOAL (Guided Opportunities for Affective Learning)

Originally developed to help handicapped children in Irvine, California. Has also been used with non-handicapped elementary children. Introduces them to the Inner Self that can guide them in decision-making and in deciding right and wrong. *See* New Age Movement.

Project Self-esteem (PSE)

Educational curriculum written in 1985, which uses mystical guided imagery exercises. *See* New Age Movement.

Project Volunteer

Charitable program. *See* Unification Church.

Prophet, Mark L., and Elizabeth Clare Wulf

Mark founded the Church Universal and Triumphant. Elizabeth is the present spokesman. Together they wrote

Climb the Highest Mountain. Elizabeth claims to have channeled messages from Jesus, which were published as *The Lost Teachings of Jesus*. *See* Church Universal and Triumphant.

A Prophet Without Honor
Book by Ellen Gould White. *See* Seventh-day Adventism.

Prosperity, Your Divine Right
Written by Terry Cole-Whittaker. *See* Science of Mind Church International.

The Prosperos
Background is Islam (Sufism) and New Thought. There is only the One Mind; God is just the capacity to create and control thoughts. Founded in 1956 by Thane Walker (a student of Georgei I. Gurdjieff) and Phez Kahlil. Based in El Monte, California. An inner circle of those who have completed three classes is called the High Watch.
General: Ellwood, pp. 164-68; Melton, *Encyclopedia*, p. 691.

Psychic Healing
Employs the use of "healing energy" directed from the healer to the client by direct touch, waving hands over the body or calling up spirit guides to do the healing. *See* Holistic Health.

Psychic Seminar
Taught by Dick Sutphen. *See* New Age Movement.

Psychic Surgery
Supposedly bloodless way to operate without instruments. The surgeon makes an imaginary incision, some internal tissue appears, and the patient gets up and walks away. Famous psychic surgeons include the late Arigo of Brazil and Carlita of Mexico. Apparently fraud is involved. *See* New Age Movement *and* Spiritualism.

Psychokinesis
Movement of objects using mental or psychic powers usually displayed by tricks such as spoon bending, table tipping, and levitation. *See* Spiritualism.

Psychometry
Spiritualist art of divining information about a person by concentrating on an object he owns. *See* Divination.

Psychorientology
Alternate cult name. *See* Silva Mind Control.

Purification: An Illustrated Answer to Drugs
Book by L. Ron Hubbard that is the basis for the Narconon International drug detoxification centers. *See* Scientology.

Purification Program
Drug detoxification program described by L. Ron Hubbard in his book *Purification: An Illustrated Answer to Drugs.* *See* Scientology.

Purim
Feast commemorating Queen Esther's saving of the Jews in Persia. *See* Judaism.

Purnell, Benjamin
Cult founder known as King Benjamin. *See* Israelite House of David.

Pursel, Jach
One of the most well-known channelers; claims to channel a spirit known as Lazaris. *See* Lazaris *and* Channeling.

Pyramidology
Belief that pyramids force cosmic energy on whatever or whoever is placed under them. Claims to produce healing, prevent food spoilage, sweeten water, sharpen razor blades, etc. *See* New Age Movement.

Pyromancy
Spiritualist method of divination by reading the flame of a fire or candle. *See* Divination.

Q

Quartus Foundation for Spiritual Research
Non-profit organization devoted to researching the divinity of man. John Randolph Price, author of *Practical Spirituality,* is president. *See* New Age Movement.

QUEST
Common reference to *Skills for Adolescence,* an educational curriculum written in 1985 that teaches self-esteem to youth in grades 6-8. Approaches values from a secular viewpoint and introduces students to visualization. *See* New Age Movement.

Quest Books
Publishing house of the Theosophical Society in America. *See* Theosophy.

Questions and Answers by the Royal Order of Tibet
Written by George Adamski in 1936. *See* George Adamski Foundation.

Quimby, Phineas Parkhurst
Spiritual healer; father of three cults. *See* Christian Science, New Thought, *and* Unity School of Christianity.

Qur'an (Koran)
One of four sacred books for Muslims. Written by Muhammad. *See* Community of Islam in the West, Islam, *and* Sufism.

R

Radiant Heart World Healing Ministry
Spiritualist cult-sponsored ministry. *See* International Church of Ageless Wisdom.

"Radiant Light Interfaith Church"
Typical name for a New Age church. *See* New Age Movement.

Radical Faerie Movement
Group of homosexuals who connect their sexual choices with pagan nature religion. *See* Witchcraft.

Radiesthesia
Spiritualist method of divination by reading the way a pendulum swings. *See* Divination.

Radio Church of God
Former cult name. *See* Worldwide Church of God.

Rainan, William
Channeler of Dr. Peebles, a nineteenth-century Scottish physician. *See* Channeling *and* Dr. Peebles.

Rainbow Girls
Common name for International Order of the Rainbow for Girls, a Masonic organization for girls aged twelve to twenty. *See* Freemasonry.

Rajneesh, Bhagwan Shree
Sect founder. Author of *Beyond and Beyond, The Book,* and *Above All, Don't Wobble. See* Rajneesh International Foundation.

Rajneesh International Foundation

Begun in Poona, India, by Bhagwan Shree Rajneesh, who called it the Main Rajneesh Meditation Center. In the early 1980s he brought his followers to the United States seeking permanent residence as a "religious teacher."

Based on Tantra. "Combines major religions with Esalen-style psychological therapy." "Disciples practice sexual rites, wear orange robes, refrain from smoking and eating meat, and appear willing to make even greater sacrifices." Followers seek enlightenment through participating "actively and joyfully in life." Considered Bhagwan to be God. Aligned with the New Age movement.

Authoritative texts include Hindu scriptures and Rajneesh's books *Beyond and Beyond*, *The Book*, and *Above All, Don't Wobble*. The Chidvilas Foundation publishes the books and tapes of Rajneesh and a newspaper, *The Rajneesh Times of India*.

Operates a commune called Sambodhi, near Essex, Massachusetts. In 1981 Bhagwan settled on a 100-square-mile ranch near Antelope, Oregon, later taking over the town as well, renaming it Rajneeshpuram. The "bare necessity" communal life-style of his followers was a marked contrast to Bhagwan's own lavish life-style, which included twenty-seven Rolls Royces, a hotel, a bakery, and a nightclub in Portland. In 1985 Bhagwan was deported on immigration fraud charges. He died in 1990.

General: Ellwood, pp. 207-12; Larson, *New Book*, pp. 372-76; Martin, *Kingdom*, pp. 353-61; Tucker, *Another Gospel*, pp. 372-75.

Eastern Mysticism: Brooke.

Ram Dass

Background is Hinduism. Everyone is on the same spiritual journey, seeking the oneness of all world religions. Yoga, sex, meditation, and drugs are used to achieve enlightenment. Hindu scriptures are the authoritative text.

Founded by Baba Ram Dass, formerly Richard Alpert, in 1968. Headquarters is at the Lama Foundation, a New Age commune in San Cristobel, New Mexico. In 1974 Alpert formed the Hanuman Foundation, which recognizes the Hindu monkey-god as an example of devoted service. He also founded the Seva Foundation. Alpert has written three books: *Be Here Now* (autobiography), *The Only Dance There Is*, and

Grist for the Mill. Fits in the mainstream of the New Age movement.

General: Larson, *New Book*, pp. 339-41.

New Age: Newport, p. 47.

Rama, Swami

Sect founder. *See* Himalayan International Institute.

Rama, Zen Master

Controversial New Age guru, formerly named Frederick Lenz. Claims to be one of twelve enlightened masters on earth. *See* New Age Movement.

Ramanda, Azena

Channeler of St. Germaine, eighth-century French occultist. *See* Channeling.

Ramayana

One of two epic tales of India revered by Hindus. *See* Hinduism.

Rampa, Tuesday Lobsang

Sect founder. *See* T. Lobsang Rampa.

Ramtha

Spiritualism is the background. J. Z. Knight claims to be the channeler for this 35,000-year-old Lemurian warrior-king, an "enlightened master" who speaks words of wisdom through her.

Knight teaches reincarnation. When asked about murder, she replied, "If we're gonna live forever, how can murder be wrong?" Among other things she owns a stable called "Messiah Arabians." The *Ramtha White Book* is her sacred writing. *Windworks* is her newsletter.

Ramtha's followers include Shirley MacLaine, Linda Evans (from the television series "Dynasty"), Burt Reynolds, and Phillip Michael Thomas (from the television series "Miami Vice"). Knight grew up as Judy Hampton, who friends say was possessed by a demon known as Demias. Knight charges $400 per person per trance session for what ex-believers say is "collective, mass hypnotism." *See also* Channeling.

New Age: Larson, pp. 106-7; Miller, pp. 149-52.

Ramtha White Book

Sacred writing. *See* Ramtha.

Rand, Ayn

Late objectivism philosopher. Author of several books including *Anthem*, *Atlas Shrugged*, *The Fountainhead*, *Virtue of Selfishness*, and *We the Living*. *See* Ayn Rand.

Rand, Howard B.

Founder of the Anglo-Saxon Federation of America in Haverhill, Massachusetts. *See* Identity Movement.

Randolph, Pascal Beverly

Occult group founder whose sex magic influenced Aleister Crowley. *See* Fraternitas Rosae Crucis.

Rastafarianism

Also called Ethiopianism. "White men are devils. Black men will be free only when they are back in Africa. Some believe in reincarnation and a few claim to remember their journeys in the slave ships."

God (Jah) became man, not as Jesus but as Ras Tafari, who was called "King of Kings," "Lord of Lords," and "Conquering Lion of Judah." God, the Israelites, and early Christians were all black. Rastamen are the true Jews. Many Rastamen refuse to drink, though they often smoke marijuana to help them "meditate." Only natural food is eaten but not pork or shellfish. Marriage is sinful; a couple need only to live together as long as they want to.

Founded in the early 1900s by Marcus Garvey, who prophesied that an African king would become the black messiah. Ras Tafari (later crowned King Haile Selassie of Ethiopia) was proclaimed the messiah in 1930. Ras Tafari didn't really die in 1975; he went to live in another dimension.

Present head is Premier Michael Manley in Kingston, Jamaica. Many Rastamen carry a picture of Haile Selassie or put a red, black, green, and gold tag or sticker on their cars. Some have in their yards a shrine painted in those four colors. They usually wear their hair braided in "dreadlocks," to instill fear in white men, and wear a woolen hat in the four Ethiopian colors.

The late Bob Marley and his group "The Wailers" helped develop reggae ("to the king") music and have used it to spread Rastafarian ideas through concert tours and astronomical record sales in England and America.

General: Larson, *New Book*, pp. 342-46; Melton, *Encyclopedia*, pp. 677-78.

Ravenwood Church of Wicca
Witchcraft group in Atlanta, Georgia. *See* Witchcraft.

Rawlins, Paul
Splinter group cofounder. *See* The Way International.

The Reappearance of Christ and the Masters of Wisdom
Written in 1980 by Benjamin Creme, a popular New Age speaker. Based largely on Alice A. Bailey's *The Reappearance of the Christ*. *See* New Age Movement.

The Reappearance of the Christ
Written by Alice A. Bailey. Published in 1948. *See* New Age Movement.

Rebirthing
New Age practice of recalling the moment of birth and releasing its trauma. *See* New Age Movement.

Reconstructionism
Lesser Jewish branch that regards religion, culture, and ethics equally. *See* Judaism.

Reflections on the Christ
Important book for New Agers written by David Spangler in 1977. *See* New Age Movement.

Reflexology
Also called zone therapy. Practice of massaging certain points on the sole of the foot (peditherapy) or palm of the hand to relieve disease of the corresponding organs in the body. *See* Holistic Health.

Reform Judaism
Liberal segment of the three main Jewish branches. *See* Judaism.

Reggae Music
Music style popularized by the late Bob Marley to honor "the King" Ras Tafari, or Haile Selassie. *See* Rastafarianism.

Reiki
Belief that healing can be psychically transmitted to someone in a distant place. Teaches the balancing of the seven chakras (psychic energy centers). *See* Holistic Health.

Reincarnation
Belief that the soul will be reborn into this life (in human form) as many times as it takes to reach perfection or salvation. Similar to transmigration (rebirth as things as well as people). *See* Hinduism *and* New Age Movement.

Religious Research Foundation of America (RRFA)
Stresses psychic phenomena and experiences.
Occult: Unger, p. 18.

Renaissance Community
New Age group in Massachusetts. *See* New Age Movement.

Reorganized Church of Jesus Christ of Latter-day Saints (RLDS)
Rejects the leadership of the Utah LDS, the revelations of Brigham Young, and the name *Mormon*. Claims to be the continuation of the original church founded by Joseph Smith, Jr., in Seneca County, New York, in 1830. Formed in 1860 by Joseph Smith III.

Follows the teachings in *The Book of Mormon* and *Doctrine and Covenants*. Believes that Independence is the location of the Garden of Eden and future City of Zion, where Christ will return. No distinction is made in the priesthood because of race or color. Has always taught monogamy.

Its "Messiah Choir" performs Handel's Oratorio annually. Owns the following institutions in Independence: Herald Publishing House; the School of the Restoration; the main relief organization, the Social Service Center; the Independence Sanitarium and Hospital; and Resthaven, a retreat for the aged. Graceland College in Lamoni, Iowa, is the institution of higher learning. Current president of the church is Wallace B. Smith, grandson of the founder. Headquartered in the Auditorium at Independence, Missouri.

General: Larson, *New Book*, pp. 347-51; Melton, *Encyclopedia*, pp. 491-92; Starkes, pp. 115-16; Tucker, *Another Gospel*, pp. 375-76.

Resthaven
Retreat for the aged in Independence, Missouri. *See* Reorganized Church of Jesus Christ of Latter-day Saints.

Retrospection and Introspection
Doctrinal review book by Mary Baker Eddy. *See* Christian Science.

Rev. Ike
Cult founder. *See* United Christian Evangelistic Association.

Revelation: The Birth of a New Age
Book by David Spangler published in 1976. Considered something of a Bible by New Agers. *See* New Age Movement.

Revell, Randy
Human potential seminar cooriginator. *See* Lifespring.

ReVision
Scholarly journal. *See* New Age Movement.

Rhabdomancy
Spiritualist practice of finding water, lost articles, treasure, human bodies, and archaeological sites using a forked rod. Also called dowsing or water witching. *See* Divination.

Rhapsodamancy
Spiritualist method of divination based on a line in a sacred book that strikes the eye when the book is opened after the diviner meditates or invokes the help of spirits. *See* Divination.

Right On
Regular publication. *See* Christian World Liberation Front.

Rinpoche, Chogyam Trungpa
Buddhist sect leader. *See* Vajradhatu.

RLDS
Cult acronym. *See* Reorganized Church of Jesus Christ of Latter-day Saints.

The Road Less Traveled
Written in 1980 by M. Scott Peck, New Age teacher, explaining how to grow toward godhood. *See* New Age Movement.

Roberts, Jane
One of the channelers for Seth. Author of *The Seth Material* and *Seth Speaks*. *See* Channeling.

Roberts, Jimmie T.
Founder of an unnamed cult, sometimes called the "garbage eaters." *See* A Cult with No Name.

Roberts, Oral
Faith healer and televangelist based in Tulsa, Oklahoma. *See* Positive Confession.

Roberts, Robert
Current cult leader. *See* Christadelphians.

Rock of Ages Festival

Annual convention of The Way that meets in New Knoxville, Ohio. *See* The Way International.

Rodegast, Pat

Channeler of a spirit named Emanuel. *See* Channeling.

Rolfing

Also called structural integration. Could be called "massage with a vengeance," since trained rolfers administer painful pressure to the body with their hands and elbows to relieve energy blockages caused by previous traumatic experiences. Rolf therapists are trained at the Institute of Structural Integration in Boulder, Colorado. *See* Holistic Health.

Rolling Ball of Fire

Book by Benjamin Purnell. *See* Israelite House of David.

Rollinson-Huss, Barbara

Channels dolphins and an Oriental spirit who speaks in a Chinese-American accent. *See* Channeling.

Romney, Rodney R.

Pastor of the First Baptist Church, Seattle. Author of *Journey to Inner Space: Finding God-in-Us*, which espouses the New Age view of "realizing one's own godhood." *See* New Age Movement.

Rose-Croix University

School established by Harvey Spencer Lewis in San Jose, California. *See* Ancient Mystical Order Rosae Crucis.

Rose of Sharon Press

Publishing house in Tarrytown, New York. *See* Unification Church.

Rosenberg, John Paul

Cult founder, born Werner Erhard. *See* est.

Rosenkreutz, Christian

Occultic group founder. *See* Rosicrucianism.

Rosh Hashanah

Jewish New Year. *See* Judaism.

Rosicrucian Anthroposophic League

Formed in the 1930s by S. R. Parchment, former member of the Rosicrucian Fellowship. His books *Astrology, Mundane and Spiritual* (an astrological classic), *The Just Law of Compensation*, *The Middle Path*, *Operative Masonry*, and

Steps to Self Mastery convey his views. The League published *Rosicrucian Quarterly* for a while. *See* Rosicrucianism.

Rosicrucian Cosmo-Conception
Occultic textbook written by Max Heindel in 1937. *See* Rosicrucian Fellowship.

Rosicrucian Digest
Official monthly magazine. *See* Ancient Mystical Order Rosae Crucis.

Rosicrucian Fama
Former magazine. *See* Societas Rosicruciana in Civitatibus Foederatis.

Rosicrucian Fellowship
Traces its roots back to the Chaldeans. Background is Theosophy and mythology. The central tenet: esoteric wisdom about life beyond the grave has been preserved through the ages and is revealed only to those within the secret brotherhood. The cross is the symbol of man's evolutionary development, past, present, and future. God is an impersonal being composed of seven spirits. Jesus was a man, the highest luminary possible, and one of several incarnations of the Christ-Spirit. The Holy Spirit is the highest initiate of the moon. One is saved by overcoming all evil; its motto is "Try."

The lost continent of Atlantis is included in its speculation as described in the book *Lemuria: The Lost Continent of the Pacific*, by Wishar S. Cerve. Teaches universal brotherhood.

Founded in 1907 by Max Heindel. Based in Oceanside, California, on Mt. Ecclesia. The *Rosicrucian Magazine* is its publication. The basic textbook is *The Rosicrucian Cosmo-Conception* by Heindel. Publishes the *Ephemeris*, an annual astrological table. *See* Rosicrucianism.

Rosicrucian Forum
Publication for members. *See* Ancient Mystical Order Rosae Crucis.

Rosicrucian Magazine
Official magazine. *See* Rosicrucian Fellowship.

Rosicrucian Quarterly
Former publication. *See* Rosicrucian Anthroposophic League.

Rosicrucian Research Library
  Established by Harvey Spencer Lewis in San Jose, California. *See* Ancient Mystical Order Rosae Crucis.

Rosicrucianism
  Rosicrucian orders are occultic, and their teachings are available only to members. Supposedly founded by Christian Rosenkreutz in 1407 in Germany after he had studied occultic arts in Damascus, Egypt, and Morocco for fourteen years. The Order of the Rose Cross nearly died out after his death. It was renewed in 1604 when his tomb was discovered. It almost disappeared again in the eighteenth century, but it became a major component in the occult revival in the West in the nineteenth century.
  Orders include Ancient Mystical Order Rosae Crucis (AMORC), Ausar Auset Society, Fraternitas Rosae Crucis, Lectorium Rosicrucianum, Rosicrucian Anthroposophic League, Rosicrucian Fellowship, Societas Rosicruciana in America (SRIA), and Societas Rosicruciana in Civitatibus Foederatis (SRICF).
  General: Larson, *New Book*, pp. 355-59; Martin, *Kingdom*, pp. 507-12; McDowell, pp. 221-24; Melton, *Encyclopedia*, pp. 593-97; Tucker, *Another Gospel*, pp. 376-78.

Rota, Eileen
  Channeler for Pretty Flower. *See* Channeling.

RRFA
  Psychic group acronym. *See* Religious Research Foundation of America.

Rumi, Melvana Celaleddin
  Muslim sect founder. *See* Sufi Order.

RuneQuest®
  Fantasy role-playing game similar to Dungeons and Dragons® that teaches occultic practices. *See* Occult.

Runes
  Spiritualist method of divination using tiles inscribed with letters from the Viking Rune alphabet. Runes are cast and interpreted from these twenty-four characters. It is considered a magical alphabet and is used by occultists to write their pacts with Satan. *See* Divination.

The Runestone
  Quarterly newspaper of a Norse neopagan group. *See* Asatru Free Assembly.

Russell, Arthur James

Author of *For Sinners Only* in 1932. *See* Moral Rearmament.

Russell, Charles Taze

Cult founder. *See* Jehovah's Witnesses.

Rutherford, Joseph Franklin "Judge"

Former cult president. *See* Jehovah's Witnesses.

Ryan, Dom Mark

Sect founder. *See* Followers of Jesus.

Ryerson, Kevin

One of the best-known channelers, who claims to channel John (a member of the Essene community in Jesus' day), Tom McPherson (a mischievous Irishman), and other disembodied spirits who are trying to make the world a better place. He claims 75 percent accuracy for channeled messages, charging $250 for a private session. He has written *Spirit Communication of the Soul*. *See also* Channeling.

New Age: Miller, pp. 153-55.

S

The Sacred Journey: You and Your Higher Self
Written by Lazaris, the ascended master channeled by Jach Pursel. *See* Channeling *and* Lazaris.

"The Sacred Name Broadcast"
Radio program originating in Bethel, Pennsylvania, featuring Jacob O. Meyer. *See* Assemblies of Yahweh.

Sacred Name Broadcaster
Monthly magazine published in Bethel, Pennsylvania. *See* Assemblies of Yahweh.

The Sacred Scriptures
Translation of the Bible published in Bethel, Pennsylvania. *See* Assemblies of Yahweh.

The Sacred Sword
Book by Betty Bethards, psychic. *See* Inner Light Foundation.

Sadanaga
Current Buddhist sect leader. Real name is George M. Williams. *See* Nichiren Shoshu of America.

Sadler, Dr. Bill
UFO cult founder. *See* Urantia Brotherhood.

Sadvipra
Monthly sect newspaper. *See* Ananda Márga Yoga Society.

SAI Foundation
Also known as the Spiritual Advancement of the Individual Foundation. Background is Hinduism. Founded by Sai

Baba in India in the early 1900s. Succeeded by Sathya Sai Baba. Headed in America by Indra Devi. The Sai Baba Center and bookstore are in Los Angeles. Baba claims to be an avatar of Shiva and Shakti. He has reportedly performed miracles.

General: Ellwood, pp. 212-15; Larson, *New Book*, pp. 360-64; Melton, *Encyclopedia*, pp. 723-24.

Eastern Mysticism: Brooke.

New Age: Khalsa, p. 118; Newport, p. 46.

St. Germain
Eighteenth-century French occultist channeled by Azena Ramanda and others. Guy Ballard, founder of the I AM Movement, was greatly influenced by St. Germain. *See* Channeling *and* I AM Movement.

St. Germain Foundation
Corporation. *See* I AM Movement.

Saint's Blessing
Popular occult magic spell book. *See* Magick.

Sambodhi
Commune near Essex, Massachusetts. *See* Rajneesh International Foundation.

Sanders, Alexander and Maxine
Teachers of Alexandrian Witchcraft. *See* Witchcraft.

Sanford, Agnes
Christian author who writes on New Age themes, such as past-life regression, in her book *The Healing Gifts of the Spirit*. *See* New Age Movement.

Santeria
Offshoot of Voodoo. Came from Nigeria when Yoruba natives were brought to America as slaves. They were baptized as Catholics by their owners and not allowed to worship their gods. They named their gods after Catholic saints and gave them Christian characteristics so they could continue their pagan worship. Some examples: Ekggua became St. Anthony, the Guardian Angel; Obatalla became Our Lady of Las Mercedes; Chango became St. Barbara; Babalu-aye was named St. Lazarus.

Present followers are mostly Hispanics in Cuba and other Caribbean islands. One group is called the Church of the Lukumi Babalu Aye in Hialeah, Florida. Another branch called Palo Mayombe, or Palo Monte, was responsible for the murders in Matamoros, Mexico, in 1989.

General: Larson, *New Book*, pp. 459-63.

Occult: Haynes, p. 20; Larson, pp. 183-84; Wedge, pp. 156-71.

The Satanic Bible

Sacred occultic text written in 1969 by Anton Szandor LaVey. *See* Satanism.

The Satanic Rituals

Important occultic text written in 1972 by Anton Szandor LaVey. See Satanism.

Satanism

Worship of Satan. A Satanic revival began in 1966 when Anton LaVey formed the Church of Satan. Has been popularized by movies such as *Rosemary's Baby* and *The Exorcist*, by occultic heavy metal rock music groups like Black Sabbath and Iron Maiden (*see* Heavy Metal Music) and by fantasy role-playing games such as Dungeons and Dragons® (*see* Occult).

There are three types of Satanists: (1) self-styled—usually teenagers who create their own version of Satanism using words and symbols seen in books and movies and heard in music; (2) religious—those who organize churches to formally worship Satan; and (3) cultic—very secretive Satanists involved in criminal activities such as drug trafficking, kidnapping, pornography, prostitution, and ritual sacrifices.

The Satanic Bible and *The Satanic Rituals* are used by all Satanists, as are manuals of occult magic spells (grimoires). Since copies of grimoires are rare, Satanists may write their own book of spells using the Rune alphabet.

The best known Satanic churches are the Church of Satan in San Francisco, California, headed by Anton LaVey, the Temple of Set, also in San Francisco, headed by Michael A. Aquino, and the Worldwide Church of Satanic Liberation in New Haven, Connecticut, headed by Paul Valentine. Other groups have come and gone, such as the Church of Satanic Brotherhood and Ordo Templi Satanas.

The main ritual is the Black Mass, a perversion of the Catholic Mass, which leads worshipers to blaspheme God and ridicule Christianity.

General: McDowell, pp. 236-39; Tucker, *Another*, pp. 378-79.

Occult: Koch, pp. 194-200; Larson; Unger.

Satchidananda, Swami

Cult leader. *See* Integral Yoga Institute.

Satin, Mark

Author of *New Age Politics*. A New Age activist. *See* New Age Movement.

Savoy, Eugene Douglas

Contemporary cult founder. Author of *The Decoded New Testament, The Essaei Document, Jamil: The Child Christ, Jamilians,* and *The Lost Gospel of Christ. See* International Community of Christ.

Saxon Witchcraft

Witchcraft group in Charlottesville, Virginia, headed by Raymond Buckland. Operates the Seax-Wicca Seminary and publishes the *Seax-Wica Voys* newsletter. *See* Witchcraft.

School of Enlightenment

Offers training in Zen and Vipassana meditation and other Buddhist studies. *See* American Buddhist Movement.

School of Spiritual Science

Teaches metaphysical and New Age concepts. *See* National Spiritual Science Center.

School of the Restoration

Located in Independence, Missouri. *See* Reorganized Church of Jesus Christ of Latter-day Saints.

Schucman, Helen

Using automatic writing she took the dictation of an inner voice claiming to be Jesus. The result of the seven-year project was *A Course in Miracles. See also* A Course in Miracles *and* New Age Movement.

Schuller, Robert

Pastor of the Crystal Cathedral in Garden Grove, California. Televangelist on "The Hour of Power." Prolific author. *See* Positive/Possibility Thinking.

Schulz, William F.

National cult president. *See* Unitarian Universalist Association.

SCI

Acronym for the Science of Creative Intelligence, alternate sect name. *See* Transcendental Meditation.

Science and Health with Key to the Scriptures

Cult scripture written in 1883 by Mary Baker Eddy. *See* Christian Science.

Science and Reality

Book by Annie C. Bill, cult founder. *See* Church of the Universal Design.

Science of Creative Intelligence (SCI)

Alternate sect name. *See* Transcendental Meditation.

Science of Happiness

Human potential program offered by the Ken Keyes Center. *See also* New Age Movement.

Science of Mind

Cult textbook by Ernest Holmes published in 1926. *See* Church of Religious Science.

Science of Mind Church International

Founded by Terry Cole-Whittaker. She was trained in the Church of Religious Science using *A Course in Miracles*, the teachings of Ernest Holmes, and est. She also borrowed from Christian Science the notion that anything negative is illusion. Her book *Prosperity, Your Divine Right* teaches a gospel of success, as does her other book *How to Have More in a Have-Not World*. Her latest book, *The Inner Path from Where You Are to Where You Want to Be*, has a New Age flavor.

This cult uses group rebirthing, body massage, nutrition, and affirmations in "worship." Adherents are taught to "dress to win," "visit only beautiful places," and "associate with those who are prosperous and happy." The purpose is to "bring you into oneness with God where you can have the direct experience of being limitless." Teachings include visualization, channeling, and goddess and Mother Earth energies.

General: Larson, *New Book*, pp. 185-88.

New Age: Larson, p. 237.

Scientology

Also called the Church of Scientology, or Dianetics. Founded in 1954 by the late L. Ron Hubbard, sometimes called Elron. Background is science fiction and Buddhism.

God is irrelevant. Thetans (men's souls) are all gods. Jesus was not God, but He had a "strong energy glow." Man is good, "utterly incapable of error." Man's reason will produce perfect behavior. The Bible is of no use.

Scientology teaches reincarnation; the Thetan has existed for trillions of years and has gone through countless bodies in countless solar systems. Salvation comes only through its psychoanalysis therapy sessions (auditing) with a crude lie detector; the series of sessions can cost up to $30,000.

The authoritative book is Hubbard's *Dianetics: The Modern Science of Mental Health*. Hubbard also wrote *The Way to Happiness*. Publishes *Freedom* magazine, *Advance*, *The Auditor*, and *Source*.

International headquarters is in Sussex, England. North American headquarters is in Tampa, Florida. Its International Training and Retreat Center is in Clearwater, Florida.

Narconon International drug detoxification centers in several cities use Hubbard's Purification Program, emphasizing vitamins, sauna, auditing, and exercise to help the drug user rid himself of the need for drugs. This program is described in *Purification: An Illustrated Answer to Drugs* by Hubbard. Kirstie Alley, of "Cheers" television series fame, is an adherent, having gone through the Narconon program.

Applied Scholastics, a firm connected to the Church, offers communications courses to corporations using techniques developed by the Church. Other front groups include Flag Service Organization in Florida, Owl Management, Singer and Associates, Steller Management, Sterling Management, Uptrends, Way of Happiness ("Set a Good Example Contest"), and WISE (World Institute of Scientological Enterprises).

Since Hubbard's death in 1986, the Church of Scientology has republished his works, including his science fiction books.

General: Larson, *New Book*, pp. 365-69; Martin, *Kingdom*, pp. 345-50; Melton, *Encyclopedia*, pp. 572-74; Robertson, pp. 124-31; Tucker, *Another Gospel*, pp. 299-318.

New Age: Newport, pp. 83-97.

See also Miscellaneous.

Scripture Research Association

Founded in the 1940s by A. B. Traina. Publishes *The Holy Name Bible*. *See* Assemblies of Yahweh.

Scroll of Set

Occultic newsletter. *See* Temple of Set.

Séance

Ceremony of invoking the dead in order to communicate with them. Sessions are led by a medium. *See* Spiritualism.

Search for Truth

Book by Ruth Montgomery, whose works are widely read by New Agers. *See* New Age Movement.

Seax-Wica Voys

Newsletter published by Saxon Witchcraft in Charlottesville, Virginia. *See* Witchcraft.

Seax-Wicca Seminary

School operated by Saxon Witchcraft in Charlottesville, Virginia. *See* Witchcraft.

The Secret Doctrine

Written by Helena Petrovna Blavatsky. Published in 1888. Considered theosophical canon. *See* Theosophy.

The Secret Doctrines of Jesus

Cult scripture by Harvey Spencer Lewis. *See* Ancient Mystical Order Rosae Crucis.

The Secret Life of Plants

Book by Peter Tomkins and Christopher Bird. Espouses the view that plants have feelings and intelligence. Promotes the worship of the "nature elementals." *See* Plant Communication.

The Secret of Life and Death

Written by Roy Masters in 1964. *See* Foundation of Human Understanding.

Seekers After Truth

Human potential group. *See* New Age Movement.

Seicho-no-Ie

Teaches four principles: (1) one truth, one God, one religion; (2) man a child of God; (3) reconciliation to everything in the universe; and (4) gratitude to everybody and everything.

Founded by Masaharu Taniguchi in Japan. Based in Gardena, California. Influenced by New Thought. The revered scripture is the *Holy Sutra, Nectarean Shower of Holy Doctrine*, delivered to Taniguchi in 1931 by an angel while he meditated.

General: Melton, *Encyclopedia*, pp. 525-26.
Eastern Mysticism: Ellwood, pp. 147-77.

Sekai Kyusei Kyo

Alternate sect name. *See* Church of World Messianity.

Self-hypnosis

Used for relaxation, visualization, past life regression, and altering the state of consciousness. Subliminal devices are available to help the subject achieve a hypnotic state. Opens the person to the possibility of use as a channel. *See* Spiritualism.

Self-mastery Training Seminar

Ancient wisdom training. *See* Coptic Fellowship of America.

Self-realization Fellowship Foundation

Background is Hinduism and Tantra. It "aims to disseminate definite scientific (concentration) techniques [actually Kriya Yoga meditation] for attaining direct personal experience of God; to teach that the purpose of life is the evolution into God-Consciousness; to reveal the complete harmony between original Christianity and original yoga; and to show how to serve mankind as one's large Self." Founded by the late Paramahansa Yogananda in 1935. He wrote *Autobiography of a Yogi*. Headquarters is in Los Angeles. Related to the New Age movement.

General: Ellwood, pp. 188-94; Larson, *New Book*, pp. 370-71; Melton, *Encyclopedia*, p. 725; Robertson, p. 122.

Self-revelation Church of Absolute Monism

Founded in 1928 by Swami Premananda. (Premananda is the only swami in the world to become a 33rd degree Scottish Rite Mason.) He was succeeded in 1975 by Srimati Kamala. Background is Eastern mysticism.

The headquarters was dedicated in 1952, the Golden Lotus Temple in Washington, D.C. Worship is at eleven o'clock on Sunday mornings. The service consists of prayer, hymns, offering, and a discourse. The children have church school. Operates the Gandhi Memorial Center next to the Temple. Aligned with the New Age Movement.

General: Melton, *Encyclopedia*, pp. 725-26.

Sensory Deprivation Device

Also referred to as an isolation tank or flotation tank. The practitioner floats in a special salt water solution in a closed tank in a weightless state, completely shut off from the world. Used in psychic research or for meditation. *See* New Age Movement.

Set

Ancient Egyptian deity comparable to Satan. *See* Temple of Set.

Seth

Spirit channeled by several trance channelers, most notably by Jane Roberts and most recently by Jean Loomis. *See* Channeling.

The Seth Material
Written in 1970 by the late Jane Roberts, one of the channelers of Seth, to tell of her encounters. *See* Channeling.

Seth Speaks
Written in 1972 by the late Jane Roberts, one of the channelers of Seth. *See* Channeling.

Seva Foundation
Founded by Baba Ram Dass. *See* Ram Dass.

The Seven Church Ages
Book by William Branham, cult founder, in which he set the year 1977 for the beginning of the millennium. *See* Branhamism.

Sevenoaks Center
New Age community and retreat center near Madison, Virginia. Offers training in New Age practices.

New Age: Khalsa, p. 122.

Seventh-day Adventism
This group has been treated by some as a non-Christian cult, probably because its beliefs have been misunderstood and its leaders have often been quoted out of context. A study of its doctrines indicates that it should be considered Christian; it shares some of the beliefs of orthodox Christianity. Believes in the Trinity and the deity of Christ. Salvation is by grace through faith in Jesus.

Observes Saturday as the Sabbath, the day of worship, and refrains from eating certain foods. But these are not done to secure salvation.

The Bible is the only guide for faith and practice, though the writings of F. D. Nichol, L. E. Froom, and Ellen Gould White are highly respected. Mrs. White is not regarded in the same category as writers of Scripture. But Adventists do place her alongside Miriam and Deborah as a prophetess.

Adventism began in Europe in the nineteenth century; was brought to America in 1818 under the leadership of William Miller. Headquarters is in Washington, D.C.

Has 52 publishing houses printing literature in 173 languages. Operates 587 medical facilities, 27 food factories, and 5,300 schools. In 1989 published *Seventh-day Adventists Believe . . .*, "a biblical exposition of 27 fundamental doctrines," which was sent to ministers of all faiths across the country.

General: Boa, pp. 90-96; Martin, *Kingdom*, pp. 409-500; Melton, *Encyclopedia*, pp. 435-36; Rice, pp. 92-104; Tucker, *Another Gospel*, pp. 93-116, 390-91.

Seventh-day Adventists Believe . . .

Biblical exposition of twenty-seven fundamental doctrines published in 1988. *See* Seventh-day Adventism.

Sex and Psychic Energy

Book by Betty Bethards, psychic. *See* Inner Light Foundation.

Sex and Spirituality

Written by M. Scott Peck, a New Age teacher. *See* New Age Movement.

Sex: The Substitute Love

Published by Foundation Press. *See* Foundation of Human Understanding.

Shah, Indries

Leading speaker and author. *See* Sufi Order.

Shakers

Formally known as the United Society of Believers in Christ's Second Coming. Background is Spiritualism. Founded by James and Jane Wardley, who preached that Christ would return in the form of a woman. Greatly influenced Ann Lee who later taught that she was "the Christ second-come" and the "Mother of the new creation."

Believers must renounce "the lust of the flesh, the lust of the eyes, and the pride of life." Celibacy is encouraged. Worship consists of each believer dancing, singing, speaking in tongues, jumping, laughing, whatever he feels led to do, whenever he feels led to do it.

Communal living in "ideal" communities with a simple life-style is a major characteristic. These communities have all but died out, with only two "living" settlements in the Northeast. Its communal practices have been the model for many other groups.

General: Rice, pp. 27-46.

Eastern Mysticism: Ellwood, pp. 74-84.

Shamanism

Occultic religious practice by those who claim to have direct communication with the spirit world. The shaman at times is possessed by the spirits who enter him and speak through him. His purpose is "to reconnect people with the sacred, as mystic mediator, guide, and healer." Blends animism (spirit contact) and pantheism, harmonizing spiritual and natural worlds within the self.

Carlos Castaneda has written many books that have aroused renewed interest in shamanism. Michael Harner has written *The Way of the Shaman*, teaching shamanistic techniques, and *Hallucinogens and Shamanism*. Another modern-day shaman, Lynn Andrews, is called "the Beverly Hills medicine woman." *See* Spiritualism.

Shambhala Training

Growth seminar designed to raise the level of human potential using Buddhist principles. *See* Vajradhatu.

Shanti Nilaya

Teaching and healing center founded by Elisabeth Kübler-Ross, a New Age spokesperson. *See* New Age Movement.

Share International

Official publication of the Tara Center founded by Benjamin Creme to promote the teachings of Lord Maitreya and provide a training ground for New Agers on the emerging political, social, and economic order. *See* New Age Movement.

Shariyat-Ki-Sugmad

Sacred scriptures. *See* ECKANKAR.

Shavuot (Pentecost)

Jewish feast observed fifty days after Passover commemorating the giving of the law to Moses. *See* Judaism.

Shia, or Shiite

Militant minority branch of Islam, predominate in Iran. *See* Islam.

Shiatsu

Similar to zone therapy. Areas massaged are close to the affected organ. This manipulation causes the diseased organ to be healed. *See* Holistic Health.

Shiloh's Messenger of Wisdom

Monthly cult newsletter. *See* Israelite House of David.

Shiva

Hindu deity, the destroyer. *See* Hinduism.

Showers of Blessing

Sect newsletter. *See* House of Prayer for All People.

Siddha Yoga Dham of America

Founded by the late Paramahansa Muktananda in Mangalore, India. Background is Tantra. Hindu scriptures are the authoritative text. By pressing his fingers on the eyes, Muktananda claimed to waken the elemental energy force of Shakti (the Hindu Supreme Mother goddess lying at the base of the spine). By directing one's devotion and meditation toward Muktananda, a person can receive God-realization.

Based in Oakland, California. The meditation community is in a Miami Beach hotel.

General: Larson, *New Book*, pp. 318-20; Melton, *Encyclopedia*, p. 726.

Eastern Mysticism: Brooke.

Siddhachalam

Founded by Acharya Sushil Kumarji Maharaj near Blairstown, New Jersey. Background is Jainism. Offers retreats, seminars, and summer camps teaching subjects such as chakras, chromotherapy, kundalini, meditation, psychic sciences, sound vibration, and yoga.

New Age: Khalsa, pp. 26-27.

Sikh Dharma

Alternate cult name. *See* Healthy, Happy, Holy Organization.

Sikhism

Third major branch of Hinduism; an attempt to harmonize Hinduism and Islam. Founded by Guru Nanak in 1472. Sacred scripture is the *Granth Sahib*, though it is nonessential to a Sikh's religious training.

There is one God who is absolute but not personal, the true Guru. Salvation is knowing God, or absorption into God. The Golden Temple in Amritsar, India, is a symbol of the Sikh religion.

Khalsa Sikhs (even older children) are distinguished by five symbols worn on their person: uncut hair, comb to keep the hair clean, metal bangle, knee-length underwear, and a kirpan or dagger.

General: Boa, pp. 22-24; McDowell, pp. 400-405.

Comparative Religions: Beaver, pp. 197-206.

Silent Unity

Prayer ministry. *See* Unity School of Christianity.

Silva, Jose

Contemporary cult founder and hypnotist. *See* Silva Mind Control.

Silva Mind Control (SMC)

Also known as Psychorientology. Background is parapsychology and Spiritualism. Considered to be part of the New Age movement.

According to SMC, God is not interested in man's day-to-day life. Its theology is deism—that is, God set the universe in motion and is no longer personally concerned. Man is fundamentally good. A person can reach Christ-awareness through the Silva method. Uses ESP and hypnotism and borders on possession by evil spirits.

SMC is promoted as a technique that teaches how to gain conscious control of subjective levels of mind normally thought of as the subconscious. The technique is taught in a 40-hour course costing about $200. It leads people to believe that self can solve all problems.

Founded in 1963 by Jose Silva, a hypnotist, in Laredo, Texas. Owns Silva Sensor Systems and a Mind Control bookstore. The White Sox baseball team and Richard Bach, author of *Jonathan Livingston Seagull*, have been known to be adherents.

General: Larson, *New Book*, pp. 379-81; Martin, *New Cults*, p. 237; Tucker, *Another Gospel*, pp. 380-81.

New Age: Newport, pp. 98-99.

Occult: Koch, pp. 24-26.

Silva Sensor Systems

Cult-related corporation. *See* Silva Mind Control.

Sims, Jamie

Channeler of Leah, a woman from Venus. *See* Channeling.

Sinclair, Lilith

Cofounder of one of the three main Satanic churches. *See* Temple of Set.

Singer and Associates

Front group. *See* Scientology.

Singh, Sant Thakar

Contemporary cult founder. *See* Kirpal Light Satsang, Inc.

Sirius Community

New Age commune near Amherst, Massachusetts. Cofounded by Corinne McLaughlin and Gordon Davidson in 1978. Sponsors week-long workshops incorporating meditation and dance into a daily routine of seminars on holistic health, mythology, and other New Age topics. Publishes *The New England Network of Light Directory* and distributes *Builders of the Dawn*, written by the founders. *See* New Age Movement.

The Sixth and Seventh Books of Moses
Grimoire, or occult magic spell book, dating from 1503. *See* Magick.

Skill Builder
Time management tool. *See* Metamorphosis, Inc.

Skills for Adolescence
Educational curriculum developed in 1985 to teach self-esteem to youth in grades 6-8. Approaches values from a secular viewpoint and introduces students to visualization. Sometimes referred to as QUEST. *See* New Age Movement.

Skutch, Robert, and Judy
Parapsychological investigators who founded the Foundation for Inner Peace, which published *A Course in Miracles*. *See* New Age Movement.

"The Sleeping Prophet"
Nickname for Edgar Cayce. *See* Association for Research and Enlightenment.

Small, Alethea Brooks
Cult cofounder. *See* Divine Science Federation International.

Smith, Joseph, Jr.
Cult founder. Author of *The Book of Mormon, Doctrine and Covenants*, and *The Pearl of Great Price*. *See* Mormonism.

Smith, Wallace B.
Current cult president. *See* Reorganized Church of Jesus Christ of Latter-day Saints.

Snow, L. D.
Cofounder of the Assembly of Yahvah in 1945. *See* Assemblies of Yahweh.

So Be It
Occultic group publication. *See* Foundation Faith of God.

SOAR (Set Objectives, Achieve Results)
Educational curriculum formerly used in Los Angeles schools that teaches that we are inherently good and can achieve anything we imagine ourselves achieving because of

our goodness. Teaches children how to contact the dead. Based on the book *Beyond Hypnosis: A Program for Developing Your Psychic and Healing Power*. The course was withdrawn when parents protested. *See* New Age Movement.

Social Service Center

Relief organization in Independence, Missouri. *See* Reorganized Church of Jesus Christ of Latter-day Saints.

Societas Rosicruciana in America (SRIA)

Begun in 1907 by members of Societas Rosicruciana in Civitatibus Foederatis who wanted to open the teachings of Rosicrucianism to the public, including non-Masons. The group was led by Sylvester C. Gould. George Winslow Plummer succeeded him and founded Mercury Publishing Company. He formed the Holy Orthodox Church in America in 1934.

Plummer was succeeded by his widow, called Mother Serena, then by his widow's second husband, Stanislaus Witowski. When Witowski died, Mother Serena became head of the Church. *See* Rosicrucianism.

Societas Rosicruciana in Civitatibus Foederatis (SRICF)

Founded in 1880 with Charles E. Meyer serving as the first Supreme Magus. One of the smallest Rosicrucian groups. Only Masons may join. Until 1973 it published a magazine, *The Rosicrucian Fama*. *See* Rosicrucianism.

Soka Gakkai

Lay organization of a Buddhist sect. *See* Nichiren Shoshu of America.

Solid Rock Church

Street preachers entice passers-by to attend Bible studies without telling them about the high pressure that will gradually be applied. Ex-members report being forced to sit through the three-hour church services. Considered a destructive cult because of its excessive use of deception, coercion, and manipulation. (Denny Gulick, "Destructive Cults Eliminate Freedom of Thought," *The Diamondback*, U. of Maryland, April 18, 1988.)

Songs of Divine Joy

Written by Swami Kriyananda (J. Donald Walters) and used in worship services. *See* Ananda.

Sons of Liberty

Publishing company. *See* New Christian Crusade Church.

Soul Travel

Practice of projecting the soul to another location. Also called astral projection. *See* Spiritualism.

Source

Periodical of Flag Service Organization. *See* Scientology.

Spalding, Baird T.

Author of the five-volume *Life and Teachings of the Masters of the Far East* containing many of the beliefs central to modern I AM cults. *See* I AM Movement.

Spangler, David

His books *Emergence: The Rebirth of the Sacred*, *Revelation: The Birth of a New Age*, and *Reflections on the Christ* are very important to the New Age movement. Was a codirector of the Findhorn Foundation and is president of the Lorian Association and member of Planetary Citizens. Considered a prophet by New Agers. *See* New Age Movement.

Spectrum

Quarterly New Age movement newsletter published by the Unity-in-Diversity Council. *See* New Age Movement.

Spirit Communication of the Soul

Written in 1989 by Kevin Ryerson, a channeler. *See* Channeling.

Spirit Guide

Spirit entity who "guides," or gives information to, a seeker through mediums, channelers, or automatic writing or drawing. *See* Channeling.

Spiritism

Belief that spirits inhabit objects such as rocks and trees. Sometimes it is used to refer to Spiritualism. *See* Spiritualism.

Spiritual Advancement of the Individual Foundation

Formal sect name. *See* SAI Foundation.

Spiritual Frontiers Fellowship

Founded in 1956 in Chicago by Arthur Ford and several other Christian clergymen and laymen to encourage and interpret to the churches the rising tide of interest in mystical and paranormal activities. Based in Evanston, Illinois. Background is Spiritualism.

Teaches ESP, biofeedback, holistic health, all that metaphysics has to offer. Several leaders of mainline denominations are involved. Martin Ebon is popular with this group as a lecturer on parapsychology and the occult.

Occult: Koch, p. 212.

Spiritual Healing Bulletin
UFO cult periodical. *See* Aetherius Society.

Spiritual Regeneration Movement
Former sect name. *See* Transcendental Meditation.

Spiritual Science
Alternate cult name. *See* Anthroposophical Society.

Spiritual Science Digest
Spiritualist periodical. *See* Universal Harmony Foundation.

Spiritual Sciences Institute
Founded by Verna Yater, channeler of Indira Latari. Based in Santa Barbara, California. *See* Channeling.

The Spiritual Shield
Popular occult magic spell book. *See* Magick.

Spiritual Sky
Label put on products made by the International Society for Krishna Consciousness. *See* Hare Krishna.

Spiritual Traveler
Said to be the guiding force in a person's life. *See* Movement of Spiritual Inner Awareness.

Spiritual Workshops
Offered around the country. *See* ECKANKAR.

Spiritualism
Also known as Necromancy and Spiritism. Background is the occult. The modern Spiritualist movement was begun by Leah, Kate, and Margaret Fox in Hydesville, New York, in 1848. The heart of Spiritualism is the séance, a practice designed to conjure up spirits of the dead, and necromancy, the art of making the dead appear.

Its beliefs have been codified into "Seven Principles" and "Nine Articles." The Trinity is nonsense. God is a force for good, the "Central Force." Jesus was not God. We are children of God at birth. There is no heaven or hell, only astral spheres. Claims to believe in the scriptures of all religions. Teaches reincarnation ("after death we incarnate again for the further progress of our souls").

Other features include prophecy and divination using astrology, biorhythms, cartouche, chiromancy, crystal gazing,

ESP, *I Ching*, metoposcopy, numerology, Ouija boards, palm reading, physiognomy, Runes, Tarot cards, tea leaf reading, and other forms of divination; psychic healing including biofeedback, chromotherapy, crystal therapy, occult magic charms, peditherapy, and psychic surgery; and treasure hunting using "peeping" stones and dowsing.

Automatic writing and drawing are sometimes used to receive messages from spirit guides. Fire walking, levitation, neurolinguistic programming, psychokinesis, parapsychology, self-hypnosis, and shamanism are practiced.

Channeling is offered by some who claim to be the channels for ancient masters to speak to people today. Three of the more notorious channelers are J. Z. Knight (Ramtha), Jach Pursel (Lazaris), and Kevin Ryerson. (*See also* Channeling.)

The authoritative book is the *Spiritualist Manual.* Also used are books by Andrew Jackson Davis, *OAHSPE*, by John Newbrough, *The Aquarian Gospel of Jesus the Christ*, by Levi Dowling, and the works of self-styled prophets such as Edgar Cayce, Jeane Dixon, and Nostradamus. Bishop James A. Pike was known to be a Spiritualist.

There are nearly twenty Spiritualist denominations including the National Spiritualist Association of Churches (oldest and largest), the International General Assembly of Spiritualists, the National Spiritual Alliance, the Universal Church of the Master, and the Universal Harmony Foundation. Ministers may be ordained by attending the Morris Pratt Spiritualist Institute in Whitewater, Wisconsin.

Shirley MacLaine made Spiritualism popular in 1987 by "going public" with her experiences in the occult. Her six-volume memoirs describing her "unique personal odyssey" have been best-sellers: *Don't Fall Off the Mountain, You Can Get There from Here, Out on a Limb* (made into a television miniseries), *Dancing in the Light, It's All in the Playing*, and *Going Within.*

Spiritualism is a predecessor of the New Age movement. *See also* Theosophy.

General: Boa, pp. 130-53; Larson, *New Book*, pp. 386-95; Martin, *Kingdom*, pp. 227-45; McDowell, pp. 181ff; Robertson, pp. 147-55.

Occult: Koch.

See also New Age.

Spiritualist Manual

Authoritative book. *See* Spiritualism.

Spoken Word Publishers
    Publishes the sermons of William Branham. *See* Branhamism.

The Spring Book
    Popular occult magic spell book. *See* Magick.

Sri Chinmoy Centers
    Founded in 1964 by Sri Chinmoy. Background is Hinduism. Yoga is at the heart of their salvation system. Students practice Hatha Yoga, vegetarianism, and meditation. By devotion and surrender to Chinmoy one may get to God. He claims a prolific creative talent, reportedly completing 16,000 paintings in one day, and writing 843 poems on another day. He has published *Chinmoy Family* and *Aum*.
    General: Larson, *New Book*, pp. 396-98; Melton, *Encyclopedia*, p. 711.

SRIA
    Occultic group acronym. *See* Societas Rosicruciana in America.

SRICF
    Occultic group acronym. *See* Societas Rosicruciana in Civitatibus Foederatis.

Srimad Bhagavatam
    Interpretation of the *Bhagavad Gita*, by A. C. Bhaktivedanta Swami Prabhupada. First published in 1972. Sold by followers in public places. *See* Hare Krishna.

Star of the West
    Official Muslim sect periodical. *See* Baha'i World Faith.

Starhawk, Miriam
    Self-described witch. *See* Covenant of the Goddess.

Stearn, Jess
    Author of *Edgar Cayce: The Sleeping Prophet*. *See* Association for Research and Enlightenment.

Steiner, Rudolph
    Cult founder and author. *See* Anthroposophical Society.

Stelle Community
    New Age commune in Illinois. *See* New Age Movement.

Steller Management
    Cult front group. *See* Scientology.

Steps to Christ
Written by Ellen Gould White in 1892. *See* Seventh-day Adventism.

Steps to Self Mastery
Book by S. R. Parchment. *See* Rosicrucian Anthroposophic League.

Sterling Management
Front group. *See* Scientology.

Stevens, John Robert
Cult founder. Author of *The First Principles*, *To Every Man That Asketh*, and *Living Word for . . .*, a collection of his utterances. *See* Church of the Living Word.

Stormbringer®
Fantasy role-playing game that teaches occultic practices. *See* Occult.

Strang, James Jesse
Cult founder. *See* Strangites.

Strangites
Founded in 1845 by James Strang in Voree, Wisconsin, who claimed to have been named successor to Joseph Smith, Jr., by Smith himself. This appointment was verified by an angel in a vision Strang had on the day of Smith's death. There were an estimated ten thousand followers.

Soon some of them deserted Strang, believing he was a charlatan. He moved to Beaver Island in Lake Michigan and crowned himself king. In 1852 he was elected to the Michigan legislature and tried to use this office to create a self-governed Mormon territory. He was assassinated in 1856 by some disgruntled members.

Members today deny the virgin birth of Christ, the substitutionary atonement of Christ, and the authority of Utah Mormonism. They keep Saturday as the Sabbath. They attempt to keep the law of Moses, including animal sacrifices.

General: Melton, *Biographical Dictionary*, pp. 282-84; Melton, *Encyclopedia*, p. 494; Tucker, *Another Gospel*, pp. 46-47.

Straughn, R. A.
Cult founder known as Ra Un Nefer Amen. *See* Ausar Auset Society.

Structural Integration
More commonly known as rolfing. Could also be called "massage with a vengeance," since trained rolfers administer painful pressure to the body with their hands and elbows to relieve energy blockages caused by previous traumatic experiences. Rolf therapists are trained at the Institute of Structural Integration in Boulder, Colorado. *See* Holistic Health.

Students International Meditation Society
Sect division. *See* Transcendental Meditation.

Studies in the Scriptures
Seven-volume theology written by Charles Taze Russell. Formerly titled *The Millennial Dawn. See* Jehovah's Witnesses.

Subud
God is divine energy. Worship services are called "latihan." Practitioners shout, croon, weep, leap, speak in tongues, or chant as loud as they want to and all at the same time. Men and women have latihan in separate rooms.

Founded by Muhammed Subuh (Bapak) in Java in 1933. Headquarters is in Los Angeles. Background is Islam and New Consciousness.

General: Ellwood, pp. 253-58; Larson, *New Book,* p. 402; Melton, *Encyclopedia,* pp. 691-92.

New Age: Newport, pp. 74-78.

Subuh, Muhammed
Muslim sect founder. *See* Subud.

Sufi Order
"Sufi techniques portray the universal process by which man can attain truth, beauty, and God." A person reaches God not through the observance of the Five Pillars of Islam but by entering trances induced by twirling dances. Worship is highly emotional and is characterized by this "whirling dervish." The *Koran* is the authoritative text. Indries Shah is a leading speaker and author. Omar Khayyam was an adherent.

Mystical sect of Islam, founded by Melvana Celaleddin Rumi in Turkey in 1273. Brought to America by Pir Hazrat Inayat Khan. The present leader is Pir Vilayat Inayat Khan. Its Abode of the Message headquarters and community are near Lebanon Springs, New York. Related to the New Age movement.

General: Larson, *New Book*, pp. 97-99; McDowell, pp. 383-84; Melton, *Encyclopedia*, pp. 692-93.

New Age: Miller; Newport, pp. 66-70.

Sufism Reoriented, Inc.

Also known as Baba Lovers. Founded in 1921 in India by the late Merwan Sheriar Irani, later known as Meher Baba. World headquarters is Meherabad, India, near Poona. United States headquarters is in Walnut Creek, California. The largest Meher Baba Spiritual Center is at Myrtle Beach, South Carolina. Background is Islam.

Sacred scripture is *God Speaks*. *The Awakener* is a regular publication. The five-volume *Discourses* containing Baba's teaching, *Universal Message*, and *Listen Humanity* have also been published. Operates several bookstores.

Meher Baba was God: "I am the Christ." Man's soul progresses through reincarnation.

General: Ellwood, pp. 216-20; Larson, *New Book*, pp. 405-8.

New Age: Newport, p. 70.

Sugrue, Thomas

Author of *There Is a River*, official biography of Edgar Cayce. *See* Association for Research and Enlightenment.

Sukkoth (Feast of Tabernacles)

Jewish celebration of the harvest. *See* Judaism.

Summit Lighthouse

Publishing house in Malibu, California. *See* Church Universal and Triumphant.

Summit University

School in Malibu, California. *See* Church Universal and Triumphant.

Summit Workshop

Human potential seminar. *See* New Age Movement.

Sun Bear

Medicine man and New Age teacher. *See* New Age Movement.

Sunburst

Front group. *See* Unification Church.

Sunburst Communities

New Age communities. *See* New Age Movement.

Sung, Li
Eighth-century small-town philosopher in northern China channeled by Alan Vaughan. *See* Channeling.

Sunnis
Major branch of Islam, the traditional branch. *See* Islam.

Sunrise
Periodical of the Theosophical Society. *See* Theosophy.

Sunset Corps
Senior adult training program. *See* The Way International.

Supreme Temple for North and South America
Cult headquarters in San Jose, California. *See* Rosicrucian Fellowship.

Surrey Community
Communal group. *See* Johannine Daist Communion.

Sutphen, Dick
Author and seminar leader for the New Age movement. His seminars include "Higher Self Potential," "Psychic Seminar," and "Past-Life Therapy Professional Training." He owns Valley of the Sun Publishing Company, which produces a video cassette hypnosis series teaching things like how to balance chakras, develop psychic powers, and achieve financial success. Its audio cassettes help listeners quit nail biting, lose weight, control temper, and communicate telepathically with animals. Some titles contain subliminal messages. *See* New Age Movement.

Swedenborg, Emmanuel
Cult founder. Author of more than thirty books, including *Arcana Coelestia*, *Conjugal Love*, *The Divine Providence*, *The Four Doctrines*, *Heaven and Hell*, *Miscellaneous Theological Works*, and *The True Christian Religion*. *See* Church of the New Jerusalem.

Swedenborg Foundation
Distributes the writings of Emmanuel Swedenborg. *See* Church of the New Jerusalem.

Swedenborgianism
Alternate cult name. *See* Church of the New Jerusalem.

Swetland, David
Channeler of Matea, a 35,000-year-old "six-foot eight-inch black female spice trader." *See* Channeling.

Swift, Wesley A.

Founder of the Church of Jesus Christ Christian, Aryan Nations shortly after World War II. Claims to be a "white racial theopolitical movement" designed to establish Aryan sovereignty over areas where Aryans have settled based on what they believe God teaches. *See* Identity Movement.

SyberVision

Producer of self-improvement tapes with New Age themes. *See* New Age Movement.

Synanon Foundation

Founded by Chuck Dederich in Marin County, California, as a rehabilitation center for drug and alcohol addicts. Now located in Badger, California. Desexualizes followers by requiring the men to have vasectomies and the women to shave their heads. Operates the mail-order company Advertising Gifts and Premiums.

Charges of authoritarianism, child abuse, and violence have been levied at them. During an investigation of this cult, rattlesnakes were used in an attack on the opposition's lawyer, Paul Moranz. (Dave Mitchell, Cathy Mitchell, and Richard Ofshe, *Light on Synanon* [New York: Seaview, 1980].)

General: Appel; Enroth, *Lure*, p. 29.

Synetics

Human potential seminar developed by a Boston firm that takes employees on "mental excursions." *See* New Age Movement.

T

T. Lobsang Rampa
Background is "Tibetan Buddhism which includes Bon, a practice of devil worship and witchcraft." "Emphasized astral travel and seeing auras." Founded by Tuesday Lobsang Rampa, "a Tibetan monk-doctor-pilot who supposedly, at the time of his death, left his own body and persuaded an Englishman, Cyril Hoskins, to allow him to take over and possess his body." (Gene Aven, *My Search* [Seattle: Life Messengers, n.d.].)

Tablets
Sacred writings by Bahá'u'lláh, which take precedence over the Bible. *See* Baha'i World Faith.

Tae Kwon Do
Korean version of kung fu. *See* Martial Arts.

Tafari, Ras (Haile Selassie)
Late cult messiah. *See* Rastafarianism.

T'ai Chi Ch'uan
One of the variations of kung fu. *See* Martial Arts.

Talks with Christ
Written by Elwood Babbitt, the "medium of Massachusetts" and channeler of Mark Twain, Einstein, Jesus, Vishnu, and others. *See* Channeling.

Taniguchi, Masaharu
Cult founder. *See* Seicho-no-Ie.

Tantra
Root of nearly all Eastern religious expressions in the West and all aspects of the New Age movement. Its emphasis

on the sexual aspect of life sets it apart from other Eastern religions. Was begun between A.D. 600 and 900.

Teaches that individual and social ills can be cured by balancing the right and left hemispheres of the brain, in other words by emphasizing the feminine aspect of a person to affect the masculine extreme. Seen most clearly in Tibetan Buddhism, though tantric beliefs find their place in Hindu, Sikh, Jain, Taoist, and Islamic traditions.

Reality is One; the One is the only real. Offers a shortcut to enlightenment in one lifetime. Uses sexual imagery to portray enlightenment. A person can achieve certain states of consciousness by controlling bodily functions: sex, posture, sight, breathing, speech, and hearing. Hatha Yoga is used to achieve this control.

Right-hand, or white, tantrics interpret the sex ritual figuratively; left-hand, or red, tantrics interpret the ritual literally, engaging in concrete sexual acts.

New Age: Hoyt, pp. 131-57.

Tantric Hinduism

Employs kundalini yoga. Affirms the body and its significance for religious understanding. Followers use mandalas and mantras to aid their yogic meditation, which is supposed to raise the kundalini, a nucleus of vital energy, from its position at the base of the spine up the full length of the spinal column.

In this process, chakras are opened. These are centers of dormant psychic energy located in seven places in the body. The result is a remarkable state of awareness.

New Age: Newport, pp. 41-45.

See also Eastern Mysticism.

The Tao of Physics

Written by Fritjof Capra in 1975 to explore the similarities between Eastern mysticism and quantum physics. *See* New Age Movement.

Tao Te Ching (The Way and Its Power, or The Way and Moral Principle)

Central scripture of Taoism written by Lao-tzu, its legendary founder. *See* Taoism.

Tao Tsang

Authored by Chuang-tzu in the third century B.C. The 1,120 volumes compose the Taoist canon. *See* Taoism.

Taoism (pronounced "dow-ism")
Nature is composed of conflicting elements or opposites called yin and yang, which perfectly balance one another. Taoists seek this balance. Teaches that mankind should live passively, avoiding stress and violence, and should commune with nature. This results in a life that flows with the Tao, the "sum total of all things which are and which change," the principle of the universe.

There is no personal Creator-God. Immortality is sought through yoga and meditation.

Legend has it that Lao-tzu, or Lao-tse, founded Taoism about 550 B.C. He wrote his philosophy in the *Tao Te Ching (The Way and Its Power*, or *The Way and Moral Principle)*, the central scripture.

Chuang-tzu, who died in the early third century B.C., developed and spread the teachings of Lao-tzu and wrote commentaries on his philosophy. The resulting *Tao Tsang* is the 1,120-volume Taoist canon.

General: Boa, pp. 41-44; Larson, *New Book*, pp. 84-88; McDowell, pp. 339-48.

Comparative Religions: Beaver, pp. 251-54.

Tara Center
Founded in 1980 by New Age leader Benjamin Creme to promote the teachings of Lord Maitreya and to provide a training ground for New Agers on the emerging political, social, and economic order. *Share International* is their publication. *See* New Age Movement.

Tarot Cards
Spiritualist method of divination that dates back to ancient Egypt and the *Book of Toth*. The French popularized it in the eighteenth century. By reading the cards, a person's "unconscious powers are awakened," and the "inner forces of fate can be controlled." Forerunner of our modern playing cards. *See* Divination.

Tasseography
Spiritualist practice of reading tea leaves or coffee grounds. *See* Divination.

Taylor, Robert
Founder of the First Community Church of America. *See* Fundamentalist Fringe Movements.

The Teachings of Don Juan: A Yaqui Way of Knowledge
Written by occultist Carlos Castaneda in 1969. Popularized American Indian philosophy and peyotism. *See* Occult.

Teens for Christ
Cult-sponsored group. *See* Children of God.

Telekinesis
Spiritualist practice of moving or bending an object by mind power alone. *See* Spiritualism.

Temple of Set
One of three main Satanist churches. Founded by Michael A. Aquino and Lilith Sinclair in San Francisco. Broke off from the Church of Satan in 1975. Established as a religious society dedicated to Set, an Egyptian deity and counterpart to Satan. Teachings are found in *The Book of Coming Forth by Night*. Publishes a newsletter, *Scroll of Set*. *See also* Satanism.
General: Melton, *Encyclopedia*, p. 665.
Occult: Larson, pp. 142-43.

The Temple Reporter
Newsletter. *See* Peoples' Temple Christian Church.

Tendzen, Osel
Second in command of a Buddhist sect. *See* Vajradhatu.

Tenri-kyo
Japanese faith-healing sect founded by Miki Nakayama. God is called Parent, Divine Lord of Heavenly Wisdom, and Moon-Sun. Its scripture is the *Ofudesaki*. Happiness and prosperity are achieved by mastery of human failures. Reincarnation is taught. The first U.S. church was founded in 1927 in San Francisco; based in Los Angeles since 1934.
General: Melton, *Encyclopedia*, pp. 779-80.
Eastern Mysticism: Ellwood, pp. 37-68.

The Testament of Solomon
One of the best-known grimoires, or occult magic spell books. *See* Magick.

Testimonies for the Church
Written by Ellen Gould White in 1882. *See* Seventh-day Adventism.

A Textbook of Masonic Jurisprudence
Book used by Masons. *See* Freemasonry.

Thant, U.

Former Secretary-General of the United Nations. New Age political action group cofounder. *See* Planetary Citizens.

Theosophical Company

Publishing arm of the United Lodge of Theosophy. *See* Theosophy.

Theosophical Publishing House

Publishing arm of the Theosophical Society in America in Wheaton, Illinois. *See* Theosophy.

Theosophical Society

One of the three major theosophical groups. Based in Altadena, California. *See* Theosophy.

Theosophical Society in America

One of the three major theosophical groups. Based in Wheaton, Illinois. *See* Theosophy.

Theosophical University Press

Publishing arm of the Theosophical Society in Altadena, California. *See* Theosophy.

Theosophy

Also called Divine Wisdom. The aims of the society are: "(1) to form a nucleus of Universal Brotherhood of Humanity, without the distinction of race, creed, sex, caste, or colour, (2) to encourage the study of comparative religion, philosophy, and science, and (3) to investigate the unexplained laws of nature and the powers latent in man."

Its Trinity is Power (or Will), Wisdom, and Activity, plus a "fourth Person . . . the Mother." God is impersonal. Jesus is the fifth reincarnation in the Aryan race of the "Supreme Teacher of the World." Man is part of God; in time all men become Christs. Denies Christ's sacrifice for atonement. Teaches a refined version of reincarnation, that one comes back as another person, never as an animal. We suffer now for sins done in a former existence. Followers are urged to participate in occult and paranormal phenomena.

There are three major theosophical groups: (1) The Theosophical Society and its Theosophical University Press are in Altadena, California; follows W. Q. Judge; publishes *Sunrise*, a periodical. (2) The Theosophical Society of America, the Theosophical Publishing House, and Quest Books are in Wheaton, Illinois; current president is Dorothy Appenhouse; follows Blavatsky; publishes the *American Theosophist and Discovery*. (3) The United Lodge of Theosophy and the

Theosophical Company (the publishing arm) are located in Los Angeles; publishes the monthly *Theosophy*. International headquarters is in Adyar, India.

Theosophy was founded in 1875 by Madame Helena Petrovna Blavatsky, Colonel Henry Steel Olcott, and William Quan Judge in New York City. The greatest successor to Helena was Annie Besant. Background is Spiritualism, Hinduism, Buddhism, and gnosticism. Considered the most influential Hindu/occult group in America.

Blavatsky's two books are considered sacred: *Isis Unveiled* and *The Secret Doctrine*. Also publishes *The Golden Book of the Theosophical Society* and the writings of C. W. Leadbeater and Jiddu Krishnamurti. Writers talk about the unity of all life.

Abner Doubleday, Sir Arthur Conan Doyle, Thomas A. Edison, Jawaharlal Nehru, George Bernard Shaw, Lord Tennyson, and William Butler Yeats were attracted to this movement. Related groups are the Arcane School, the I AM Movement, the Liberal Catholic Church, and the Rosicrucian Fellowship. Predecessor to the New Age movement.

General: Boa, pp. 102-7; Larson, *New Book*, pp. 411-16; Martin, *Kingdom*, pp. 246-60; McDowell, pp. 86-89; Robertson, pp. 157-60.

Theosophy

Monthly periodical of the United Lodge of Theosophy. *See* Theosophy.

Therapeutic Touch

One of the practices in holistic health. Teaches that illness is caused by poorly distributed energy. The practitioner passes his hands over the body in a flowing motion to balance this energy. Involves four steps: centering (becoming relaxed), assessment (scanning energy fields with the hands), unruffling (decongesting the energy flow), and transfer (balancing the energy). *See* Holistic Health.

Theravada Buddhism

Original, conservative branch of Buddhism in India. *See* Buddhism.

There Is a River

Official biography of Edgar Cayce written by Thomas Sugrue in 1942. *See* Association for Research and Enlightenment.

Third Force
   New Age-related group. *See* New Age Movement.
Third Wave
   New Age-related group. *See* New Age Movement.
Thomas, John
   Medical doctor; cult founder. Author of *Christendom Astray*, *Elpis-Israel*, and *Eureka*. *See* Christadelphians.
Thought
   Cult publication. *See* Unity School of Christianity.
The Three Pillars of Zen
   Buddhist sect publication. *See* Zen Buddhism.
3HO Foundation
   Alternate cult name. *See* Healthy, Happy, Holy Organization.
Tilton, Robert
   Pastor of the Word of Faith Church in Dallas; televangelist. *See* Positive Confession.
Tindall, Alice
   New Age cult founder. *See* National Spiritual Science Center.
Tkach, Joseph W., Jr.
   Overseer of congregations in the United States. *See* Worldwide Church of God.
Tkach, Joseph W., Sr.
   Pastor General of the Worldwide Church of God, named by Herbert W. Armstrong as his successor before his death in 1986. *See* Worldwide Church of God.
To Every Man That Asketh
   Book by John Robert Stevens. *See* Church of the Living Word.
Today's World
   Cult periodical. *See* Unification Church.
Toffler, Alvin
   Futurist; one of the New Age "significant thinkers." *See* New Age Movement.
Tomkins, Peter
   Coauthor of *The Secret Life of Plants*. *See* Plant Communication.
Tomorrow's World
   Former magazine title. *See* Worldwide Church of God.

Torah
First five books of the Old Testament. One of four sacred scriptures for Muslims. Considered the law by Jews. *See* Islam *and* Judaism.

Torres, Penny
Channeler for Mafu, a first-century Greek leper who claims to be a member of the "brotherhood of light" in the "seventh dimension." *See* Channeling.

Tower of Silence
Open burial area where bodies of the dead are laid so that the vultures may pick their bones. *See* Zoroastrianism.

Traill, Stewart
Cult founder. *See* Church of Bible Understanding.

Traina, A. B.
Founded the Scripture Research Association in the 1940s. Wrote a translation of the Bible called *The Holy Name Bible. See* Assemblies of Yahweh.

Trance Channeling
One method of communicating with the spirit world. *See* Channeling.

Trans Tech
Short name for Transformational Technologies, which trains corporate executives in yoga, hypnosis, visualization, and positive thinking. *See* est.

Transcendental Meditation (TM)
Also called Science of Creative Intelligence (SCI). TM is a form of Tantra that has been greatly sanitized for the public. Hindu Vedic scriptures are used. Our source of power does not lie in a personal God but in man's heart. Forgiveness comes through meditation, providing salvation. The Beatles and Mia Farrow became adherents; many thousands of respected businessmen, athletes, and clergymen practice it. TM was taught in high schools and colleges until it was declared a religion by a U.S. District Court in 1977.

Founded by Maharishi Mahesh Yogi in Rishikesh, India, in 1958. Brought to America in 1959 as the Spiritual Regeneration Movement. World headquarters is in Seelisberg, Switzerland, with TM centers in 140 countries and 400 United States cities. Background is Hinduism and Tantra. Aligned with the New Age movement. Used as a holistic health method.

Control is through the World Plan Executive Council. Operates out of 350 teaching centers of the American Foundation for the Science of Creative Intelligence. Also operates as International Meditation Society, and Students International Meditation Society.

Owns 465 acres in the Catskill Mountains of New York with a hotel, printing shop, and broadcasting station; the Maharishi International University (MIU) in Fairfield, Iowa; and Mentmore Towers in England, bought in 1977; as well as several other English mansions. Annual income is around $40 million. Plans to build the "City of Immortals" in Austin, Texas, providing "a crime-free, anxiety-free lifestyle" for the occupants of the up to two hundred homes. Leaders have met with developers in Oklahoma to plan a housing project there.

General: Boa, pp. 156-66; Larson, *New Book*, pp. 421-29; Martin, *Kingdom*, pp. 362-63; McDowell, pp. 80-85; Robertson, pp. 110-14.

New Age: Newport, pp. 20-29.

Transformational Technologies (Trans Tech)

Offshoot of est aimed at training executives of large corporations in how to use yoga, hypnosis, visualization, and positive thinking to improve sales. *See* est.

Transmigration

Belief that the soul will be reborn into this life (as objects, animals, or people) as many times as it takes to reach perfection or salvation. Similar to reincarnation (rebirth only in human form). *See* Hinduism.

Transpersonal Psychology

Relatively new field that teaches the worldview that all people are part of a "divine oneness." Promoted by the Association for Transpersonal Psychology. A leading figure in this field is Ken Wilber. *See* New Age Movement.

Treat, Casey

Pastor of Seattle's Christian Faith Center. *See* Positive Confession.

Tree of Life

Graphic depiction of God's ten creative emanations. *See* Kabbalah.

Tremaine, Kit

Author of *The Butterfly Rises*, which features dialogues with Indira Latari, a nineteenth-century Hindu woman channeled by Verna Yater, as well as other channeled spirit entities. *See* Channeling.

Trevelyan, George
Popular speaker among New Agers. Author of *A Vision of the Aquarian Age* and *Operation Redemption*. *See* New Age Movement.

Tripitaka
Group of three writings sacred to Theravada Buddhism. *See* Buddhism.

The True Art of Creation
Textbook on which is based the Cosmic Study Center, a UFO cult in Potomac, Maryland. *See* UFO Cults.

True Centuries
Prophetic quatrains of Nostradamus, fourteenth-century astrologer and physician. *See* Spiritualism.

The True Christian Religion
Book by Emmanuel Swedenborg, cult founder. *See* Church of the New Jerusalem.

True Father and True Mother
Titles of Sun Myung Moon and his wife. *See* Unification Church.

True Grimoire
Former newsletter for OTS and the Church of Satanic Brotherhood. *See* Ordo Templi Satanas.

Trujillo, Immanuel
Founder of the Peyote Way Church of God. *See* Native American Religions.

Truth Journal
Hindu sect publication. *See* Center for Spiritual Awareness.

The Truth That Leads to Eternal Life
Published by the Watchtower Bible and Tract Society in 1968. Used in recruiting new members. *See* Jehovah's Witnesses.

Tulku, Chogyam Trungpa
Buddhist sect founder. *See* Vajradhatu.

Tunnels and Trolls®
Fantasy role-playing game similar to Dungeons and Dragons® that teaches occultic practices. *See* Occult.

The Turning Point—Science, Society, and the Rising Culture
Manifesto on New Age ideology written by Fritjof Capra in 1982. Shows the relationship of Eastern mysticism and modern physics. *See* New Age Movement.

Tucson Tabernacle
Worship center for followers of Branhamism in Arizona. *See* Branhamism.

Twig
Local congregation of The Way. *See* The Way International.

Twin Oaks
New Age commune in Virginia. *See* New Age Movement.

Twitchell, Sri John Paul
Cult founder, "971st ECK Master." *See* ECKANKAR.

2001: A Space Odyssey
Science fiction book written by Arthur C. Clarke in 1968 and made into a movie depicting evolution, contact with extraterrestrials, a New Age millennial concept, and evolving consciousness. *See* New Age Movement.

2010: Odyssey Two
Sequel to *2001: A Space Odyssey*, by science fiction writer Arthur C. Clarke. Depicts contact with extraterrestrials and a New Age millenial concept. Expresses devotion to Lucifer, the Light Bearer. Later made into a movie. *See* New Age Movement.

U

UBF

Acronym for University Bible Fellowship, a cult that uses "chance encounters on campuses to invite students to Bible studies without mentioning the high pressure to conform that will come later." *See* Fundamentalist Fringe Movements.

UFO Cults

Not just a casual belief in the existence of unidentified flying objects, but a religious fervor and reliance on the beings that inhabit them rather than on God. There is no God; there is an Ultimate: the "Infinite Intelligence," or "Great Guiding Force." Jesus came here from Venus and will return on a UFO. There is no sin; therefore, there is no need for salvation. The Bible has to be rewritten. Oriental religious teachings must be incorporated into Western religious thought. Reincarnation must be reintroduced.

The inhabitants of UFOs are holy, sinless beings who communicate with us through psychics and mediums. Their mission is to help earthlings evolve spiritually, since our progress affects the universe.

Teach that there are four kinds of close encounters with UFOs: the first kind—actual sighting; the second kind—finding impressions left on the ground or fragments of the UFO; the third kind—contact with the aliens; and the fourth kind—abduction and/or examination by the aliens.

This belief shows up in many separate groups, such as the following: Aetherius Society in Hollywood, California; Amalgamated Flying Saucer Clubs of America, in Los Angeles, California; CE 3K Skywatchers, in New York City;

Center for UFO Studies, in Evanston, Illinois; Cosmic Study Center, in Potomac, Maryland; George Adamski Foundation; Mark-Age, in Fort Lauderdale, Florida; UFO Education Center, in Valley Center, California; Understanding, Inc., in Oregon; and Urantia Brotherhood, in Chicago, Illinois, and Santa Barbara, California.

Often UFO cults are connected with a Spiritualist group, though not all are. UFO believers gather annually at the Giant Rock Space Convention near Yucca Valley, California. *Cosmic Masters* is one of their publications.

General: Larson, *New Book*, pp. 430-36; Melton, *Encyclopedia*, pp. 559-66.

Miscellaneous: Allan; Scheaffer.

New Age: Brooke, pp. 24-27.

Occult: Koch, pp. 340-45.

UFO Education Center

Founded by Charlotte Blob in Valley Center, California, to perpetuate the work of George Adamski. *See* George Adamski Foundation.

The Ultimate Formula of Life

Written by H. Charles Berner in 1968. *See* Abilitism.

Umbanda

Alternate name for Macumba, spirit worship practiced in South America, primarily in Brazil. Also called Candomblé. *See* Voodoo.

Understanding, Inc.

A UFO cult with headquarters in Oregon. Emphasizes occult knowledge, mental telepathy, and hypnosis. The goal is to prepare people of all races and needs to live in harmony in the space age. There are about sixty "units" around the country that hold regular meetings. Founded in 1955 by Daniel Fry, who wrote *White Sands Incident* following an encounter with a UFO. *See also* UFO Cults.

General: Ellwood, pp. 121-23; Melton, *Encyclopedia*, p. 565.

Unification Church

Official name is the Holy Spirit Association for the Unification of World Christianity. Also called the Moonies. Founded in 1954 by Sun Myung Moon in Korea. Brought to the United States in 1972. Its sacred writing is *Divine Principle*. Background is Taoism and Korean Messianity.

There is no Trinity. God is a syncretistic oriental deity; the real god is Moon himself. Jesus meant well but was a total failure; He was crucified before He could accomplish His mission. Moon is the third Adam, the Lord of the Second Advent, the Messiah.

Salvation must come by a process of blood purification provided by Moon and by doing good works for Moon. The Bible must be translated in light of *Divine Principle*. The Unification Church is the true church, joining all churches together.

Marriage is a special theological union that is arranged by the Church. These marriages help create perfect families. Moon regularly performs mass weddings; the largest was 6,512 couples in October 1988.

Fund raising is the chief activity with an average take per person of $150 per day. It all goes to Moon. Adherents are trained to lie ("heavenly deception") to get money out of people or to get them to join.

In 1982 Moon was found guilty of conspiracy to defraud the federal government and filing false income tax returns. He was sentenced to eighteen months in prison. In 1985, as he served his sentence, the organization sent "a gift" to more than 300 thousand ministers—a packet of three video tapes explaining their theology, a copy of *Divine Principle*, and a copy of *God's Warning to the World* containing Moon's "message from prison."

In 1988 the Church reported that Moon's deceased son Heung Jin Nim had been reincarnated as a black convert from Zimbabwe. Periodicals include *Unification News*, *Today's World*, and *CARP Monthly*, which are widely distributed, and *Principle Life* and *Blessing Quarterly*, which are for members only.

Front groups through which it does fund raising, recruiting, public relations work, and lobbying include American Constitution Committee, American Freedom Coalition (AFC), Collegiate Association for the Research of Principles (CARP—the college recruiting arm), Council for Unified Research and Education, and Creative Community Project. Others are D.C. Striders Track Club, Freedom Leadership Foundation, Global Congress of the World's Religions, International Conference on the Unity of the Sciences (ICUS), International Cultural Foundation (ICF), International Relief Friendship Foundation, International Religious Foundation,

Korean Folk Ballet, Korean Little Angels, Korean National Folk Dance Company.

Also works through National Council for the Church and Social Action, NEW ERA, New Hope Singers International, One World Crusade, Sunburst, Professors World Peace Academy, Project Volunteer, Unification Thought Institute, Universal Ballet Academy, and World Media Conference. The goal is to establish a one-world government with Moon at the head and church and state united.

Owns several choice estates on the Hudson River in New York including the $2 million, sixty-acre International Training Center at Tarrytown; property in all fifty states; the $5 million Hotel New Yorker; the *Washington Times* newspaper and its publisher, Newsworld Communications; Paragon House publishing firm in New York; Panda Motors Corporation of Vienna, Virginia; and in Korea, the Il Haw Pharmaceutical Company and Tong Il Industries (which makes firearms, ammunition, and automobile parts). Operates the Unification Theological Seminary in Tarrytown, New York, and Camp New Hope in Ulster County, New York.

There are plans to build the International Peace Highway from Tokyo to London. The first leg will be the 140-mile undersea road and rail Japan-Korea Tunnel. The Church has already bought land in both countries and has bored the initial shafts.

Headquarters is in Washington, D.C. Current president is James A. Baughman. Col. Bo Hi Pak is the Chief Lieutenant to Moon.

Not affiliated with the New Age movement.

General: Boa, pp. 167-77; Larson, *New Book*, pp. 437-45; Martin, *Kingdom*, pp. 338-44; McDowell, pp. 99-104; Passantino, pp. 121-38; Robertson, pp. 24-86; Tucker, *Another Gospel*, pp. 245-66, 396-97.

New Age: Newport, pp. 119-39.

See also Miscellaneous.

Unification News
  Periodical. *See* Unification Church.

Unification Theological Seminary
  School in Tarrytown, New York. *See* Unification Church.

Unification Thought Institute
  Front group. *See* Unification Church.

Unitarian Universalist Association

"God" refers to "natural processes such as the power of love in the universe." "We do not need to believe that Jesus was God." "Unitarians refuse to acknowledge Jesus as their Lord and God." Salvation is by works, an ethical life, and caring for fellow men. The doctrine of the death of Christ for our sins is "offensive, unbiblical, even immoral." Man can save himself.

The Bible is not divinely inspired. Heaven and hell are conditions within the human spirit. Man is potentially good and capable of being perfect.

Formed in 1961 as a merger of Unitarian and Universalist churches. William F. Schulz is national president with headquarters in Boston. Beacon Press is its publishing house.

Famous adherents include John Adams, John Quincy Adams, Louisa Mae Alcott, Susan B. Anthony, Ralph Waldo Emerson, Millard Fillmore, Bret Harte, Nathaniel Hawthorne, Oliver Wendell Holmes, Thomas Jefferson, Henry Wadsworth Longfellow, James Russell Lowell, Horace Mann, Samuel Morse, Adlai Stevenson, William Howard Taft, and Henry David Thoreau.

The Covenant of Unitarian Universalist Pagans in Cambridge, Massachusetts, combines goddess religion (witchcraft) with UUA principles.

General: Larson, *New Book*, pp. 446-47; Martin, *Kingdom*, pp. 501-6; Melton, *Encyclopedia*, pp. 473-74; Starkes, pp. 97-107.

United Christian Evangelistic Association

Born Frederick Eikerenkoetter, Rev. Ike says, "The lack of money is the root of all evil." A mixture of black pentecostalism and Christian Scientism. Based in Boston. Publishes *Action* magazine.

The Bible is a book of psychology. Satan is "negative thoughts." Deity is "the Presence of God in you." Heaven is out; instead Ike teaches "the eternal now." Those who give generously to his cause will receive great benefits from the god-who-is-in-you. "Your only Savior is your own realization that you are the Christ."

Rev. Ike demonstrates his "prosperity gospel" by owning many diamonds and sixteen Rolls Royces.

General: Larson, *New Book*, pp. 352-54.

United Lodge of Theosophy
   One of the three major theosophical groups. *See* Theosophy.

United Order Effort
   Fundamentalist spinoff. *See* Mormonism.

United Society of Believers in Christ's Second Coming.
   Formal name. *See* Shakers.

Unity: A Way of Life
   Cult magazine. *See* Unity School of Christianity.

Unity Correspondence School
   Cult-related school. *See* Unity School of Christianity.

Unity-in-Diversity Council
   Network of more than 200 New Age organizations. Promotes global cooperation and an interdependence of all nations of the world. *See* New Age Movement.

Unity Ministerial School
   Program of Unity School for Religious Studies. *See* Unity School of Christianity.

Unity School of Christianity
   Works through Unity Tract Society and the Unity Correspondence School. Sponsors a prayer ministry called Silent Unity. Unity School for Religious Studies was established to help people achieve "the self-realization of their own divine potential." It offers a Continuing Education Program for adults, Unity Village Vacation Retreats, and the Unity Ministerial School.
   Background is Christian Science, Eastern mysticism, and gnosticism. Contrasted with Christian Science: there is less emphasis on the negation of matter and more emphasis on the latent powers within. Prayer releases these powers, producing peace of mind, inner harmony, good health, and success.
   There is no Trinity. God is the impersonal "Father Principle." Jesus was not the Christ. He was a good man who had part of the Christ principle as we all do. He was the elder teacher, the way-shower. The Holy Spirit "is the executive power of the Father and the Son." Jesus' death was a pagan concept. "Being born again . . . is the establishment of that which has always existed as the perfect man idea of divine mind."
   As for reincarnation, "the repeated incarnations of man is a merciful provision of our loving Father to the end that all

240

may have opportunity to attain immortality through regeneration as did Jesus.''

Founded by Charles S. and Myrtle Fillmore in 1889; based on the teachings of Phineas Parkhurst Quimby. Was one of the New Thought groups known in the early days as Modern Thought. Charles Rickert Fillmore became president in 1972. Charles R. Fillmore is the current president. Headquartered at Unity Village in Lee's Summit, Missouri. Individual Unity congregations are related through the Association of Unity Churches.

Charles S. Fillmore wrote *Jesus Christ Heals* and *Metaphysical Bible Dictionary*. Publications include *Daily Word*, *Good Business* (for the working man), *Thought*, *Unity: A Way of Life*, *Wee Wisdom* (for children), and *Weekly Unity* (a devotional magazine). Frequently seen by Americans is the ''word for today is . . .'' spot on television.

General: Boa, pp. 97-101; Larson, *New Book*, pp. 448-51; Martin, *Kingdom*, pp. 279-302; McDowell, pp. 131-35; Robertson, pp. 160-62; Tucker, *Another Gospel*, pp. 177-90, 394.

Miscellaneous: Barron.

Unity Tract Society
Publishing division. *See* Unity School of Christianity.

Unity Village
Cult headquarters in Lee's Summit, Missouri. *See* Unity School of Christianity.

Unity Village Vacation Retreat
Program of Unity School for Religious Studies. *See* Unity School of Christianity.

Universal Ballet Academy
Cultural front group in Washington, D.C. The Prima Ballerina of its Universal Ballet Company is Julie Hoon Sook Moon, daughter of Col. Bo Hi Pak and daughter-in-law of Sun Myung Moon. She was married to Moon's deceased son after his death. *See* Unification Church.

Universal Brotherhood
Disembodied spirits who have reached the highest level of spiritual consciousness and now guide the spiritual evolution of mankind. Also called ascended masters, enlightened masters, and Great White Brotherhood. *See* New Age Movement *and* Spiritualism.

Universal Brotherhood Movement, Inc.
Teaches a oneness of life philosophy. New Age group founded in 1976 by Rick and Jen-i Prigmore in Fort Lauderdale, Florida.
New Age: Khalsa, p. 141.

Universal Brotherhood of Humanity
One of the theosophical aims. *See* Theosophy.

Universal Church of the Master
Formed in 1908 in Los Angeles by a group of Spiritualists. Headquarters is now in San Jose, California. *See also* Spiritualism.
General: Melton, *Encyclopedia*, pp. 545-46.

Universal Faith Church
Teaches the "Way of Divine Radiance." Seeks to establish a single world faith that will unite all humanity in God-Realization. Founded by Mishael, Enlightened World Teacher. Headquartered at the Universal Faith Temple in Tulsa, Oklahoma.
Mishael has written *Pools in Parched Ground*. Publishes *Celebration* quarterly.
New Age: Khalsa, p. 141.

Universal Faith Temple
Cult headquarters in Tulsa, Oklahoma. *See* Universal Faith Church.

Universal Harmony Foundation
Formed in 1942 as the Universal Psychic Science Association. J. Bertran and Helene Gerling were the founders. Headquarters is in Seminole, Florida. Background is Spiritualism and New Thought.
Operates a seminary. Publishes a periodical called *The Spiritual Science Digest. See also* Spiritualism.
General: Melton, *Encyclopedia*, p. 546.

Universal Life Church
ULC "only believes in what is right, and that all people have the right to determine what beliefs are right for them, as long as they do not interfere with the rights of others." "After a person has become an ordained minister, he or she can join with two other people and form their own ULC." The minister then channels all his income through the "church" and does not pay income tax. The property where the church meets is tax exempt. Each member can deduct from his in-

come tax up to 50 percent of his outside income. The adults of Hardenburg, New York, became ULC ministers.

Kirby J. Hensley founded ULC in 1962 in his garage in Modesto, California, ordaining ministers for $1 by mail. (Keith E. L'Hommedieu, "The Fastest Growing Church in the World," *Consumer Life* 3, No. 3.)

General: Melton, *Encyclopedia*, pp. 478-79.

Universal Message

Muslim sect publication. *See* Sufism Reoriented, Inc.

Universal Psychic Science Association

Original cult name. *See* Universal Harmony Foundation.

University Bible Fellowship (UBF)

Uses "chance encounters on campuses to invite students to Bible studies without mentioning the high pressure to conform that will come later." Considered a destructive cult because of its excessive use of deception, coercion, and manipulation. (Denny Gulick, "Destructive Cults Eliminate Freedom of Thought," *The Diamondback*, U. of Maryland, April 18, 1988.) *See also* Fundamentalist Fringe Movements.

University of Life

Teaches New Age concepts and practices. *See* Mark-Age.

Unveiled Mysteries

Written by Godfré Ray King (Guy Ballard) in 1934. *See* I AM Movement.

Up from Eden: A Transpersonal View of Human Evolution

Written in 1981 by Ken Wilber, leading figure in transpersonal psychology. *See* New Age Movement.

Up with People

Internationally-known singing group originally sponsored by Moral Re-armament. Now they are not related to any religious or political group. *See* Moral Re-armament.

The Upanishads

Sacred writing of Hinduism; collection of speculative treatises. *See* Hinduism *and* Yoga.

Uptrends

Cult front group. *See* Scientology.

Urantia Book

Sacred writing published in 1955 after it was channeled to Bill Sadler by seven celestial beings. Includes a section called "The Life and Teachings of Jesus," an adulterated re-telling of the biblical account. *See* Urantia Brotherhood.

Urantia Brotherhood

Based on the Urantia Book supposedly written by seven celestial beings and communicated to Bill Sadler by automatic handwriting. It includes a section called "The Life and Teachings of Jesus," an adulterated retelling of the biblical account. Background is UFO cults, Spiritualism, and the occult.

Its aim is to improve man's "comprehension of Cosmology and the relation of the planet on which we live to the universe of the genesis and destiny of man and his relation to God, and of the true teachings of Jesus Christ." Is organized into societies made up of ten or more followers.

Prayer is "not to be attempted until one has exhausted the human capacity for human adjustment." The blood atonement of Christ is an unnecessary encumbrance. Marriage is not a sacred state.

The Urantia Book teaches that there are many gods and many Paradise Sons of God. "Jesus is not about to die as a sacrifice for sin. . . . The salvation of God for the mortals of Urantia [earth] would have been just as effective and unerringly certain if Jesus had not been put to death." Seven Paradise personalities raised Jesus' Morontia form and personality from the dead. Gabriel gave the body of Jesus a "dignified and reverent disposal of near-instantaneous dissolution."

Begun in 1950 by Bill Sadler and a group called The Forum. John Nales is the current president. Headquarters are in Chicago, Illinois, and Santa Barbara, California. The Urantia Foundation publishes its works.

General: Larson, *New Book*, pp. 452-56; Melton, *Encyclopedia*, p. 590.

Urantia Foundation

Publisher and custodian of the *Urantia Book*. *See* Urantia Brotherhood.

V

Vajradhatu

Background is Tibetan Buddhism. Its practices "aim at direct experience of the enlightened self through symbols, visual images, repetition of sounds, prescribed movements, breath control, and ritualized sexual intercourse."

The Nalanda Institute spreads the message of Vajradhatu throughout the world. The Naropa Institute is the think tank. Karme-Choling is a commune farm near Barnet, Vermont. The Rocky Mountain Dharma Center is used for meditation retreats. Dorje Khyung Dzong in southern Colorado is a private center for individual retreats. The Maitri Therapeutic Community treats neurosis with Buddhist practices. The Mudra Theatre Group is a drama group that portrays Buddhist concepts. Shambhala Training is a growth seminar designed to raise the level of human potential.

Founded by Chogyam Trungpa Tulku, a Buddhist in Tibet. Current leader is Chogyam Trungpa Rinpoche. Osel Tendzen is the second in command. U.S. headquarters is in Boulder, Colorado. Dharmadatus are local centers located across the United States. *Garuda* and *Vajradhatu Sun*, a bimonthly newspaper, are periodicals.

General: Ellwood, pp. 236-41.

New Age: Newport, p. 62.

Vajradhatu Sun

Bimonthly newspaper for a Buddhist sect. *See* Vajradhatu.

Valentine, Paul

Cult leader. *See* Worldwide Church of Satanic Liberation.

Valley of Rewards
Destination gained by achieving "peace of mind and enlightenment." *See* Astara.

Valley of the Sun Publishing Company
Owned by New Age author Dick Sutphen. Produces a video hypnosis series on such New Age subjects as how to balance chakras, develop psychic powers, and achieve financial success. Its audio cassettes help listeners quit nail biting, lose weight, control temper, and communicate telepathically with animals. Some titles contain subliminal messages. *See also* New Age Movement.

Value Creation Society
Alternate cult name. *See* Nichiren Shoshu of America.

Values Clarification
Pivotal point in transpersonal education, teaching that values emerge from within an individual and should not be imposed from without. *See* New Age Movement.

Van Rijckenborgh, J.
Cult founder. *See* Lectorium Rosicrucianism.

Vaughan, Alan
Channeler of Li Sung, an eighth-century Chinese philosopher. *See* Channeling.

Vedanta Society
A branch of the Ramakrishna movement. Heavily influenced by Tantra. Divinity is inherent in man, who has the capacity for infinite evolution. Meditation is the path to self-realization. Classes are offered in the *Upanishads* and *Bhagavad Gita*. Ralph Waldo Emerson was influenced by Vedanta as well as Unitarianism. Many of his poems express Indian mystical ideas.

First Hindu-based cult to be established in America. Founded in New York in 1894 by Swami Vivekananda. International headquarters is near Calcutta, India. There are more than a dozen centers in the United States, each governed by its members. Owns three monasteries and two convents.

General: Ellwood, pp. 184-88; Larson, *New Book*, pp. 457-58; Robertson, p. 122.

Comparative Religions: Mead, pp. 255-56; Melton, *Encyclopedia*.

New Age: Brooke, pp. 169-72.

The Vedas
Collection of wisdom books revered by Hindus. *See* Hinduism.

Vickers, Karen
Channeler for Annie Besant and twenty other spirit healers. *See* Channeling.

Villains and Vigilantes®
Fantasy role-playing game similar to Dungeons and Dragons® that teaches occultic practices. *See* Occult.

Virtue of Selfishness
Book by Ayn Rand. *See* Ayn Rand.

Vishnu
Major Hindu deity, the preserver. Sometimes one of his ten incarnations is worshiped, such as Krishna, Rama, or Buddha. *See* Hinduism.

Vision Mound
Communal group. *See* Johannine Daist Communion.

A Vision of the Aquarian Age
Written in 1984 by George Trevelyan, a popular New Age speaker. *See* New Age Movement.

VISN
Vision Inter-faith Satellite Network, distributed through nearly four hundred cable systems in America. Programming is provided by Roman Catholicism, Eastern Orthodoxy, Judaism, Mormonism, Mennonites, Seventh-day Adventism, the Salvation Army, and fifteen smaller groups.

Visualization
Also called guided imagery. Involves relaxation techniques, self-hypnosis, and meditation. The person concentrates on an image in his mind in an effort to make something happen. The image may be suggested by a therapist. *See* New Age Movement.

Vivekananda, Swami Ramakrishna
Sect founder. *See* Vedanta Society.

Voice of Astara
Monthly publication. *See* Astara Foundation.

Voices of Spirit
Written by Elwood Babbitt, the "medium of Massachusetts" and channeler of Mark Twain, Einstein, Jesus, Vishnu, and others. *See* Channeling.

Von Grasshoff, Carl Louis

Birth name of Max Heindel, occultic group founder. *See* Rosicrucian Fellowship.

Voodoo

Spirit worship that originated in Africa and spread to the Caribbean. Each believer is assigned a spirit at birth, a guardian who will protect and guide him throughout his life. If the believer treats his guardian well, he is ensured a good life. Believers use sorcery, fetishes, and séances.

In Brazil it is called Macumba, Candomblé, or Umbanda; in the Caribbean it is Santeria.

General: Larson, *New Book*, pp. 459-63; McDowell, p. 267.

Occult: Larson, pp. 178-83.

W

Wakea

"Sky father" god. *See* Polynesian Religions.

Waldorf Schools

Established to awaken spiritual consciousness in children. *See* Anthroposophical Society.

The Walk

Alternate cult name. *See* The Church of the Living Word.

Walker, Thane

Muslim sect cofounder and dean. *See* The Prosperos.

Walters, J. Donald

Sect founder now known as Swami Kriyananda. Wrote *Songs of Divine Joy*, used in worship, and *The Path: A Spiritual Autobiography. See* Ananda.

Wardley, James and Jane

Cult founders who preached that Christ would return as a woman. *See* Shakers.

Warhammer®

Fantasy role-playing game that teaches occultic practices. *See* Occult.

Warlock of Firetop Mountain®

Fantasy role-playing game that teaches occultic practices. *See* Occult.

Warner, James K.

Sect founder. *See* New Christian Crusade Church.

Washington Times
Cult-owned newspaper. *See* Unification Church.

The Watchman
Identity Movement group publication. *See* Church of Israel.

The Watchtower
Cult periodical. *See* Jehovah's Witnesses.

Watchtower Bible and Tract Society
Cult headquarters and publishing house in Brooklyn, New York. *See* Jehovah's Witnesses.

The Way
Semi-monthly magazine. *See* The Way International.

The Way and Its Power
English title of *Tao Te Ching*, the central scripture of Taoism. Also translated as *The Way and Moral Principle*. *See* Taoism.

The Way College
School in Emporia, Kansas. *See* The Way International.

The Way College of Biblical Research
School in Rome, Indiana. *See* The Way International.

The Way Corps
Basic training program. *See* The Way International.

The Way Family Corps
Family training program. *See* The Way International.

The Way International
Founded by the late Victor Paul Wierwille in 1953. Only the New Testament epistles are of any value to the Christian. The Trinity concept is a pagan belief confirmed by a scribe's error in translating the Bible. God is one in substance, one in person. Jesus was not God; He was a perfect man. In his book *Jesus Christ Is Not God*, Wierwille declared that God used sperm to make the body of Jesus. In *Jesus Christ Our Passover*, he used astrology to figure out the exact time of Jesus' birth. The Holy Spirit is not God. The Bible is not the Word of God but only contains the word of God. Wierwille claimed to have rediscovered the long lost "true" teachings of the apostles. Uses *The Holy Bible from Ancient Eastern Manuscripts*, by George M. Lamsa.

Recently The Way released a shareware computer program called "Wordworker," a topical cross-referenced Bible program. It cites reference works that are their own publications including *Jesus Christ Is not God.*

As to the church, "No one has the real Truth like we have the real Truth." Bible study classes meet; the meeting place is sometimes called the Abundant Life Church. Teaches how to speak in tongues. They do not oppose drinking, dancing, or using curse words.

The organization is modeled after a tree: the trunk is international headquarters, the root is the board of directors, the limbs are the state organizations, branches are city and county ministries, twigs are local fellowships, and leaves are individual believers.

Headquarters is in New Knoxville, Ohio. Craig Martindale is now the leader. In 1988 some followers became disillusioned over Wierwille's alleged adultery and plagiarism and challenged Martindale's leadership. They splintered into three groups: American Fellowship Services, Pacific West Fellowship, and Great Lakes Fellowship.

The Way magazine is its semimonthly publication; *Heart* is a bimonthly periodical. The American Christian Press is the publishing arm. Works through "Power for Abundant Living" classes (fee is about $200), Bible fellowships, The Way Corps, The Way Family Corps, WOW Ambassadors, Way Productions, Sunset Corps, and Biblical Research Centers.

Operates The Way College, in Emporia, Kansas; The Way College of Biblical Research, in Rome, Indiana; Camp Gunnison, The Way Family Ranch, at Gunnison, Colorado; Lead Outdoor Academy, in Tinnie, New Mexico; the Cultural Center, in New Bremen, Ohio; and The Way International Fine Arts and Historical Center, at Sidney, Ohio. "The Rock of Ages" is its annual convention in New Knoxville.

General: Boa, pp. 196-203; McDowell, pp. 105-13; Passantino, pp. 159-82; Robertson, pp. 97-105; Tucker, *Another Gospel*, pp. 217-30, 395-96.

Miscellaneous: Williams.

New Age: Newport, p. 146.

The Way International Fine Arts and Historical Center

Houses historical records in Sidney, Ohio. *See* The Way International.

Way of Happiness

Front group that promotes a "Set a Good Example" contest. *See* Scientology.

The Way of the Shaman
Written by Michael Harner in 1982 to teach shamanistic techniques. *See* Shamanism.

Way Productions
Dedicated to developing the arts following biblical principles. Based at the Cultural Center, in New Bremen, Ohio. *See* The Way International.

The Way to Happiness
Written by L. Ron Hubbard in 1984. *See* Scientology.

"We Are the World"
Song published in 1985 that expressed the New Age concept of one world unity. Words and music by Michael Jackson and Lionel Richie. *See* New Age Movement.

We the Living
Ayn Rand's 1936 novel that propagated capitalism as God. *See* Ayn Rand.

Wee Wisdom
Monthly publication for children, first published in 1893. *See* Unity School of Christianity.

Weekend Trainings in Focusing
Sponsored training sessions. *See* Focusing Institute.

Weekly Unity
Cult periodical. *See* Unity School of Christianity.

Weiner, Robert
Founder of a fundamentalist fringe movement. *See* Maranatha Christian Church.

Wells, Alice
Daughter of George Adamski, UFO contactee. Founded the George Adamski Foundation to carry on his work and publish his books. *See* George Adamski Foundation.

Wells, H. G.
Wrote *The Open Conspiracy: Blueprints for a World Revolution* read by New Agers. *See* New Age Movement.

Western Yoga
Also called Functional Integration, the Feldenkrais method, and Awareness Through Movement. Holistic health method of using one thousand physical and meditative exercises related to yoga. Developed by Moshe Feldenkrais, Israeli scientist. *See* Holistic Health.

Westminster Theatre
　　In London. *See* Moral Re-armament.

Wheels of Life: A User's Guide to the Chakra System
　　Written by Anodea Judith in 1987. *See* Church of All Worlds.

White Eagle, Chief
　　Spirit entity of a Cherokee medicine man channeled by Verna Yater. He produces "powerful healing sounds." *See* Channeling.

White, Ellen Gould Harmon
　　Her writings are considered prophecy. She wrote more than eighty books, including *Almost Armageddon*, *America in Prophecy* (previously titled *The Great Controversy*), *The Desire of Ages*, *Health and Happiness*, *Hidden Treasures*, *A Prophet Without Honor*, *Steps to Christ*, and *Testimonies for the Church*. *See* Seventh-day Adventism.

White Sands Incident
　　Written by Daniel Fry in 1954 describing his encounter with a UFO. *See* Understanding, Inc.

Whitman, Walt
　　American poet who expressed the New Age concept of personal divinity in his "Song of Myself": "Divine am I inside and out, and I make holy whatever I touch or am touch'd from." *See* New Age Movement.

Whitten, W. Roy
　　Episcopal priest and cofounder of a human potential seminar. *See* Life Training.

Whole Life Times
　　Periodical. *See* New Age Movement.

W.I.C.C.A.
　　Acronym for Witches International Coven Council Association. A coalition of witches whose aim is to coordinate efforts of diverse groups of witches. *See* Witchcraft.

Wicca, or Wicce
　　Other terms for witch, preferred by some. Also refers to witchcraft itself. *See* Witchcraft.

Wierwille, Victor Paul
　　Cult founder. Author of *Jesus Christ Is Not God* and *Jesus Christ Our Passover*. *See* The Way International.

Wilber, Ken

Leading figure in transpersonal psychology. Author of *The Atman Project* and *Up from Eden.* One of the New Age "significant thinkers." *See* New Age Movement.

Williams, George M.

Current Buddhist sect leader called Sadanaga. *See* Nichiren Shoshu of America.

Windam Hill

Largest distributor of New Age music. *See* New Age Movement.

Winds of Change

Autobiography of ECK Master Harold Kemp. *See* ECKANKAR.

Windstar Foundation

New Age group begun in 1976 by John Denver near Aspen, Colorado, to promote global awareness, ecology, citizen diplomacy, and conflict resolution. Publishes the *Windstar Journal. See* New Age Movement.

Windstar Journal

Periodical. *See* Windstar Foundation.

Windworks

Newsletter. *See* Ramtha.

WISE

Acronym for World Institute of Scientological Enterprises, a front group. *See* Scientology.

Witchcraft

Occultic practice motivated by the lust for power, knowledge of the future, and control over opposing forces. Often called "the old religion"; also called the craft, wicca, or wicce. Today's witchcraft is attributed to Gerald B. Gardner of England, who wrote *Witchcraft Today.* Some of his students introduced it to America in the 1960s. Gardnerian witchcraft was taught by Raymond and Rosemary Buckland. Alexandrian witchcraft was spread by Alexander and Maxine Sanders.

Most witches are solitary. Some band together in a coven, usually six men, six women, and a high priest or priestess. Some prefer to be called wicca, pagans, or neopagans. A group called W.I.C.C.A. (Witches International Coven Council Association) is trying to coordinate efforts of all the diverse groups of witches.

Witches worship gods and goddesses, claiming that their power comes from them. They practice what they call "white magic" as opposed to Satanists' black magic. They meet for regular semimonthly "services" called esbats and for the eight major solar festivals called sabbats.

Rituals, spells, and charms in grimoires are followed to the letter in order to achieve the desired results. Ceremonies include sexual rituals and drug use. Reincarnation and lycanthropy are taught.

Sybil Leek wrote *Diary of a Witch* and *The Complete Art of Witchcraft*. *The Book of Shadows*, Margo Adler's *Drawing Down the Moon*, and *A Book of Pagan Rituals*, by Donna Cole and Ed Fitch, are also used by witches.

There are four major national witchcraft organizations: (1) Church of Circle Wicca in Mt. Horeb, Wisconsin, is the largest. Publishes *Circle Network News*. (2) Covenant of the Goddess in Berkeley, California, the second largest, is headed by Miriam Starhawk. (3) Gardnerian Wicca in Wheeling, Illinois, publishes *The Hidden Path* periodical. (4) Saxon Witchcraft based in Charlottesville, Virginia, headed by Raymond Buckland. Operates the Seax-Wicca Seminary and publishes the *Seax-Wica Voys* newsletter.

Other witchcraft organizations include the following: Asatru Free Assembly, in Breckenridge, Texas; Church and School of Wicca, in New Bern, North Carolina, founded by Gavin and Yvonne Frost; Church of the Eternal Source, in Burbank, California; Coven of Arianhu, in Dimmitt, Texas; Cymry Wicca, in Smyrna, Georgia, founded by Rhuddlwm Gawr; Georgian Church, in Bakersfield, California; and Mother Earth Church. The Radical Faerie Movement is made up of homosexuals who connect their sexual choices with the old pagan nature religions.

Covens are located from coast to coast. Most do not advertise. However, the Ravenwood Church of Wicca in Atlanta, Georgia, does. Some have received tax-exempt status; others have been recognized by the ministerial alliance in their area; and Laurie Cabot has been named the official witch of Salem, Massachusetts.

General: Larson, *New Book*, pp. 464-67; McDowell, pp. 260-70; Melton, *Encyclopedia*, pp. 639-61; Rice, p. 209.

Occult: Larson, pp. 160-74; Wedge, pp. 172-92.

Witchcraft Today
Written by Gerald B. Gardner in 1954. *See* Witchcraft.

Witches International Coven Council Association (W.I.C.C.A.)

Coordinates efforts of the diverse groups of witches. *See* Witchcraft.

Witowski, Stanislaus

Late occultic group leader. *See* Societas Rosicruciana in America.

Women's Welfare Department

Seeks to strengthen women physically and spiritually. *See* Ananda Márga Yoga Society.

Word of Faith Movement

Also called "Health and Wealth Gospel" and "Name It and Claim It Gospel." *See* Positive Confession.

"Wordworker"

Topical cross-referenced Bible program for computers, which cites reference works that are published by The Way, including *Jesus Christ Is Not God. See* The Way International.

World Goodwill

One of the Bailey-oriented groups sponsored by Lucis Trust, with roots in the Arcane School. A political lobby at the United Nations. *See* New Age Movement.

World Institute of Scientological Enterprises (WISE)

Front group. *See* Scientology.

"World Monitor"

Nightly news program produced by Christian Science and aired on the Discovery Channel. *See* Christian Science.

World Mother

Another name for Elizabeth Clare Prophet. *See* Church Universal and Triumphant.

World Plan Executive Council

Controlling entity. *See* Transcendental Meditation.

World Teacher

Former title of Jiddu Krishnamurti. *See* Krishnamurti Foundation of America.

"The World Tomorrow"

Television and radio program. *See* Worldwide Church of God.

Worldwide Church of God

Also known as The World Tomorrow, the Radio Church of God, Armstrongism, and Anglo-Israelism. Background is Seventh-day Adventism with some doctrines borrowed from Mormonism and Jehovah's Witnesses. Its teachings are polytheistic; humans become God. "The heresy of the Trinity; this limits God to three persons." God is thought of as a "family of persons." "We grow spiritually more and more like God till at the time of the resurrection we shall be instantaneously changed from mortal to immortal. We shall then be God."

"People have taught falsely that Christ completed the plan of salvation on the cross when actually it was only begun there." "The blood of Christ does not save any man." Members must keep the laws of Sabbath and feast days, abstain from unclean foods, and tithe three times.

"For eighteen and a half centuries the gospel was not preached" until the Armstrongs came along. "There is no other work on earth proclaiming to the whole world this very same gospel that Jesus taught and proclaimed." It opposes military service, public education, and voting. Modern use of prescription drugs and physicians is discouraged.

Recently the Worldwide Church of God has been revising its doctrinal statement, but there is no indication that it will reject its position on the Trinity and the deity of Christ.

Founded by Herbert W. Armstrong in 1934. Headed by Joseph W. Tkach, Sr., named successor by Armstrong before his death in 1986. His son, Joseph W. Tkach, Jr., oversees all churches in the United States. Headquarters is in Pasadena, California, with offices in Big Sandy, Texas, and in England, Australia, Canada, and South Africa.

Works primarily through broadcasting and the Ambassador International Cultural Foundation. Built an $11 million Ambassador Auditorium to be used mostly by the foundation. Owns Ambassador College in Pasadena, California.

The Plain Truth is the free monthly publication; *Tomorrow's World* magazine was a former publication. Also publishes *The Good News*, *Youth*, and *The Worldwide News*. Its publishing division is Ambassador College Press.

On July 8, 1978, the *Los Angeles Times* reported that Herbert had ordered his son, Garner Ted, to take a six-month leave of absence and stripped him of all titles in the church. Garner Ted did not come back. He called it a "fear-ridden" organization. Instead, he founded his own organization, the Church of God International, in Tyler, Texas. *See also* Identity Movement.

General: Larson, *New Book*, pp. 468-72; Martin, *Kingdom*, pp. 303-37; McDowell, pp. 114-22; Robertson, pp. 87-96; Starkes, pp. 44-55; Tucker, *Another Gospel*, pp. 191-216, 394-95.

Miscellaneous: Martin.

Worldwide Church of Satanic Liberation

One of the three main Satanist churches. Headed by Paul Valentine in New Haven, Connecticut. *See* Satanism.

The Worldwide News

Periodical for members only. *See* Worldwide Church of God.

WOW Ambassadors

Missionaries for The Way. *See* The Way International.

Wright, Machaell Small

Leader of Perelandra, a natural learning center near Washington, D.C. The eighteen gardens offer residence for the spirits. Students are taught how to communicate with plants. *See* New Age Movement.

Y

Yano, Jiro

   Cult leader. *See* Perfect Liberty.

Yantra

   Visual equivalent to a mantra. The practitioner stares at a geometric design as an aid to meditation. *See* New Age Movement.

Yater, Verna V.

   Founder of Spiritual Sciences Institute in Santa Barbara, California. Channeler of Indira Latari, a nineteenth-century Hindu woman, and Chief White Eagle, a Cherokee medicine man. *See* Channeling.

"Year of Sunday"

   Song by Seals and Croft, which espouses Baha'i views. *See* Baha'i World Faith.

Yin and Yang

   Conflicting elements, or opposites, in nature that perfectly balance one another, such as light and dark, male and female. *See* Taoism.

Yoga

   Background is Hinduism. The practice of yoga, with its various postures and exercises, leads man to self-liberation and god-realization. The purpose of all yoga is to unite man with the Cosmic Consciousness, or that spark of divinity that each possesses. Teaches reincarnation.

   There are four forms of yoga: (1) Karma Yoga teaches spiritual union by right conduct; (2) Bhakti Yoga teaches union with the Absolute by devotion to a guru; (3) Juana Yoga teaches access to God through knowledge; and (4) Raja Yoga teaches god-realization through mental control.

The most familiar in the West is Hatha Yoga, a subdivision of Raja Yoga. Its eight stages are: body purification, postures, postures to produce psychic energy, breath control, stilling the mind, concentration, meditation, and union with God. Sacred writing is the *Upanishads* and other Hindu Vedic scriptures.

General: Ellwood, pp. 198-201; Larson, *New Book*, pp. 473-78; Tucker, *Another Gospel*, pp. 385-87.

New Age: Newport, p. 18.

See also Eastern Mysticism.

Yoga Fellowship
Corporation that operates Swami Kriyananda's business ventures, grossing 2 million dollars a year. *See* Ananda.

Yoga Journal
Bimonthly publication of the California Yoga Teachers Association. *See* New Age Movement *and* Yoga.

Yoga Teacher Training Program
Offers training in how to teach yoga techniques. *See* Ananda.

Yogananda, Paramahansa
Former cult leader. Author of *Autobiography of a Yogi*. *See* Self-realization Fellowship Foundation.

Yogi, Maharishi Mahesh
Cult founder. Formerly known as Mahesh Prasad Warma. *See* Transcendental Meditation.

Yom Kippur (Day of Atonement)
Jews' most solemn day, observed ten days after Rosh Hashanah. *See* Judaism.

You Are the World
Written by Jiddu Krishnamurti in 1973. *See* Krishnamurti Foundation of America.

You Can Get There from Here
Written by Shirley MacLaine in 1975. *See* Spiritualism.

Young, Brigham
Mormon prophet who led followers to Utah after Joseph Smith's death. *See* Mormonism.

Your Heritage
Church in San Diego, California. *See* Identity Movement.

Your Right to Know
Explanation of ECKANKAR written in 1979 by Darwin Gross, late ECK Master. *See* ECKANKAR.
Youth
Cult periodical. *See* Worldwide Church of God.

Z

Zabin: Psalms of David
One of four sacred Muslim books. *See* Islam.

Zain, C. C.
Pen name of Elbert Benjamine, author of the *Brotherhood of Light Lessons* and occultic group founder. *See* Church of Light.

Zamoro, Michael Valentine
Occultic group president. *See* Church of Universal Brotherhood.

Zarephath-Horeb
Survivalist commune near the Arkansas-Missouri border. *See* The Covenant, the Sword, the Arm of the Lord.

Zell, Tim
Neopagan cult cofounder. *See* Church of All Worlds.

Zen Buddhism
There is no God or sin and, therefore, no need for salvation. Self-understanding is the goal. Haiku poetry and gardens of moss, gravel, and gnarled trees promote meditation. "The goal of meditation is Satori, or self-awakening." Zen uses "a koan, or nonsensical statement or sound, to nudge the mind into perception of truth." The aim is to reach ultimate enlightment.

Sect of Mahayana Buddhism widely known in the West. Founded in 600 B.C. by Bodhidharma. Headquarters is in California. *The Three Pillars of Zen* is a publication. There are a dozen Zen centers across the country.

General: Larson, *New Book*, pp. 79-83; Martin, *Kingdom*, pp. 261-70; McDowell, pp. 317-20; Starkes, pp. 84-89; Tucker, *Another Gospel*, pp. 387-88.

New Age: Newport, pp. 53-55.

See also Eastern Mysticism.

Zend-Avesta

Sacred Zoroastrian scripture with an added commentary. *See* Zoroastrianism.

Zero Population Growth

Shares ideologies with the New Age movement. *See* New Age Movement.

Zone Therapy

Method of manipulating certain areas of the skin to cure distant organs. Reflexology is a related form in which certain areas of the palms of the hands and soles of the feet are massaged. *See* Holistic Health.

Zoroaster, Spitoma

Founded Zoroastrianism in Persia in the seventh century B.C. In his native language his name was Zarathushtra. *See* Zoroastrianism.

Zoroastrianism

Founded in Persia (present-day Iran) in the seventh century B.C. by Spitoma Zoroaster. His name in the *Avesta*, sacred scriptures, was Zarathushtra. Zoroastrians are known today as Parsis.

Zoroaster received a series of visions and, as a result, elevated one of the Persian gods, Ahura Mazda, to supremacy. He finally succeeded in converting the king and eventually the nation to his beliefs.

To the *Avesta* was added a commentary, and the whole volume is called the *Zend-Avesta*. Ahura Mazda is the good god; Angra Mainyu is the evil god. They are coequal and coeternal. Salvation is by works and high moral standards.

Fire is considered sacred, and the flame that burns in each secluded fire-temple must not be allowed to go out. Priests of Zoroastrianism are called magi. Haoma, a hallucinogenic, is drunk as an act of worship. Believers wear a sacred cord and sacred vest at all times. When a Parsi dies, his body is laid on an open Tower of Silence where vultures pick the bones clean.

General: Boa, pp. 32-40; McDowell, pp. 356-63.

Comparative Religions: Beaver, pp. 80-87.

Bibliography

GENERAL

LITERATURE

Andres, Rachel, and James R. Lane, eds. *Cults & Consequences*. Los Angeles: Commission on Cults and Missionaries of the Jewish Federation Council of Greater Los Angeles, 1988.

"The definitive handbook." Sections of it are written from a Jewish perspective. Deals with the "deceptive proselytizing and unethical conduct" of cults. "Why do cults attract? What can parents do when their child becomes involved in a cult?"

Appel, Willa. *Cults in America*. New York: Holt, Rinehart and Winston, 1985.

"Programmed for paradise." What attracts people to cults? What goes on inside cults? What dangers do they represent? A study of brainwashing.

Boa, Kenneth. *Cults, World Religions, and You*. Wheaton: Victor, 1977.

Covers the major cults from the East and the West, including some of the newer ones. Also includes the major non-Christian Eastern religions.

Brooks, Keith L., comp. "The Spirit of Truth and the Spirit of Error 1." Revised by Irvine Robertson. Chicago: Moody, 1985.

"What God has said on seven fundamentals and what men are now saying." A fold-out chart comparing the "scriptures" of six major cults with the Word of God.

Ellwood, Robert S., Jr., and Harry B. Partin. *Religions and Spiritual Groups in Modern America.* Englewood Cliffs, N.J.: Prentice Hall, 1988.

Who are these groups, and why do they appeal to some?

Enroth, Ronald M. *The Lure of the Cults and New Religions.* Downers Grove, Ill.: InterVarsity, 1987.

Deals with the sociological aspect of the cults from a Christian perspective. Looks at why people join cults.

————. *What Is a Cult?* Downers Grove, Ill.: InterVarsity, 1989.

Explains the meaning of the word "cult" and gives examples of modern-day cults.

————, and J. Gordon Melton. *Why Cults Succeed Where the Church Fails.* Elgin, Ill.: Brethren, 1985.

"Why do young people join? Do cults make positive contributions to their members? How should Christians relate to cultists?"

———— et al. *A Guide to Cults and New Religions.* Downers Grove, Ill.: InterVarsity, 1983.

Describes the challenges cults bring because of their contradiction of biblical doctrines. Surveys ten of the most notable cults.

Gruss, Edmond Charles. *Cults and the Occult.* Grand Rapids: Baker, 1982.

Brief descriptions of several cults designed to be the basis for a group study.

Hassen, Steven. *Combatting Cult Mind Control.* Rochester, Vt.: Park Street, 1988.

The author was a member of the Unification Church for more than two years until he was deprogrammed in 1976. He explains mind control and how cults use it to recruit.

Hexham, Irving, and Karla Poewe. *Understanding Cults and New Religions.* Grand Rapids: Eerdmans, 1986.

A fresh approach to the study of cults. "This book presents a convincing account of what it is about our society that has helped create these communities."

Hoyt, Karen, ed. *The Cults Explosion*. Irvine, Calif.: Harvest House, 1987.

Hunt, Dave. *Beyond Seduction*. Eugene, Oreg.: Harvest House, 1987.

Irvine, William. C. *Heresies Exposed*. Neptune, N.J.: Loizeaux Brothers, 1987.

"An examination of the prevailing cults of today."

*Larson, Bob. *Larson's New Book of Cults*. Wheaton: Tyndale, 1989.

"An encyclopedia of flourishing cults."

———. *Strange Cults in America*. Wheaton: Tyndale, 1986.

*Martin, Walter R. *The Kingdom of the Cults*. Minneapolis: Bethany, 1985.

"The history, teachings, and tragic errors of the cults of our age." This is the classic survey of major cults.

———. *The New Cults*. Ventura, Calif.: Regal, 1980.

"What these cults believe, how to respond to them as Christians, and how to share with them the good news of Jesus Christ."

*McDowell, Josh, and Don Stewart. *Handbook of Today's Religions*. San Bernardino, Calif.: Campus Crusade, 1983.

"A reference work written for Christians who desire a more discerning knowledge of the major cults." Includes cults, occultism, secular religions, and non-Christian religions.

Melton, J. Gordon. *Biographical Dictionary of American Cult and Sect Leaders*. New York: Garland, 1986.

*———. *Encyclopedia of American Religions*. Second edition. Detroit: Gale Research, 1987.

Not written from a distinctly evangelical position, but an outstanding reference book.

*Use of an asterisk denotes a recommended resource.

Passantino, Robert and Gretchen. *Answers to the Cultist at Your Door*. Eugene, Oreg.: Harvest House, 1981.

"A clear, concise, step-by-step guide to answering the questionable doctrines of cultists." Includes testimonies of people who have escaped cults. Provides information on how to help loved ones in cults.

Rice, Edward. *American Saints and Seers*. New York: Four Winds, 1982.

"Discusses a variety of religions that were nurtured . . . on this continent."

Robertson, Irvine. *What the Cults Believe*. Chicago: Moody, 1983, 1991.

"A guide to the teachings of the major modern cults. The author explains exactly what they teach and where they misinterpret."

Ross, Joan Carol, and Michael D. Langone. *Cults: What Parents Should Know*. Weston, Mass.: American Family Foundation, 1988.

"A practical guide to help parents with children in a destructive cult."

Sire, James W. *Scripture Twisting*. Downers Grove, Ill.: InterVarsity, 1980.

"Twenty ways the cults misread the Bible." Shows how cults use the Bible to support their doctrines and practices.

Starkes, M. Thomas. *Cults at the Close of the 80s*. Chattanooga, Tenn.: Global, 1987.

Tucker, Bruce. *Twisting the Truth*. Minneapolis: Bethany House, 1987.

"Recognizing how cult groups subtly distort basic Christian doctrines."

*Tucker, Ruth A. *Another Gospel*. Grand Rapids: Academie, 1989.

"Alternative religions and the New Age movement." Explains how these and other alternative religions seem to meet peoples' needs.

AUDIOVISUAL RESOURCES

(These media presentations are on film/video unless otherwise noted.)

"The Counterfeits." Eden Prairie, Minn.: Christian Ministries International.

> Dr. Ron Carlson gives biblical answers to the cults. The six tapes in the series are titled: Confusion of the Cults; Jehovah's Witnesses and the Trinity; Transcendental Meditation, Yoga and Reincarnation; Mormonism: Christian or Cult?; Spiritism: UFOs and the Occult; and Secular Humanism, Evolution and the Decline of America. Each tape is fifty min.

"Cult Awareness Library." St. Louis: Personal Freedom Outreach.

> A filmstrip series. Includes Jehovah's Witnesses: the Christian View, Mormonism: the Christian View, The Way International: the Christian View, The Unification Church: the Christian View, and Patterns in the Cults. Also includes fifty copies of the outline tracts for each title.

"The Cults." Eden Prairie, Minn.: Christian Ministries International.

> A set of nineteen cassette tapes on such cults as Jehovah's Witnesses, Mormons, New Age movement, Occult, Freemasonry, Worldwide Church of God, Christian Science, Unity, The Way International, Unitarian Church, Eastern mysticism/Transcendental Meditation, and on related topics such as Prosperity Theology, Humanism, Evolution, Roman Catholicism, and true Christian meditation.

"Kingdom of the Cults." Huntington Beach, Calif.: Growth Resources International.

> Fifteen one-hour presentations by the late Walter Martin. Includes: Introduction, Hare Krishna, Unification Church, Christian Science, Mormonism, Worldwide Church of God, Jehovah's Witnesses, Freemasonry, Rajneesh, Trancendental Meditation, and the Occult. Features interviews with former members and experts on the different cults.

"Martin Speaks Out on the Cults." Santa Ana, Calif.: Vision House Films.

> The late Walter Martin is featured in this six-part series featuring Mormonism, Jehovah's Witnesses, the occult, and others. Each tape is fifty min.

"Patterns in the Cults." St. Louis: Personal Freedom Outreach.

> An introduction to major cults. Describes four "patterns" found within the cults. 37 min.

"The World of the Cults." Santa Ana, Calif.: Vision House.

> Each volume contains six cassette tapes by Walter Martin. Vol. I: Introduction, Jehovah's Witnesses, Mormons, Christian Science, Spiritism, and Worldwide Church of God. Vol. II: Baha'ism, Black Muslims, Scientology, Unity, Unitarianism, and Zen Buddhism/ Hare Krishna/Meher Baba.

TEACHING KITS

"The Christian Confronting the Cults I, Revised." Nashville: Baptist Sunday School Board.

> "Examines the teachings of Jehovah's Witnesses, Mormons, Worldwide Church of God, Unification Church, and Christian Science and equips adults for a Christian witness." Six sessions.

"The Christian Confronting the Cults II." Nashville: Baptist Sunday School Board.

> "Profiles the beliefs of Hare Krishna, The Way International, Transcendental Meditation, Scientology, Baha'i, and the New Age movement." Seven sessions.

Resource Packets. Weston, Mass.: American Family Foundation.

> Each packet contains fifty to eighty pages of articles on the group you select. These packets are available for $10: Ananda Márga; Bible Speaks; Church of Bible Understanding; Church Universal and Triumphant; Children of God; Da Free John; Divine Light Mission; ECKANKAR; est; Hare Krishna; Healthy, Happy, Holy (3HO); LaRouche, Lyndon; Lifespring; Maranatha; Masters, Roy; Nichiren Soshu Soka Gakkai; Rajneesh; Scientology; Transcendental Meditation; Unification Church; The Way International; Worldwide Church of God.

COMPARATIVE RELIGIONS

*Beaver, R. Pierce, ed. *Eerdman's Handbook to the World's Religions*. Grand Rapids: Eerdmans, 1982.

"A comprehensive, clear, and stimulating guide to the world's religions, past and present."

Cory, Steven, comp. "The Spirit of Truth and the Spirit of Error 2." Chicago: Moody, 1986.

A fold-out chart describing "world religions. The truths of Christianity compared to: Buddhism, Hinduism, Islam, Judaism and Primitive Religion."

Martinson, Paul Vare. *A Theology of World Religions*. Minneapolis: Augsburg, 1989.

"Interpreting God, self, and world in Semitic, Indian, and Chinese thought."

Mayer, F. E. *Religious Bodies of America*. St. Louis: Concordia, 1987.

*Mead, Frank S., and Samuel S. Hill. *Handbook of Denominations in the United States*. Nashville: Abingdon, 1985.

The 8th edition.

Muck, Terry. *Alien Gods on American Turf*. Wheaton: Victor, 1990.

"How world religions are evangelizing your neighborhood."

Neill, Stephen. *Christian Faith and Other Faiths*. Downers Grove, Ill.: InterVarsity, n.d.

Describes the essential features of the religions of the world and emphasizes the uniqueness of Jesus.

Rausch, David A., and Carl Hermann Voss. *World Religions*. Minneapolis: Augsburg, 1989.

"Our quest for meaning."

Starkes, M. Thomas. *Today's World Religions*. Chattanooga, Tenn.: Global, 1986.

EASTERN MYSTICISM

LITERATURE

Brooke, Tal. *Riders of the Cosmic Circuit.* Batavia, Ill.: Lion, 1987.

An account of what makes gurus like Rajneesh, Sai Baba, and Muktananda tick.

Ellwood, Robert S., Jr. *The Eagle and the Rising Sun.* Philadelphia: Westminster, 1974.

Several American cults that have roots in Japan.

Hubner, John, and Lindsey Gruson. *Monkey on a Stick.* San Diego, Calif.: Harcourt, Brace, Jovanovich, 1989.

"Murder, madness, and the Hare Krishnas."

Johnson, David L. *A Reasoned Look at Asian Religions.* Minneapolis: Bethany House, 1989.

"A critical analysis of Eastern thought." Examines Islam, Buddhism, Hinduism, Confucianism, and Chinese Marxism.

Maharaj, Rabindranath, and Dave Hunt. *Death of a Guru.* Eugene, Oreg.: Harvest House, 1986.

A former Hindu guru tells the story of his conversion to Christ.

Miller, William McElwee. *A Christian Response to Islam.* Nutley, N.J.: Presbyterian and Reformed, 1976.

Milne, Hugh. *Bhagwan: The God That Failed.* New York: St. Martin's, 1987.

Shinn, Larry D. *The Dark Lord.* Philadelphia: Westminster, 1987.

"Cult images and the Hare Krishnas in America."

Shorrosh, Anis A. *Islam Revealed.* Nashville: Thomas Nelson, 1988.

"A Christian Arab's view of Islam."

AUDIOVISUAL RESOURCE

"Fear Is the Master." Jeremiah Films.

Describes how Rajneesh, the counterfeit messiah, "controlled hundreds of thousands of followers" and took over a town in Oregon. Warns us to learn from history and prevent this from happening again. Fifty-eight min. Available on film or video.

JEHOVAH'S WITNESSES

LITERATURE

*Ankerberg, John, and John Weldon. *The Facts on Jehovah's Witnesses.* Eugene, Oreg.: Harvest House, 1988.

"Answers to the 30 most frequently asked questions about the Watchtower Society."

Bowman, Robert M., Jr. *Jehovah's Witnesses, Jesus Christ, and the Gospel of John.* Grand Rapids: Baker, 1988.

Uses John 1:1 and 8:58 to refute errors made by Jehovah's Witnesses.

————. *Why You Should Believe in the Trinity.* Grand Rapids: Baker, 1990.

"A brief refutation of claims made recently by the Jehovah's Witnesses that the Trinity is an apostate concept which should be rejected by all Christians."

*Cetnar, William I. *Questions for Jehovah's Witnesses.* Kunkletown, Pa.: Personal Freedom Outreach, 1989.

*Chretien, Leonard, and Marjorie. *Witnesses of Jehovah.* Eugene, Oreg.: Harvest House, 1988.

"A shocking exposé of what Jehovah's Witnesses really believe" by former Jehovah's Witnesses.

Countess, Robert H. *The Jehovah's Witnesses' New Testament.* Phillipsburg, N.J.: Presbyterian and Reformed, 1982.

"A critical analysis of the New World Translation of the Christian Greek scriptures."

Duggar, Gordon E. *Jehovah's Witnesses: Watch Out for the Watchtower!* Grand Rapids: Baker, 1985.

A former Jehovah's Witness reveals the deception in their teachings.

Franz, Raymond. *Crisis of Conscience.* Atlanta: Commentary, 1983.

"The struggle between loyalty to God and loyalty to one's religion. . . . A penetrating view of a religion's supreme council and their dramatic power over human lives." Written by a former member of the Jehovah's Witnesses Governing Body.

Magnani, Duane. *A Problem of Communication*. Clayton, Calif.: Witness, 1989.

"A compact 'How-to' guide to winning Jehovah's Witnesses to Christ."

_____. *The Watchtower Files: Dialogue with a Jehovah's Witness*. Minneapolis: Bethany House, 1985.

"Startling, eye-opening information for Jehovah's Witnesses and the Christians who talk with them."

*Martin, Walter R. *Jehovah's Witnesses*. Minneapolis: Bethany House, 1988.

"A summary of the ancestry, cardinal teachings, and activities of this zealous and rapidly growing movement."

Morey, Robert A. *How to Answer a Jehovah's Witness*. Minneapolis: Bethany House, 1980.

"Dealing with the Jehovah's Witness who comes to your door."

*Quick, Kevin R. *Pilgrimage Through the Watchtower*. Grand Rapids: Baker, 1989.

"The inner workings of the Watchtower organization, the Jehovah's Witness mindset, and Christian counter-cult apologetics. . . . An intimate, personal account of a typical Jehovah's Witness."

Reed, David A. *How to Rescue Your Loved One from the Watchtower*. Grand Rapids: Baker, 1989.

This former Jehovah's Witness gives helpful guidance to a concerned family member who wants to deliver a loved one from Watchtower captivity.

_____. *Jehovah's Witnesses Answered Verse-by-Verse*. Grand Rapids: Baker, 1987.

Answers their misinterpretations of Scripture. Explains how to use these Scriptures in witnessing to Jehovah's Witnesses.

Schnell, William J. *Jehovah's Witnesses' Errors Exposed*. Grand Rapids: Baker, 1988.

A study of the basic teachings of Jehovah's Witnesses in the light of the Bible.

Zuck, Roy B. *Open Letter to a Jehovah's Witness*. Chicago: Moody, 1989.

AUDIOVISUAL RESOURCES

"Doctrines unto Destruction." Arlington, Tex.: Watchman Fellowship.

James Walker describes the alterations that have been made in Watchtower theology that most Jehovah's Witnesses don't realize have been made. Cassette tape and manual.

"Effective Witnessing to the Witnesses." La Canada Flintridge, Calif.: Frontline Ministries.

How to share your faith with Jehovah's Witnesses. A sixty-min. cassette tape.

"Evaluating the New World Translation." St. Louis: Personal Freedom Outreach.

A slide set that critiques Jehovah's Witnesses' "Bible." Thirty-five min.

*"Witnesses of Jehovah." Jeremiah Films.

"The real story behind those uninvited door-to-door visitors." Describes their beliefs. Helps you know what to say when they knock on your door. Fifty-six min. Available on film or video.

MISCELLANEOUS

Alexander, Brooks, and Dean C. Halverson, eds. *Scientology: The Technology of Enlightenment*. Berkeley, Calif.: Spiritual Counterfeits Project, 1982.

Allan, John. *The Gospel According to Science Fiction*. Grand Rapids: Baker, 1986.

Exposes UFO Cults.

Andres, Rachel, and James R. Lane. *Astrology*. Eugene, Oreg.: Harvest House, 1989.

"Do the heavens rule our destiny? . . . Thoroughly researches astrology's claims, assesses its occult aspects, and emphasizes the personal consequences of its use."

*Ankerberg, John, and John Weldon. *The Secret Teachings of the Masonic Lodge*. Chicago: Moody, 1990.

"Reveals how Masonry conflicts with the very foundations of Christianity."

Atack, Jonathan. *A Piece of the Blue Sky: Scientology, Dianetics, and L. Ron Hubbard Exposed*. New York: Carol, 1990.

Barron, Bruce. *The Health and Wealth Gospel*. Downers Grove, Ill.: InterVarsity, 1987.

"A fresh look at healing, prosperity, and positive confession." A study of New Thought and Unity School of Christianity.

Beckwith, Francis. *Baha'i*. Minneapolis: Bethany House, 1985.

"A Christian response to Baha'ism, the religion which aims toward one world government and one common faith."

Biermans, John T. *The Odyssey of New Religions Today*. Lewiston, N.Y.: Edwin Mellen, 1988.

"A case study of the Unification Church."

Bjornstad, James. *Sun Myung Moon and the Unification Church*. Minneapolis: Bethany House, 1984.

"A careful look at the history, theology and claims of the Moonies."

Byers, Dale A. *I Left the Lodge*. Schaumburg, Ill.: Regular Baptist, 1989.

A former Mason "shows that Masonry is neither as innocent nor as noble as it appears, that it is essentially a religion in its own right, and holds a power of fear over its members."

Chambers, Roger R. *The Plain Truth About Armstrongism*. Grand Rapids: Baker, 1989.

The second edition of an exposé of the Worldwide Church of God.

Davis, Deborah. *The Children of God*. Grand Rapids: Zondervan, 1984.

The inside story of this cult by the daughter of the founder, Moses David Berg.

Gordon, Ruth. *Children of Darkness*. Wheaton: Tyndale, 1988.

An ex-adherent of the Children of God tells how she joined and ultimately escaped.

Harm, Frederick R. *How to Respond to the Science Religions*. St. Louis: Concordia, 1981.

Discusses Christian Science, Unity, Church of Religious Science, Divine Science, and Scientology.

*Horton, Michael, ed. *The Agony of Deceit*. Chicago: Moody, 1990.

"What some TV preachers are really teaching." Exposes the false doctrine of the "Health and Wealth" gospel, also called the Word of Faith Movement.

Lawrence, Troy. *The Secret Message of the Zodiac*. San Bernardino, Calif.: Here's Life, 1990.

"What you don't know might hurt you." Written by a former New Ager.

*Martin, Walter R. *Herbert W. Armstrong and the Worldwide Church of God*. Minneapolis: Bethany House, 1985.

"The rise of Herbert W. Armstrong, his relationship to Seventh Day Adventism and Anglo-Israelism, and his main differences with orthodox Christianity."

McConnell, Dan R. *A Different Gospel*. Peabody, Mass.: Hendrickson, 1989.

A non-technical critique of New Thought. Shows how its teachings on healing, prosperity, and atonement differ from biblical teachings.

McCormick, W. J. *Christ, the Christian, and Freemasonry.* Chattanooga, Tenn.: Global, 1988.

Miller, William McElwee. *The Baha'i Faith: Its History and Teachings.* South Pasadena, Calif.: William Carey Library, 1984.

A former missionary to Iran gives the history of the Baha'i faith.

Shaw, James D., and Tom C. McKenney. *The Deadly Deception.* Lafayette, La.: Huntington House, 1988.

Shows members of Freemasonry to be "victims of a deadly deception." Written by one of the top leaders who "found the Light of the World and was set free."

Sheaffer, Robert. *The UFO Verdict.* Buffalo, N.Y.: Prometheus, 1986.

"Examining the evidence" about UFOs.

Strohmer, Charles. *What Your Horoscope Doesn't Tell You.* Wheaton: Tyndale, 1988.

"A former practitioner of astrology exposes its hidden agenda."

Weldon, John. *est.* Downers Grove, Ill.: InterVarsity, 1989.

Exposes Erhard Seminars Training and its dangers.

*Williams, J. L. *Victor Paul Wierwille and The Way International.* Chicago: Moody, 1979.

Probably the best book on The Way International.

Wooden, Kenneth. *Children of Jonestown.* New York: McGraw-Hill, 1980.

Describes life in the Peoples' Temple Christian Church and how Jim Jones came to power.

*Yeakley, Flavil R., Jr., ed. *The Discipling Dilemma.* Nashville: Gospel Advocate, 1988.

An analysis of the discipling and shepherding movements with a focus on the Boston Church of Christ.

Mormonism

LITERATURE

Benson, Jerry, and Dianna. *How to Witness to a Mormon.* Chicago: Moody, 1986.

This booklet "will make you aware of the differences between Mormonism and Christianity and better equip you to witness to" Mormons.

*Cowdrey, Wayne L., Howard A. Davis, and Donald R. Scales. *Who Really Wrote the Book of Mormon?* Santa Ana, Calif.: Vision House, 1980.

Explains the theory that Joseph Smith plagiarized the *Book of Mormon* from a Solomon Spaulding. This is the best book on this theory.

Decker, Ed. *The Mormon Dilemma.* Eugene, Oreg.: Harvest House, 1990.

"The dramatic story of a Mormon couple's encounter with Truth."

_____, and Dave Hunt. *The God Makers.* Eugene, Oreg.: Harvest House, 1984.

"A shocking exposé of what the Mormon church REALLY believes."

Douglas, S. L. *The Handbook on Mormonism.* Okemos, Mich.: Ex-Mormons and Concerned Christians, 1989.

*Geer, Thelma "Granny." *Mormonism, Mama, and Me.* Chicago: Moody, 1986.

Raised in the Mormon church, Granny Geer tells her story, including her conversion to Jesus Christ. She examines the main tenets of Mormon theology.

*Martin, Walter R. *The Maze of Mormonism.* Ventura, Calif.: Regal, 1979.

Unravels "the confused maze of Mormon doctrine and practice."

McElveen, Floyd C. *The Mormon Illusion.* Ventura, Calif.: Regal, 1980.

A study of Mormonism's history, doctrines, and sacred writings.

Morey, Robert A. *How to Answer a Mormon.* Minneapolis: Bethany House, 1983.

"Practical guidelines for what to expect and what to reply when the Mormon comes to your door."

Ropp, Harry. *Are the Mormon Scriptures Reliable?* Downers Grove, Ill.: InterVarsity, 1987.

"Cites internal inconsistencies and the absence of archaeological evidence to question their credibility." A revision of *The Mormon Papers.*

Scott, Latayne Colvett. *Ex-Mormons.* Grand Rapids: Baker, 1990.

"Why we left. . . . How does one reach a Mormon friend? What would make a Mormon decide to leave the church?"

Spencer, James R. *Beyond Mormonism.* Old Tappan, N.J.: Revell, 1984.

"An elder's story" by one who faced social rejection to follow Christ.

_____. *Have You Witnessed to a Mormon Lately?* Old Tappan, N.J.: Chosen, 1986.

A former Mormon provides "an insightful guide for sharing the Gospel with Mormons."

Tanner, Jerald. *Changes in Joseph Smith's History.* Salt Lake City: Modern Microfilm, n.d.

_____. *Changes in the Pearl of Great Price.* Salt Lake City: Modern Microfilm, n.d.

Tanner, Jerald, and Sandra. *Archaeology and the Book of Mormon.* Salt Lake City: Modern Microfilm, n.d.

Provides proof that the Book of Mormon has no archaeology.

*_____. *The Changing World of Mormonism.* Chicago: Moody, 1981.

"A behind-the-scenes look at changes in Mormon doctrine and practice." A condensed version of *Mormonism—Shadow or Reality?*

*_____. *Mormonism—Shadow or Reality?* Salt Lake City: Modern Microfilm, 1987.

A 600-page sourcebook on Mormon teachings, history, and practices.

Wardle, James D. *Selected Changes in the Book of Mormon.* Salt Lake City: Modern Microfilm, n.d.

AUDIOVISUAL RESOURCES

(These media presentations are on film/video unless otherwise noted.)

*"The Church of Jesus Christ of Latter-day Saints." Atlanta: Home Mission Board, Southern Baptist Convention.

A two-part documentary featuring Gary Leazer and Sandra Tanner. Examines the history, organization, and doctrines of the Mormon church. Each part about twenty-four min.

"Mormonism: the Christian View." St. Louis: Personal Freedom Outreach.

Examines their history, doctrines, and missionary methods. Gives witnessing suggestions. Forty-six min. Also available as a fifty-min. filmstrip.

"Witnessing to Mormons More Effectively." La Canada Flintridge, Calif.: Frontline Ministries.

How to share your faith with Mormons. A ninety-min. cassette tape.

"Witnessing with the Book of Mormon." Arlington, Tex.: Watchman Fellowship.

James Walker shows how to share the gospel with a Mormon using his own scriptures. Cassette tape and study guide.

NEW AGE

LITERATURE

Alexander, Brooks. *Spirit Channeling*. Downers Grove, Ill.: InterVarsity, 1989.

What does the Bible say about contacting spirits of the dead?

Ankerberg, John, and John Weldon. *The Facts on the New Age Movement*. Eugene, Oreg.: Harvest House, 1988.

"Answers to the 30 most frequently asked questions about the New Age movement."

Barron, Will. *Deceived by the New Age*. Boise, Idaho: Pacific, 1990.

"The story of a New Age priest" and his "encounter with the 'Mastermind' behind this growing movement and the clandestine war he is waging on Christians right in the pews of their own churches!"

Brooke, Tal. *When the World Will Be as One*. Eugene, Oreg.: Harvest House, 1989.

Examines the emerging signs of One World Order: "the World Bank, the International Monetary Fund, the Global Peace Initiative. . . . The decline of America and the West may not be historical accidents after all."

Chandler, Russell. *Understanding the New Age*. Dallas: Word, 1988.

Explores every facet of the New Age movement, featuring interviews with more than thirty proponents and critics.

Cumbey, Constance. *The Hidden Dangers of the Rainbow*. Shreveport, La.: Huntington House, 1983.

"The New Age movement and our coming age of barbarism."

Gabler, Mel, and Norma. *What Are They Teaching Our Children?* Wheaton: Victor, 1985.

Geisler, Norman L., and J. Yutaka Amano. *The Infiltration of the New Age*. Wheaton: Tyndale, 1989.

"What you need to know about magic, selfism, reincarnation, holistic health, inner healing, the global village, and more." A balanced critique of self-deification and occult practices in the New Age movement.

*Groothuis, Douglas R. *Confronting the New Age*. Downers Grove, Ill.: InterVarsity, 1988.

How to resist this growing religious movement, identify its concepts, discuss them with understanding, and combat it evangelistically.

_____. *Revealing the New Age Christ*. Downers Grove, Ill.: InterVarsity, 1990.

"Challenges to orthodox views of Christ."

*_____. *Unmasking the New Age*. Downers Grove, Ill.: InterVarsity, 1986.

Explains the difference between secular humanism and the New Age movement. Shows how New Age influence has spread in our culture.

Howard, Jay. *Confronting the Cultist in the New Age*. Old Tappan, N.J.: Revell, 1990.

"How cultists twist the truth, and how you can witness effectively to them."

Hoyt, Karen. *The New Age Rage*. Old Tappan, N.J.: Revell, 1987.

"A probing analysis of the newest religious craze." Contrasts the New Age worldview with the biblical worldview.

Hunt, Dave. *Peace, Prosperity, and the Coming Holocaust*. Eugene, Oreg.: Harvest House, 1983.

"The New Age Movement in prophecy."

Khalsa, Parmatma Singh. *The New Consciousness Sourcebook*. San Bernardino, Calif.: Borgo, 1986.

Lists cults and organizations involved in the New Age movement. Written from a New Age perspective.

*Kjos, Berit. *Your Child and the New Age*. Wheaton: Victor, 1990.

Exposes New Age practices in classrooms. Also "explores television, movies, and music, where New Age thought shows up in the most unexpected places." An excellent resource for parents—must reading!

*Larson, Bob. *Straight Answers on the New Age*. Nashville: Thomas Nelson, 1989.

Describes terms, names, and titles associated with the New Age movement, which most of us tend to naively accept as harmless.

Marrs, Texe. *Ravaged by the New Age*. Austin, Tex.: Living Truth, 1989.

"Satan's Plan to destroy our kids." Exposes the television shows, cartoons, movies, comic books, fantasy games, and toys that introduce our children to the occult.

Martin, Walter R. *The New Age Cult*. Minneapolis: Bethany House, 1989.

A concise, readable overview.

*Melton, J. Gordon. *New Age Encyclopedia*. Detroit: Gale Research, 1989.

An exhaustive reference work on the New Age movement.

*Miller, Elliot. *A Crash Course on the New Age Movement*. Grand Rapids: Baker, 1989.

"Describing and evaluating a growing social force. . . . Shares his experience as a former New Ager, explains how to present the gospel to New Agers, and . . . offers understandable, concise information on the New Age movement." Technical but comprehensive.

Morey, Robert A. *Battle of the Gods*. Nashville: Wolgemuth and Hyatt, 1988.

"Exposing the foundations of the New Age movement."

Newport, John P. *Christ and the New Consciousness*. Nashville: Broadman, 1978.

"New consciousness groups in the light of Christian truth."

*Peretti, Frank E. *Piercing the Darkness*. Westchester, Ill.: Crossway, 1989.

A sequel to *This Present Darkness*. A fictional account of how New Age thought affects our educational system.

*————. *This Present Darkness*. Westchester, Ill.: Crossway, 1986.

"Not since *The Screwtape Letters* has there been a novel with as much insight into spiritual warfare and the necessity of prayer." A ficitonal account of what happens when the New Age movement comes to town.

Reisser, Paul C., Teri K. Reisser, and John Weldon. *New Age Medicine*. Downers Grove, Ill.: InterVarsity, 1987.

"A Christian perspective on holistic health." Explains methods like therapeutic touch, biofeedback, homeopathy, and psychic healing.

Sire, James. *Shirley MacLaine & the New Age Movement*. Downers Grove, Ill.: InterVarsity, 1988.

*Smith, F. LaGard. *Out on a Broken Limb*. Eugene, Oreg.: Harvest House, 1986.

"Is Shirley MacLaine right? Or is she out on a broken limb? . . . A response to Shirley . . . about the meaning of life and the afterlife."

AUDIOVISUAL RESOURCES

"The New Age—a Pathway to Paradise?"

A three-hour video documentary on New Age thought featuring interviews with leading Christian authorities including Dave Hunt, Constance Cumbey, and Martin and Deidre Bobgan.

"The New Age Movement." Arlington, Tex.: Watchman Fellowship.

A cassette tape with workbook. Describes the New Age movement as a "cult of many faces." Discusses its roots in Hinduism and its acceptance by society.

OCCULT

LITERATURE

Ankerberg, John, and John Weldon. *The Facts on Spirit Guides*. Eugene, Oreg.: Harvest House, 1988.

"How to avoid the seduction of the spirit world and demonic power."

Barger, Eric. *From Rock to Rock*. Lafayette, La.: Huntington House, 1990.

"The music of darkness [and the occult] exposed! . . . Including the original rock music rating system."

*Breese, Dave. *Satan's Ten Most Believable Lies*. Chicago: Moody, 1987.

"Learn to avoid falling into the pit of deception, as well as how to fight each lie."

Bubeck, Mark L. *The Adversary*. Chicago: Moody, 1975.

The purpose of the book is "to alert Christians to the battle they are engaged in [with Satan] and to give them specific, effective guidelines in dealing with the devil and demonic power."

_____. *Overcoming the Adversary*. Chicago: Moody Press, 1984.

"Shows you how to be strong in the Lord, appropriate the power of the Holy Spirit, and put on the whole armor of God, piece by piece."

Dickason, C. Fred. *Demon Possession and the Christian*. Westchester, Ill.: Crossway, 1989.

Shows from Scripture how Christians can be affected by demons. Emphasis is given to the power Christians have in Christ to win spiritual battles.

Elwood, Roger. *The Christening*. Eugene, Oreg.: Harvest House, 1989.

A novel depicting what happens when three boys dabble in the occult and its disastrous effects on their town. Also shows how the materialistic theology of the local pastor contributes to the spread of the occult.

Gruss, Edmond C. *The Ouija Board*. Chicago: Moody, 1989.

Haynes, Michael, and Paul W. Carlin. *What They Do Not Want You to Know*. Crockett, Tex.: Kerusso, 1989.

"Satanism in America: safety through awareness—what you don't know might destroy you!"

Johnson, Arthur L. *Faith Misguided*. Chicago: Moody, 1989.

"Exposing the dangers of mysticism. . . . Gives a warning of the dangers of giving mystical experiences authority equal to or above the authority of Scripture."

*Johnston, Jerry. *The Edge of Evil*. Dallas: Word, 1989.

Warns us of the rise of Satanism in America. Describes the warning signs of involvement in the occult.

Koch, Kurt E. *Occult ABC*. Grand Rapids: Kregel, 1981.

"Brings to the reader an awareness of occult movements and Satan's devices."

Korem, Dan. *Powers*. Downers Grove, Ill.: InterVarsity, 1988.

"Testing the psychic and supernatural." A professional magician unravels the mystery of paranormal activity. He exposes psychic "cold reading," telekinesis, and psychic detectives and takes a fresh look at old claims about Jesus' resurrection.

————, and Paul Meier. *The Fakers*. Grand Rapids: Baker, 1981.

"Exploding the myths of the supernatural." Shows how Spiritists and occultists are mostly fakers.

*Larson, Bob. *Satanism: The Seduction of America's Youth*. Nashville: Thomas Nelson, 1989.

"Examines the pervasive influence of satanic activity on youth. . . . Provides practical ways to recognize and combat Satanism."

Leithart, Peter, and George Grant. *A Christian Response to Dungeons and Dragons*. Fort Worth, Tex.: Dominion, 1987.

Presents Dungeons and Dragons® as the "catechism of the New Age—an introduction to occultism."

Maybee, Richard. *Unmasking Satan*. Wheaton: Victor, 1988.

"An exposé of the devil's schemes and God's strategies for fighting back."

Michaelsen, Johanna. *Like Lambs to the Slaughter*. Eugene, Oreg.: Harvest House, 1989.

"Your child and the occult . . ." Discusses Dungeons and Dragons, television cartoons, yoga, "Star Wars," "ET," and children's books about witches. "Are these merely innocent, fun-filled activities for kids . . . or are these the subtle influences" that lead our children to destruction?

Parker, Russ. *Battling the Occult*. Downers Grove, Ill.: Inter-Varsity, 1990.

"How can we respond to a growing danger? . . . Ouija boards . . . horoscopes . . . music glorifying Satan . . . mock séance."

Passantino, Robert, and Gretchen. *Witch Hunt*. Nashville: Thomas Nelson, 1990.

Phillips, Phil. *Turmoil in the Toy Box*. Lancaster, Pa.: Starburst, 1986.

"A shocking exposé of the toy and cartoon industry."

Unger, Merrill F. *Demons in the World Today*. Wheaton: Tyndale, 1980.

Urges the church to expose the power of demonic spirits and to use its own Holy Spirit-given powers to set men free from the power of evil.

*Wedge, Thomas W. *The Satan Hunter*. Canton, Ohio: Daring, 1988.

Reveals the diabolical battle that affects every area of society.

*Weldon, John, and James Bjornstad. *Playing with Fire*. Chicago: Moody, 1984.

"Dungeons and Dragons, Tunnels and Trolls, Chivalry and Sorcery, and other fantasy games" are exposed.

_____, and Clifford Wilson. *Psychic Forces and Occult Shock*. Chattanooga, Tenn.: Global, 1986.

An excellent resource on parapsychology.

Wrestling with Dark Angels. Ventura, Calif.: Gospel Light, 1990.

Essays by several respected Christian leaders that will help you "come to a deeper understanding of the supernatural forces in spiritual warfare."

AUDIOVISUAL RESOURCES

(These media presentations are on film/video unless otherwise noted.)

"The Fakers." Vision Video.

Dan Korem discloses how people can walk across hot coals without being burned and how fortune tellers can "read minds." He exposes the danger in using a Ouija board. Forty-one min.

"Hell's Bells." Gospel Light Video, 1989.

Describes "how the spiritual power of music is being used by the dark side in much of today's hottest groups." 185 min.

"The Occult." Muskegon, Mich.: Gospel Films.

Hal Lindsey shares the reality of Satan working through witchcraft, astrology, Ouija boards, and other occultic forms. Fifty-two min.

"Psychic Confession." Vision Video.

Dan Korem unmasks the world's leading psychic, disclosing the secrets behind the tricks that have deceived people. Forty-four min.

"Stuck in a Nightmare." Youth for Christ Productions, 1989.

The story of Sean Sellers, self-proclaimed Satanist who is on death row in Oklahoma for the murder of a store clerk and his parents. Thirty-four min.

"What Happens If You Worship Satan?" Nashville: Broadman, 1989.

This cassette tape message by Jay Strack is part of the twelve-part series "The 24-Hour Counselor, Volume IV: Youth Doubt Edition."

"The World of the Occult." Santa Ana, Calif.: Vision House.

Two volumes of six cassette tapes, each by Walter Martin. Covers all aspects of the occult including witchcraft, Satanism, astrology, divination, parapsychology, modern prophets, and Rosicrucianism.

TEACHING KIT
"Understanding the Occult." Nashville: Baptist Sunday
School Board.

"Equips adults to recognize and respond to astrology,
spiritualism, magic and witchcraft, Satanism, and Hin-
du-Occult beliefs." Six sessions.

Ministries

GENERAL MINISTRIES

American Family Foundation
Box 336
Weston, MA 02193
617-893-0930

Director: Kay H. Barney
Collects information on cultic groups and shares this with other professionals, the general public, and those needing help with cultic involvements. Publishes *The Cult Observer* and *Cultic Studies Journal.*

Answers in Action
Box 2067
Costa Mesa, CA 92628
714-957-0249

Provides information on general cults, the occult, apologetics, and theology. Publishes a newsletter.

Bob Larson Ministries
Box 36480
Denver, CO 80236
303-980-1511

Director: Bob Larson
Produces the radio program "TALK-BACK," through which former cult members are directed to counselors, pastors, and helping agencies in their areas.

Christian Apologetics: Research and Information Service (CARIS)
Box 1659
Milwaukee, WI 53201
414-771-7379

Director: Jack Roper
A research team designed to assist individuals, churches, educational institutions, and law enforcement in understanding the problem of cults and the occult.

Christian Ministries International (CMI)
7601 Superior Terr.
Eden Prairie, MN 55344
612-937-8424

Presents seminars on cults and the occult. Available also on video and audio cassette tape.

Christian Research Institute (CRI)
Box 500
San Juan Capistrano, CA 92693
714-855-9926

Does research on cults and the occult and provides this information to individuals. Produces a radio program: "Bible Answer Man." Publishes *Christian Research Journal* and *Christian Research Newsletter*.

Concordia Publishing House
3558 S. Jefferson Ave.
St. Louis, MO 63118
314-664-7000

Publishes booklets and tracts on major cults.

Cornerstone Press
4707 N. Malden
Chicago, IL 60640
312-989-2080

Publishes *Directory of Cult Research Organizations*.

Council on Mind Abuse, Inc. (COMA)
40 St. Clair Ave. E., #203
Toronto, Ontario M4T 1M9 CANADA

Director: Robert Tucker
Informs people about deceptive recruitment and indoctrination techniques used by cults in general. Publishes literature on the

cults. Counsels families with members in cults. Produces radio and television programs about mind control.

Cult Awareness Network
2421 W. Pratt Blvd., #1173
Chicago, IL 60645
312-267-7777

Helps "individuals of all ages recognize deceptive and indirect techniques of persuasion and control" practiced by "groups which promise intellectual/spiritual/self-actualization Utopias." Works with state Cult Awareness Councils.

Cult Hot-line and Clinic
1651 Third Ave.
New York, NY 10028
212-860-8533

Offers assistance to people who are in or have left a cult, family and friends of someone involved in a cult, and groups who want to know more about cults.

Home Mission Board, Southern Baptist Convention
Interfaith Witness Dept.
1350 Spring St., N.W.
Atlanta, GA 30367
404-898-7000

Director: Dr. Gary Leazer
Provides information on cults, the occult, and world religions.

Interfaith Coalition of Concern About Cults
711 Third Ave., 12th Floor
New York, NY 10017
212-983-4977

Director: Philip Abramowitz
Provides information on cults to all members of the community. Sponsors conferences on the cults.

Jewish Federation Council: Committee on Cults and Missionaries
6505 Wilshire Blvd., #802
Los Angeles, CA 90048
213-852-1234

Director: Rachel Andres
Provides education, information, referrals, and advocacy on behalf of former members, families, and others victimized by destructive groups.

Lutheran Church—Missouri Synod
Commission on Organizations
1333 S. Kirkwood Rd.
St. Louis, MO 63122
314-965-9000

Director: Philip Lochhaas
Supplies information and/or counsel regarding general cults.

Spiritual Counterfeits Project
Box 4308
Berkeley, CA 94704
415-540-0300

Provides information on all cults, especially Eastern mysticism, and the occult. Publishes the *SCP Newsletter*.

Witness Inc.
Box 597
Clayton, CA 94517
415-672-5979

Director: Duane Magnani
Witnesses to cult members and informs Christians about the dangers of cults. Provides books and training aids.

Specific Ministries

Evangelical Ministries to New Religions
Denver Seminary
Box 10,000
Denver, CO 80210

Director: Dr. Gordon Lewis
"Alert Christians to the increasing impact of pantheistic belief systems and occult activities, stimulate responsible assessments of the New Age movement, and share strategies for effective Christian ministries to those affected by New Age teachings and practices."

Ex-Mormons and Concerned Christians
Box 542
Okemos, MI 48805
517-655-3797

Director: S. L. Douglas
Provides information primarily on Mormonism, Jehovah's Witnesses, New Age movement, and evolution.

Free Minds, Inc.
Box 4216
Minneapolis, MN 55414
612-378-2528

Director: Douglas Agustin
Provides information on The Way International, Scientology, Hare Krishna, Divine Light Mission, Church Universal and Triumphant, Unification Church, and Children of God. Offers counseling to former members of cults. Affiliated with Cult Awareness Network.

Free the Masons Ministries
Box 1077
Issaquah, WA 98027

Provides information on Freemasonry.

Frontline Ministries
Box 1100
La Canada Flintridge, CA 91012
818-794-5849

Director: Wally Tope
Evangelizes Mormons. Provides information on Mormonism, Jehovah's Witnesses, Christian Science, and New Age movement.

HRT Ministries, Inc.
Box 12
Newtonville, NY 12128

Director: Harmon R. Taylor
Provides information on Freemasonry.

J.O.E.L. Ministries
Box 12638
El Paso, TX 79913

An arm of W.A.T.C.H. Network. Works with teenagers coming out of the occult and drugs.

The Master's College
Dept. of Apologetics
Box 878
Newhall, CA 91322
805-259-3540

Professor: Edmond C. Gruss
Provides books, leaflets, and lectures specifically on Jehovah's Witnesses, and on the occult and cults in general. Provides counseling for Jehovah's Witnesses.

Michael Paul & Associates
Box 1168
Crockett, TX 75835
409-544-4953

Directors: Michael Haynes and Paul Carlin
Offers seminars on the occult. Serves as a consultant to law enforcement officers.

Missionary Crusader
2451 34th St.
Lubbock, TX 79411
806-799-1040

Director: Homer Duncan
Provides books and tracts on Jehovah's Witnesses, Mormonism, Seventh-day Adventism, secular humanism, Unitarians, and evolution.

Mormonism Research Ministry
Box 20705
El Cajon, CA 92021
619-447-3873

Director: Bill McKeever
Informs the public about the error of Mormonism through a quarterly magazine, *Mormonism Researched*, distribution of tracts and books, and a talk show in the San Diego area.

New Directions Ministries
Box 2347
Burlington, NC 27216
919-227-1273

Director: J. L. Williams
Provides information about cults in general and the occult and The Way International specifically.

Parents' Music Resource Center
1500 Arlington Blvd.
Arlington, VA 22209
703-527-9466

Director: Jennifer Norwood
Provides extensive information on occult-related incidents in music concerts and lyrics containing Satanic themes.

Personal Freedom Outreach
Rt. 3 Wier Lake Rd.
Kunkletown, PA 18058
215-381-3661

Director: Bill Cetnar
Provides information about Jehovah's Witnesses, Mormonism, and others. There are five other regional offices across the country.

Probe Ministries International
1900 Firman Dr., Suite 100
Richardson, TX 75081
214-480-0240

Administrative Director: Ray Cotton
Provides leaders for seminars on Mormons and Jehovah's Witnesses. Publishes literature in the area of current issues, ethics, and Christian apologetics. Sponsors two radio talk shows: "Probe" and "Newstalk."

Saints Alive
Box 1076
Issaquah, WA 98027
206-392-2077

Director: Ed Decker
Witnesses to Mormons and provides information to Christians on the doctrinal errors of Mormonism.

The Teaching Ministry
Box 22596
Fort Worth, TX 76122

Director: Mark Stepherson
Offers seminars on Mormonism and Jehovah's Witnesses.

Utah Christian Publications
Box 21052
Salt Lake City, UT 84121

Director: Marvin W. Cowan
Publishes material for use in witnessing to Mormons. Presents seminars on Mormonism. Counsels with Mormons.

Utah Lighthouse Ministry
Box 1884
Salt Lake City, UT 84110

Directors: Jerald and Sandra Tanner
Provides information on Mormonism. Publishes the *Salt Lake City Messenger* and books. Operates a bookstore. Formerly known as Modern Microfilm.

Utah Missions, Inc.
Box 348
Marlow, OK 73055
800-654-3992

Director: John L. Smith
Educates Christians about Mormonism and how to win Mormons to Christ. Publishes *The Evangel* monthly.

Warnke Ministries
672 Pleasant Hill Rd.
Box 472
Burgin, KY 40310
606-748-9961

Director: Mike Warnke
Educates people about Satanism and the occult through humorist concerts. Publishes a newsletter. Mike and Rose have written books and recorded music and humor tapes.

W.A.T.C.H. Network
Box 12638
El Paso, TX 79913
915-581-2011

Director: Sue Joyner
Provides information and services to individuals involved in Satanism and witchcraft who are trying to get out. Offers workshops on the occult. Assists victims of satanic ritual abuse. J.O.E.L Ministries is its ministry to teenagers coming out of the occult and drugs.

Watchman Fellowship, Inc.
Columbus, GA

President: David Henke
Provides education on the Mormons, Jehovah's Witnesses, and New Age movement. Equips churches to deal with these cults. Trains Christians to witness to cult members.

Watchman Fellowship, Inc.
Box 13251
Arlington, TX 76094
817-277-0023

Director: James K. Walker
A branch of the international office in Columbus, Ga. Provides information on Mormons, Jehovah's Witnesses, and New Age movement. Publishes the *Watchman Expositor*.

Moody Press, a ministry of the Moody Bible Institute,
is designed for education, evangelization, and edification.
If we may assist you in knowing more about Christ
and the Christian life, please write us without obligation:
Moody Press, c/o MLM, Chicago, Illinois 60610.